exicon of conomic Thought

Lexicon of Economic Thought

Walter Block and
Michael Walker

Canadian Cataloguing in Publication Data

Walker, Michael, 1945-

Lexicon of economic thought

Includes index.

ISBN 0-88975-081-5 (bound). --ISBN 0-88975-077-7 (pbk.)

1. Economic policy - Dictionaries. 2. Economic development - Dictionaries. 3. Economic development - Social aspects - Dictionaries. I. Block, Walter, 1941- II. Fraser Institute (Vancouver, B.C.) III. Title.

HB61.W34 1988 c. 2 338.9'003'21 C88-091614-1

Printed in Canada.

ABOUT THE AUTHORS

WALTER E. BLOCK

Walter Block is Senior Research Fellow at the Fraser Institute in Vancouver, British Columbia, and Director of its Centre for the Study of Economics and Religion. A member of the British Columbia Association of Professional Economists, the Canadian Economics Association, the Canadian Association for Business Economics, and an ex-university professor of economics, he has worked in various research capacities for the National Bureau of Economic Research, the Tax Foundation, and *Business Week.*

Dr. Block has published numerous popular and scholarly articles on economics, is a regular contributor to *The Financial Post*, and writes a syndicated column for Sterling newspapers. An economic commentator on national television and radio, he lectures widely on public policy issues to university students, service, professional, and religious organizations.

Walter Block is the editor of the Fraser Institute books *Zoning: Its Costs and Relevance* (1980), *Rent Control: Myths and Realities* (1981), *Discrimination, Affirmative Action and Equal Opportunity* (1982), *Taxation: An International Perspective* (1984), *Theology, Third World Development, and Economic Justice* (1985), *Morality of the Market: Religious and Economic Perspectives* (1985), *Reaction: The New Combines Investigation Act* (1986), *Religion, Economics and Social Thought* (1986), *The Environmentalists versus the Economy* (1989), and is the author of *Defending the Undefendable* (1976), *Amending the Combines Investigation Act* (1982), *Focus on Economics and the Canadian Bishops* (1983), *Focus on Employment Equity: A Critique of the Abella Royal Commission on Equality* (1985), and *The U.S. Bishops and their Critics: An Economic and Ethical Perspective* (1986), and *Government Expenditure Facts* (1989).

MICHAEL A. WALKER

Michael Walker is Director of the Fraser Institute. Born in Newfoundland in 1945, he received his B.A. (summa) at St. Francis Xavier University in 1966 and his Ph.D. in Economics at the University of Western Ontario in 1969. From 1969 to 1973, he worked in various research capacities at the Bank of Canada, Ottawa, and when he left in 1973 was Research Officer in charge of the Special Studies and Monetary Policy Group in the Department of Banking. Immediately prior to joining the Fraser Institute, Dr. Walker was Econometric Model Consultant to the Federal Department of Finance, Ottawa. Dr. Walker has also taught Monetary Economics and Statistics at the University of Western Ontario and Carleton University.

Dr. Walker writes regularly for daily newspapers and financial periodicals. His articles have also appeared in technical journals, including the *Canadian Journal of Economics*, *Canadian Public Policy*, *Canadian Taxation*, and the *Canadian Tax Journal*. He has been a columnist in *The Province*, the *Toronto Sun*, the *Ottawa Citizen*, *The Financial Post*, the Sterling newspaper chain, and community newspapers across Canada, as well as a regular contributor to CBCs "As It Happens." He prepares a daily, syndicated radio programme and speaks on a regular basis to a wide variety of groups, conferences, and associations throughout Canada and the United States.

He is an author, editor, and contributor to more than 20 books on economic matters, some of which include *Balancing the Budget*; *Flat-Rate Tax Proposals*; *Reaction: The National Energy Program*; *Rent Control: A Popular Paradox*; *Unions and the Public Interest*; *Discrimination, Affirmative Action and Equal Opportunity*; *Privatization: Theory and Practice*; *Trade Unions and Society*; *Privatization: Tactics and Techniques*; and *Freedom, Democracy and Economic Welfare*.

Dr. Walker is a member of the Mont Pelèrin Society, the Canadian and American Economics Associations, and the International Association of Energy Economists.

PREFACE

There are innumerable dictionaries of economics designed to help the non-technical specialist or the layman penetrate the shorthand or jargon which economists frequently use in their communication with each other and, unfortunately, sometimes in their attempts to communicate to a broader audience. Those dictionaries and compendia of terminology serve a very useful purpose. They are, however, of almost no use to those wishing to interpret the passing economic scene and understand the implications of economic and social development.

The present volume is designed to fill the needs of those who want to have a concise view on, among other subjects, arts policy, bailouts, industrial strategy, minimum wages, rent control, Sunday shopping laws, school vouchers, and even yellow dog contracts without reading a whole volume on the subject. Within the *Lexicon of Economic Thought,* the reader will find a one- or two-page treatment of some 176 subjects of an economic or social nature.

The entries in the *Lexicon* are not meant for the in-depth researcher who is looking for a comprehensive treatment of the subject area. To attempt to provide such a treatment would defeat the whole purpose, which is to provide a concise point of view on each of the issues.

The point of view provided is essentially that of the market economist. We have attempted to consistently and conscientiously apply disciplined economic analysis and, to the extent that the issues discussed are resolvable along scientific lines, the commentaries reflect the current thinking of economists on the issue. Of course, the main theme reflected in the opinions expressed is that most issues relating to the allocation of resources and choices about how things ought to be achieved economically should be made within the context of the market system rather than at the discretion of bureaucrats.

In a recent survey of the Canadian Economics Association—an association which contains in its membership most serious professional economists in this country—the authors have discerned that the vast majority agree with this view about how resources ought to be allocated. To that extent, it can be said that most of the economic analysis contained within these pages reflects a majority opinion of the economics fraternity.

But, of course, all the issues are not purely economic—some involve value judgements and these will be more or less evident to the reader. In view of the fact that we, as authors, disagree amongst ourselves from time to time about the judgements to be adopted in particular cases, it can be predicted that readers will also find themselves at variance with some of the positions adopted.

We hope that on most occasions our readers will find themselves in agreement with the positions we present, but even if they do not, we are confident that the *Lexicon* will help readers formulate their own views, if only by reflection away from the views we express.

This work is a collaborative effort on the part of its two co-authors in the best sense of that much-abused term. Specifically, each entry has been carefully scrutinized by both; generally, the work of each has been heavily influenced by the other. In some sense, then, the entire book can be considered as being written by both contributors. However, insofar as it has been possible to segregate their separate inputs, their initials appear at the end of each entry. While this work reflects the thinking of the Director of the Fraser Institute and of the Senior Research Fellow, owing to the independence of the authors, the views expressed may or may not conform severally or collectively with those of the members of the Institute.

MAW
WEB

ABORIGINAL RIGHTS—LAND CLAIMS

If we are to approach the issue of aboriginal land claims in a systematic manner, we must view it as a subset of the more general question of justice in property rights. If we do, we can derive a methodology not only for settling aboriginal land claims but those of Japanese Canadians and any other such claimants as well.

Any complete theory of titles in property must account for how unowned virgin land can come into private ownership. First, the government can claim all the land, and then turn it over to the populace, through auction or homesteading (as was done for significant portions of the Canadian and American West) or in some other manner. Secondly, this process can take place without the intermediation of the state. (This would be the only viable method in the case of aboriginal land claims which predate the birth of the Canadian government.)

The time-honoured and traditional method of converting virgin territory to private property is that of homesteading, or "mixing one's labour with the land," in the felicitous expression of John Locke. In this view, which has precedence in natural or common law, a person becomes the owner of an unowned natural resource by transforming it in some manner—by farming it, in the case of land; or domesticating it, in the case of a wild animal;

or converting it to uses desired by consumers through mining or cutting trees and blazing paths in the forest.

How might the homesteading theory be used to resolve native land claims? First, it is clear that nothing like a claim to 100 percent of the land in Canada, or in any province, could be substantiated. The aboriginal peoples did not farm the land. The typical Indian tribe engaged in annual migratory patterns. This means that it could lay claim to both the summer and winter camps, each of no more than several square miles, plus the right to travel between them. (If one merely travels across the land, without altering the path in any way, one obtains only the right of egress, not the land itself. Similarly, if a people hunts for animals, they may achieve ownership over them—but not over the lands over which the chase took place—unless these lands were altered as well, say through the digging of pits to trap animals.)

Secondly, the native peoples must be able to offer proof that they have indeed altered nature in some manner or other. This is difficult because the longer the period of time that has elapsed between the actual homesteading and the present the more difficult it is to prove anything. In this sense, the homesteading theory is a conservative one, preserving present land titles unless there is proof that they should be changed. As well, aboriginals will have difficulty because their culture was such that they only *lived* on the land but did not seek to *alter* it in any way.

Nevertheless, even under the somewhat stringent precepts of homesteading, a small but significant proportion of what is now very valuable real estate in Canada, in justice, should revert to the native population. The canons of decency and fair play demand that these claims be adjudicated expeditiously. *W.B.*

ACADEMIC TENURE

Whenever any government seeks to end tenure in the universities, this leads to howls of outrage from virtually the entire academic community. Faculty associations, university departments, and even groups of professors from abroad, all protest vociferously along with the nations' editorialists at what they consider an affront to all that is decent and right. This should occasion little surprise, since the professors are hardly a disinterested group in this matter. Rather, they have a compelling and vested interest in the perpetuation of tenure for themselves.

In contrast, the average Joe Lunchbucket is typically highly bemused by all the fuss. If anything, he witnesses this comeuppance delivered to the high and mighty professors with a certain indifference, and even equanimity. And this is no surprise either, for it is the average citizen and taxpayer who is called upon to pay for the trough at which the professors have been so avidly feeding these many years.

What arguments do the professors make on their own behalf?

First, *tenure saves money for the university.* According to 29 faculty members of the UBC economics department, without tenure "salaries would have to be raised to continue to attract highly qualified people. Tenure can thus be regarded as a way of making B.C. universities a more attractive place to work at no additional cost to the provincial treasury." This, as a matter of fact, is true as far as it goes. Since most people, professors included, have an aversion to risk, you can usually hire people for less, other things being equal, if you guarantee them life-long employment. So what else is new?

But the argument is too clever by half. According to this logic, *everyone* should be given tenure. We could get away with paying lower wages for *all employees* in this manner.

Also, we gain out-of-pocket wage savings only at the cost of added inflexibility. Under this system, a university is liable to gather unneeded tenured professors in disciplines no longer desired by students. Nowadays, these areas would include philosophy, ancient languages, literature, and the classics. In order to meet the increased demand for courses in commerce, computers and the physical sciences, universities will have to hire additional professors in these disciplines. Thus, even with somewhat higher salaries, total costs may well be lower without tenure.

To put this point somewhat differently, these 29 professors have focused only on out-of-pocket expenses, but the relevant concept is "alternative costs." This poses the more meaningful question of whether by saving a few pennies in monetary outlays now, the province is undertaking pounds of costs further down the road.

Second, *tenure promotes independence of thought.* Without tenure, it is contended, it would be more difficult for academics to challenge the powers that be. This again, is true—so far as it goes. But academics are not the only ones who from time to time point out that the "emperor has no clothes." Other boat-rockers and watchdogs include editorialists, novelists, playwrights, essayists, rock and roll and folk song lyricists, clergymen, journalists, critics, businessmen, movie producers, TV writers, cartoonists, and whistle blowers from many other walks of life. Shall all of these callings be given tenure—the better to upset the established order?

Then there is the question of independence from whom. The professors and their apologists, as could be expected, are concerned with undue or political influence from outside academia. But that is where the paying customer—the taxpayer—resides, outside the groves of academe. Under our system of public higher education, it is the politician who is the only representative of the voter and taxpayer. This demand for freedom from outside interference is thus a demand to do as one will with the hard-earned money of other people.

But what about undue influence on scholarly independence from within the university community? Anyone even vaguely familiar with the politics of tenure grantsmanship knows how strong and undue an influence tenured professors can bring to bear on the untenured junior faculty. Let us consider an example we have already touched upon. Can anyone imagine that there were no implicit pressures brought to bear on the junior faculty to go along with that statement on behalf of tenure, signed by all 29 members of the UBC economics department? This is why the NDP in British Columbia well and truly opposed tenure in 1971-73. They feared, and rightly so, that the young and more radical junior professors would be severely weeded-out at the hands of the more conservative senior faculty.

Third, *tenure ensures a high quality, competent professorate.* According to the theory, tenure is granted—after an arduous, exhaustive, and intensive procedure—only to those who have demonstrated excellence in research and teaching. In reality, however, the process is marred by politicking, favouritism, and an "old boy" network. There are dangers even when this process works well. A young scholar who has shown great promise during a five- or six-year period may not necessarily live up to his potential. The universities become cluttered with ancient incompetents and useless time-servers in their dotage waiting for retirement.

Perhaps a better plan might be to set a 10-, 15-, or even 20-year time period before tenure is granted. Under such a plan, there would be far fewer embarrassments. Professors would have more time to demonstrate that they were not just flashes in the pan. As well, such an alteration would have favourable effects on academic industriousness. No longer could people rest on their earlier laurels. But such a change would undermine the whole logic of tenure. If it is granted later in life, fewer benefits are derived. If postponed until almost retirement, the tenure system would be virtually destroyed.

So there we have it. On the plus side, tenure can save out-of-pocket expenses, promote independence from outside forces, and increase quality. On the minus side, tenure increases costly inflexibility, cuts the tie to the paying customer, increases dependence on inside forces (the tenured professors), and runs the risk of entrenching people who later turn out to be intellectual deadwood.

So, is tenure a good or a bad system? We cannot say. There is nothing in the discipline of economics that would allow for an unambiguous answer one way or the other. This is akin to a question of managerial technique, "what is the optimum allocation of labour and capital in a given plant or industry?"

Fortunately, however, economics can supply a methodology for answering all such questions. The general answer is, *let the market work.* Allow freedom of choice. Operate a system where entrepreneurs can try different proportions of labour and capital, and the competitive system will determine which management techniques are best. This experiment must be held in the private sector, so that the financial situation of the entrepreneurs is solely dependent on allocational decision making.

It is easy to apply this to the tenure system: privatize all colleges and universities, making them directly dependent upon the choices of the paying customers. Give students vouchers instead of providing cash directly to universities. Some universities would presumably maintain tenure. Others would not. Still others might institute variations on and permutations of this system. Then, from the competition between academies using different schemes, we would be in a position to judge. Perhaps, even then, there would be no definitive answer. Tenure might work well in some institutions and badly in others. But only on the basis of the free marketplace can such a determination be made. *W.B.*

ACCURACY IN MEDIA

There is a group in the United States called Accuracy in Media that is a watchdog on the activities of the major media leaders in that country. Their main objective is to perform the role of critic on the way the media gathers the news and, in particular, to inquire as to whether or not the dragnet they employ is unbiased in its collection of fact.

For example, a number of years ago Accuracy in Media performed a very revealing exercise. They counted the number of stories, columns, and editorials on human rights in particular countries which appeared in the five most influential U.S. media, namely the *New York Times*, the *Washington Post*, and on the three major television networks. They found that there were 147 columns, stories, and editorials about human rights in Chile, 96 about human rights in South Korea, one about human rights in

North Korea, seven about human rights in Cuba, and 13 about human rights in Cambodia. The 13 about human rights in Cambodia is particularly significant, as those who saw the recent popular movie *The Killing Fields* can attest. That movie, based on a true story of a journalist's nightmare in Cambodia, is an attempt to document the hell on earth created by communist strongman Pol Pot, who is estimated to have killed more than a million Cambodians in that year when only 13 stories appeared in the U.S. media about human rights in Cambodia.

This, of course, is remarkable. It is remarkable to contrast the extent of coverage the news media accord left-wing dictatorships such as Cuba, North Korea, and Cambodia, with the overwhelming attention paid to activities in countries such as South Africa and Chile. One explanation, of course, is that Western journalists are permitted much freer access to the latter countries. In any event, such revelations should make us duly skeptical about accuracy in the media. *M.W.*

ADVERTISING

Release of the advertising figures for large corporations is often the occasion for an expression of concern by some who argue that this money is essentially wasted. What good does advertising really do anyway?

A number of years ago the humourist, John Kenneth Galbraith, taking this idea to extremes, strongly argued that the essential feature of capitalism as practised in North America is the use by oligopolistic manufacturers of a steady barrage of advertising to convince hapless consumers to purchase their products. Economists argue, however, that advertising is not only important but an essential feature of the high standard of living which we enjoy in Canada.

Don't get us wrong. We are as irritated by mind-numbing jingles as anyone. But, in a Churchillian sense, we have to acknowledge that marketing-cum-advertising is probably the worst possible way to organize communication about consumer products—except for all the other systems that have ever been devised. This is because of the central role advertising plays in ensuring sharp competition amongst rival suppliers. It is only by advertising, after all, that producers of new products or better producers of old products can make their offers known to customers.

In the process of keeping customers aware of new products and new prices, business also puts existing suppliers or their competitors on notice as to the new standard they must meet. The very size of the advertising budget of an organization like McDonald's restaurants is mute testimony to the fact they have offered a better product at a better price. That's how they got a quarter of a billion dollars to spend on advertising—by providing consumers with a product at a price they preferred to that of other products. *M.W.*

ADVERTISING AND FRAUD

Advertising which commits fraud is properly prohibited and should be severely penalized. However, much advertising of this sort is perpetrated by government—the very agency we must rely on to police the private sector. Political advertising is notorious for its untruth. Consider those Petro-Canada ads telling us that we all own this Crown corporation. Let's face it: we the citizens *don't* own Petro-Canada in any real sense. We have no evidence of ownership. We don't receive any specific benefits from this "ownership" and can assert no meaningful control over our supposed property. Were there any justice in the world, Petro-Canada would be prosecuted immediately by the Consumer Protection Branch for false advertising.

If we owned a share of stock in a private company, we would resent as wasteful an advertising campaign telling us that we own a share of XYZ Ltd. If we really own a piece of Petro-Canada, let them stop advertising and instead send us a copy of the Annual Report along with some dividends. *W.B.*

ADVERTISING—RULES OF CONDUCT

There is a storm of opposition brewing over the use of women as sex objects in advertising. Magazines as disparate as *Maclean's*, *Vogue*, and *City Woman* have been accused of using pictures of sexy women to enhance their advertised products.

According to some critics, women are increasingly used as sex objects in print and electronic advertising. And unless broadcasters and advertisers do something to turn this situation around, they threaten to lobby the Canadian Radio-Television and Telecommunications Commission to impose new government regulations.

As a result, a committee has been struck by the advertising industry itself. Called the Advertising Advisory Board, its mission is to act as a sex role educational watchdog, trying to induce the industry as a whole to make changes on a voluntary basis. The AAB has called for a more realistic portrayal of women, as well as men, in commercial advertisements. Specifically, it has asked advertisers not to exploit sexuality purely for attention-getting purposes. Rather, it should be relevant to the advertised product. For example, the Advertising Advisory Board is trying to stop the use of sexy women in irrelevant situations, such as draped over the hood of a tractor in a commercial for farm equipment.

As admirable as these efforts may appear to some, they are fraught with difficulties. First of all, there is the very important matter of rights of free speech and free association. If the advertiser can pay the female model an acceptable wage, and likewise induce the voluntary co-operation of photographers, copywriters, artists, and all other necessary personnel, then to prohibit this ad campaign is an interference with all their rights of free speech and association.

Secondly, the AAB puts its finger on the essence of advertising—grabbing the attention of the consumer. People are subjected to a bewildering array of conflicting and competitive messages. The advertiser who can grab the attention of the consumer is a step ahead of the competition.

There is a joke about mule training. There was a particularly intractable animal, the bane of his trainers. An expert was called in, and promptly hit the mule a resounding clunk on the head with a sledgehammer. When asked by the amateur mule trainers to explain this rather bizarre behaviour, the expert explained, "Well, I had to get his attention first." Precisely. This is why advertisers have to be so clever. And, students of human nature, they have learned that nothing grabs the attention of the jaded Canadian consumer as quickly as the inclusion of an attractive half-dressed model.

Of course, these contrivances are not merely humdrum descriptions of the product. Only amateur advertisers limit themselves to telling the price, quality, product specifications, directions, and operations. The professionals, like the expert mule trainer, grab the consumer's attention first. Strictly speaking, much of good advertising can most assuredly be interpreted in this manner: testimonials from actors and athletes, catchy musical jingles, headlines, and eye-catching layout in the print medium. If this essential ingredient of advertising is removed, this de-fanged industry will no longer be in a position to contribute to the consumer welfare.

Many people have swallowed whole the view of the critics that the advertising industry makes no contribution to the common weal anyway and, thus, de-fanging it will be a loss to no one—except possibly to a bunch of thieving, dollar-chasing, exploiting advertisers and capitalists, and they deserve whatever is done to them anyway. There are grave problems with this view. If advertising were limited to the cold-hearted creation and dissemination of information—price, warranties, product specification and the like—it would, paradoxically, impart far less information than it does at present. For the plain fact is that most people tune out such boring messages.

The dissemination of commercial information is well-nigh impossible unless one has first captured the attention of the consumer. A de-fanged advertising industry cannot possibly accomplish this crucial task. Without this smooth and easy flow of information, our economy would lose much of its vitality. So the advertiser, derided, excoriated, and put down though he may be, plays an essential role in our economy.

In contrast, consider these busybody do-gooders who would handcuff his efforts with a welter of prohibitory legislation. If they succeed, they will reduce our economic well-being by attacking our economy in a vulnerable spot—our information flow. Opponents of such advertising, of course, have the right, in our free enterprise system, to promulgate their own views. They may do this by creating competitive messages, and by engaging in boycotts. *W.B.*

AFFIRMATIVE ACTION (see Discrimination)

An affirmative action programme mandates that employers consider three additional characteristics in determining hiring and promotions. To the normal ones of intelligence, hard work, and experience, will now be added whether or not you are a woman, a native person, or handicapped. The inevitable consequence of this is that people who have the first three characteristics but not the latter will be discriminated against in consideration for promotion and employment opportunities. This is the inevitable consequence of an affirmative action programme.

The justification for this heavy-handed and, indeed one must say, unjust policy is the view that the reason women, native peoples, and the handicapped are not better represented in employment and management positions in the civil service is because of existent discrimination. But the fact of the matter is that the research which has been done does not support that assertion. The representation of various groups in employment is explained much better by differences in education, age, experience, attachment to the work-force, geographical location, and other specific differences between individuals.

In the particular case of women, for example, it is clear that sex role stereotyping in childhood educational and career choices is a much more powerful explanation of labour force participation than discrimination. In consequence, the affirmative action programme will not, as it applies to women, solve the problem. Rather, it will compound the problems of injustice the proponents of affirmative action see because it involves reverse discrimination against groups who have in no way been responsible for the under-representation of women and others in management and employment situations.

Why is it that females are under-represented in mathematical and hard sciences and in the professions which go along with them? The process of selection which determines this result begins in the 7th grade. It is sobering if not grim to think of teenagers as has-beens with no realistic chance of a comeback but that is precisely the situation. It is a cold fact that the serious study of science, mathematics, engineering, or economics is off-limits to most young women by the time they sct foot on a college campus, largely because they have not selected the appropriate mathematical prerequisites in high school.

The reason females do certain jobs in our society and males do others is thus not because of discrimination of one form or another. There is, therefore, no necessity to correct representational imbalances in the professions and other areas of employment. To a large extent, the representation of various groups in different jobs is a reflection of choices which individuals have made, in most cases, very early in their lives.

Affirmative action or, more properly, reverse discrimination programmes which seek to "correct representational imbalances," or quota systems in universities don't get at the core of the problem. Those who think it is desirable for females to be more active in the math and science professions must address the central issue of why females make the early choices they do.

Most disturbing about the current thrust of government policy on affirmative action is the extent to which the government is prepared simply to dismiss the evidence—evidence that while women and men are certainly paid unequally and promoted at different rates, the reason is not discrimination but factors such as education and career choice, problems which affirmative action won't resolve.

The pro-affirmative action fallback position, of course, is that even if the unequal labour force representation of females is not due to discrimination, the inequality of representation itself is an injustice which must be rectified. Aside from the fact that inequality doesn't imply anything about justice, affirmative action in this case is a form of reverse discrimination. As such there will be people in this generation who will be harmed now by the affirmative action policies of government. Nowhere in the policy statements of government or in the pleadings of special interest groups is mentioned the plight of those individuals who will be refused promotion because "the department must meet its native people quota."

Most people know about and can understand employment quotas. People know the likely effect if every employer were forced to employ a certain percentage of black, female, disabled, or other workers. People know this would mean abandoning merit as the criterion of employment and advancement.

Perhaps it is this that leads proponents of affirmative action programmes to deny their support for quotas. Almost to a person, those who react strongly against criticism of affirmative action do so on the grounds that affirmation action doesn't imply quotas. Those who care should also be warned, however, that until recently those same folks were saying that affirmative action doesn't have to be compulsory. The sad fact is that Canada is following a perfectly predictable course leading to full-blown compulsory affirmative action—quotas and all—and few Canadians are aware of this or of the implications.

Based on a superficial examination, it is hard to see why any reasonable person could oppose an affirmative action programme, a positive programme of assistance to the downtrodden, the neglected, and minority group members. Surely, it will be said, the plight of many minority groups cries out for adjustment, and any legislative endeavours in this regard which might succeed should be tried.

The reason thinking people should reconsider these programmes is because they are not positive programmes. They are not typically programmes to ensure equal opportunity. They are not programmes of positive action; they are programmes of reverse discrimination. They are programmes for excluding one group from jobs or university places to make room for other groups.

Because they are, in effect, reverse discrimination programmes, affirmative action has the effect of increasing the animosity of majority groups toward the plight of minorities, thereby worsening the ultimate position of minority groups. This was brought home with a chilling and frightening ring by the comments of one of the leaders of the infamous Ku Klux Klan in the United States. Imperial Wizard Bill Wilkinson of Danham Springs, Louisiana, when asked why his group (which is one of three major Klan organizations) has gained in membership, said without hesitation: "Affirmative action programmes, and the Weber decision by the Supreme Court have done more to make a race war possible in this country than anything the Klan has done." While Klansman Wilkinson is hardly an unbiased source of information, he certainly indicates the reaction of some American whites to the extreme forms of affirmative action now practised in the United States.

In addition, affirmative action programmes harm highly competent minority persons by making it appear that their accomplishments are not due to their own efforts but to government "largess." They harm unqualified minority persons by placing them in positions which expose their incompetence, and they harm minority persons excluded from affirmative action by increasing their frustration and lowering their motivation to attain job qualifications on their own.

A further complexity is that there is a resource almost entirely disregarded by those in the forefront of the fight against prejudice—the market test of profit and loss, which tends to eliminate from the private sector (through bankruptcy) those who indulge in discriminatory practices. In the public sector (where a profit and loss system is by definition inoperable), there may be greater need for vigilance. In non-competitive settings such as highly regulated industries, utilities, for example, to say nothing of government agencies, one might well expect to find discriminatory employment practices. In these organizations there is no market test, no pressure from competitors to ensure that productivity and not sex, age, or ethnic background is used as a guide in hiring practices. Government efforts, therefore, ought to be directed primarily toward ensuring that discrimination does not occur in the public sector. *W.B.*

AGE

King Canute ordered the waves not to come onto the beaches of his empire. In similar manner, human rights commissions of various levels of government are trying to stem the flow of time and aging—by ordering citizens to disregard their effects. Neither is likely to succeed in flaunting the laws of nature.

Consider the following items:

- A mother of a four-year-old girl is arguing in a Prairie courtroom that the local school division which admits children only after they have reached their fifth birthday is discriminating under the Human Rights Act.
- An Eastern radio station was ordered by a human rights commission to apologize to an 11-year-old girl for not allowing her to participate in a phone-in show (discussing male strippers) because of her tender years.
- A major air carrier was found guilty of discrimination by the Human Rights Commission for its policy of giving special preference to young pilot trainees between the ages of 21 and 27.

There is great difficulty with the position staked out on age by this "human rights" philosophy. Prohibiting age discrimination flies in the face of reality, nature, and common sense. The desire to age discriminate is pervasive, ranging over all sorts of human institutions and endeavours. The three cases cited above are only the tip of the iceberg.

People commonly age discriminate in their choice of marital or love partners. The personal advertisements in our newspapers offer ample evidence: "woman, age 41, seeks man, age 40-51, object matrimony" is but one example of this. Further, it is the rare client, indeed, who would voluntarily patronize a dentist, attorney, electrician, doctor, plumber, architect, or any other such professional, who was six years of age, even were he a "child prodigy" who had passed all the relevant certification requirements. Nor would it be a popular idea to allow such children to take driver licencing exams. Some might even pass, and then where would we be?

The furniture store in a Canadian west coast city is yet another blatant age discriminator. Its "ballroom"—a romper room for children filled with nothing but Styrofoam plastic balls three feet deep—prohibits entry both to children under four (a loose dirty diaper would be a tragedy) and over nine (they might frolic too roughly and squash the smaller kiddies). Don't people have a human right to discriminate in this manner?

So counter-initiative and ridiculous is the prohibition against age discrimination that even the human rights commissions themselves, thank goodness, can act sensibly upon occasion—i.e., when matters of public safety are at issue—but when it does it must renounce its own philosophy. For example, the Canadian Human Rights Commission found that ten airline pilots, who were forced to retire at age 60, were *not* victims of age discrimination. It argued that Canadian Airlines International and Air Canada, the accused airlines, were not guilty because forced retirement of airline pilots at age 60 was "normal practice" in the industry. However welcome this decision was on grounds of safety and common sense, it was clearly arbitrary and illogical. If "normal practice" can be a defence against the charge of discrimination, then any discriminator can escape being held culpable as long as there are (many) others who also follow this practice.

Age is clearly a proxy, or stand in, for other human attributes. It is almost always much cheaper and more convenient to determine a person's age, at least roughly, than these other personal qualities. If human abilities did not vary with age, there would be little sense in discrimination on this basis and little would probably occur. But they do. The reason we don't send four-year-olds to school or allow 11-year-olds to debate the merits or demerits of male strippers is because such children do not usually have the maturity to handle these experiences. The reason airlines like to train young pilots and retire old ones is that it usually takes a long time to learn this skill, which tends to deteriorate rapidly as bodily reactions slow down in old age.

There are, of course, exceptions to all such rules of thumb. *Some* three-year-old girls, conceivably, could be trusted to go to school, keep their diapers clean, discuss sexology, get married, drive an automobile, or act as a qualified doctor or lawyer. *Some* 75-year-old men could be relied upon to continue to pilot aircraft successfully. And it certainly is "unfair," in at least some sense of that much abused word, to preclude such talented people, if ever they could be found, from taking on these roles.

But the point is, shall such exceptional individuals be allowed to thrust themselves upon an unwilling society? The airline companies are, in the final analysis, only the agents of the flying public. They will not voluntarily employ even an otherwise fully qualified 75-year-old pilot because their customers will fear for their lives (however irrationally) in these few exceptional cases. Laws which force over-age pilots upon airlines are ultimately a violation of the human rights of the air passengers as well as an interference with the airline industry. *W.B.*

AGRICULTURAL LAND RESERVE

According to a recent federal task force, Canada lost 3.5 million acres of farmland in the 15 years between 1961 and 1976. This trend is scarier than even these figures reveal, in the view of many alarmists, since these are only gross figures. Underlying them is the fact that prime farmland in the East has been falling to the developer's bulldozer, while land clearing efforts in the West have added acreage of poorer quality. So, not only has Canada lost 3.5 million acres of farmland; what remains has lower fertility on average.

Has some sort of modern day Jack the Ripper been running amok, applying a scorched earth policy to Canadian farmland?

Not a bit of it—although this is the way some people look at the problem.

On the contrary, tillable soil in Canada has been "disappearing" for the very best of reasons. Millions of ordinary Canadians would rather live and work on these lands—especially those bordering on cities and towns—instead of leaving it for crops. That is to say, our people have placed a much higher value upon these properties for residential, industrial, and commercial purposes than for their use in growing food. So much so that acreage under Agricultural Land Reserve Acts commonly sells for $10,000 to $20,000 while the same property—with no restrictions—is at times worth hundreds of thousands or even millions of dollars.

Since the dawn of humankind in the Tigris and Euphrates delta there has been a continuous conflict between the use of land for food production and the use of land for habitation. While the popular rendition of this struggle in more modern times pits the land developer against the farmer or against our natural heritage, the reality, of course, is that even though he does so only in the interests of earning a profit, the developer represents all of those people who want to use urban fringe land for residential purposes. The prospect of making a profit by selling homes to new families is what motivates the developer. And the value which the developer places upon the land for its use as residential space is a direct reflection of the evaluation of that land for that purpose by the broader population to whom he will eventually attempt to sell the dwelling space.

The farmer, for his part, reflects, as our agents, the valuation which we collectively as a community place on the land in its use as a food producing asset. The prices that we are willing to pay for the produce from the land stiffen the financial spine of the farmer and cause him, in considering his own self interest, to consider our evaluation of the land in its use as an agricultural producer. The conversion of agricultural land from food production to residential use is a reflection of the fact that those who desire it for that purpose value it more highly than those who value it for food production.

Under such conditions, it should occasion no surprise that developers are anxious to convert practically worthless farmland—no matter how fertile—into uses more highly valued by the Canadian citizenry. In this way, we can really "get something for nothing." Every time agricultural land worth $10,000 is converted to building land worth $1,000,000, society gains value equivalent to $990,000.

However, there are numerous naysayers, who oppose these socially beneficial conversions. They have a whole host of reasons, none of which can withstand serious analysis. Consider the claim that Canada loses food production. Of course Canada may lose food production. But if so, it gains residential, commercial, or industrial capabilities which, in the eyes of the people involved, are worth far more than the losses in tillable soil. Should we plow under downtown Toronto, or the West End of Vancouver, or Portage and Main in Winnipeg in order to grow a few more beans? Sure, we may lose some food production, but we gain things of far greater value. Objecting to the tide of progress on this ground is penny wise—but pound (and ton) foolish.

Nor is it by any means necessary that the ALR even increase Canadian food production. True, without the agricultural land reserve, arable soil on the edge of urban areas will tend to be bid away by home builders on behalf of their clients. But farmers can relocate to more outlying areas, where land prices are much cheaper. If they till more acreage there, the result may be more food, not less.

But let us consider the worst possible scenario in this regard. Suppose Canadian food production falls off as a result of land development for housing. This will mean—given our citizenry does not decide to eat less—that the country must decrease its export of foodstuffs and/or increase its imports. Neither is a problem. If we reduce our exports of farm produce slightly, we will have less foreign exchange. Instead, we will be better housed, as a nation. This must be a preferable state of affairs—for by assumption, we want the housing more than the extra food. Moreover, farmers are free to expand their base of operations, and thereby gain foreign exchange. That they do not, in our example, indicates they see it as not worth their while.

Of course, I am aware that some environmentalists reserve their second strongest emotions for land developers. And, it must be readily admitted that this market for valuing the alternative uses of land does not work perfectly. Participants have only imperfect information. Not everybody on each side of the market gets involved in the process of casting their dollar votes and, of course, there is a very considerable non-market participant in the form of government regulation, both on the side of the farmer and on the side of the developer.

The important thing, however, is that there is a continuously working market relationship which, on an ongoing basis, assesses the value of land in alternative uses and causes an orderly and, for the most part, beneficial conversion of land which serves the public interest. It provides a resolution of the conflict between two legitimate end uses of the land. One point to note about this process is that simply by following their own interests the developer and the farmer, the two main actors in focus in these transactions, are led to reflect the wider societal interest and to ensure that there is an appropriate valuation of this scarce resource.

While there are, evidently, continuing problems with the way urban land markets function, it is noteworthy that interest in governmentally mandated solutions to these problems has abated. Government land banking and more complete public ownership are no longer seen as the panacea for land market problems. It has been observed that government solutions come with their own complement of problems. On every hand, there is interest in privatization and returning economic activities to the private sector. *W.B.*

AIRLINE DEREGULATION

Economic regulation is ofttimes in the interests of those who are regulated. This is the opposite of the usual interpretation that regulation leads to lower prices and better quality for the consumer.

It used to be argued, for example, that regulation of airline routes and strict governance of the fares charged by airlines was primarily in the interest of the consumer. How else to ensure that adequate service was provided to small communities and prevent those large airline companies from gouging the defenseless public?

Eventually, work done by Nobel Prize winner George Stigler and what grew to be an army of colleagues convinced the government in the United States that the consumer interest really was not being served by regulation but rather that regulation served to create a kind of cartel for the producers. It limited competition among existing airlines for the consumer's dollar and therefore limited the natural tendency of competition to improve the service provided. The gradual lifting of regulations has produced precisely the result Stigler predicted. Airline fares have fallen, service to small cities has increased, and in general the travelling public is far better off.

Simultaneously, the effects of competition are beginning to show on the fortunes of the airline companies. Restructuring and streamlining have been the order of the day for those companies surviving the onslaught of competition, and Canada is beginning to reflect these competitive pressures. It is now a lot cheaper to fly from coast-to-coast in Canada, regardless of how you do it.

Air Canada, in response to pressure from cost-cutting Wardair has inaugurated a $199 fare from Vancouver to Toronto. This must be regarded as a puzzling development indeed. Air Canada is a Crown corporation. As such, it is supposed to be purely concerned with the welfare of the travelling public and not at all concerned with making a profit. (At least that is the theory of Crown corporations that boosters often mention.) Why is it, then, that we had to rely on pressure from well-known Canadian capitalist Max Ward to get the cheapest possible airplane tickets? If purely economic considerations permitted Wardair to offer a drastic cut in airline prices, why didn't Air Canada do it before? Why didn't some other airline do it?

The reason is that the airline business in Canada was and still is highly regulated. Airlines can't just fly where they like—they have to get permission from the Canadian Transport Commission. Until recently, Wardair simply wasn't permitted to fly the routes offered by Air Canada and Canadian Airlines International. By the same token, Air Canada was required to fly certain routes which weren't economic, so it had to pay for flights to some areas by charging higher prices on other flights.

What is paradoxical is that Air Canada, a Crown corporation operating in a tightly regulated market, wasn't able to provide the kinds of deals to consumers that are now available when regulations are being lifted and the Crown privilege is being removed from Air Canada. Regulations and Crown corporations don't benefit consumers, but good old capitalist competition does. Now, all we need is to get Air Canada out of the public sector.

But there are objections to the airline deregulation movement. There is concern about waiting lines at airports, over-booked flights leading to disappointed travellers, increasing delays caused by crowded runways, and the hostility of travellers exposed to long lines and waiting. A typical newspaper headline of this ilk noted that "Delays Sour Joy of Low Fares for U.S. Air Travellers," while another proclaimed "Safety a Loser in Deregulation."

The message is clear, deregulation isn't all that it was cracked up to be and perhaps we in Canada are making a mistake to follow the U.S. example. But these objections are mistaken. They commit the Toots Shore fallacy. (Yogi Berra once remarked that "Toots Shore's restaurant is so crowded that nobody goes there anymore.") The reason problems are emerging for U.S. airlines is not because of deregulation but because deregulation has been so successful. The reason airports are crowded and flights are over-booked is because prices have fallen so much that people who couldn't afford air travel in 1978 take it for granted in 1987. In the year of deregulation, 274 million people flew in the U.S. Last year the number had skyrocketed to 415 million. Of course, that means that O'Hare Airport in Chicago, for example, is "so crowded that nobody wants to go there anymore," but it doesn't mean that airline deregulation is a regrettable development for the vast numbers of Americans who have had their horizons expanded by a stroke of the legislative pen.

The most serious objection to airline deregulation is that it has led to increased travel-related deaths. Nothing, however, could be further from the truth. There are two remarkable studies regarding airline regulation and accidents. The first shows that deregulation in the United States, begun in 1978, produced a prompt reduction in the cost of airline travel and also resulted in a reduction in the number of people killed in the United States. Professor Richard McKenzie found that a reduction in airline fares had the effect of causing a decrease in the number of passenger miles travelled by people in private automobiles. Rock bottom airfares made transcontinental automobile trips quite a bit less attractive, both financially and timewise. Since airline travel is much safer than automobile travel, particularly over long distances, the end result of the change has been to actually save Americans' lives.

An even more profound revelation comes from a study of Federal Aviation Administration inspection effectiveness. This research, reported by Andrew Chalk in the *Wall Street Journal*, discovered that the Federal Aviation Administration, which employs 210 inspectors, is expected to monitor the work of 50,000 mechanics employed by more than 100 airlines operating 3,000 aircraft. Even when these inspectors find violations, the top fine they can levy is $1,000, an amount that was established in 1938. The only conclusion is that FAA regulators don't do a lot of regulating, at least where airline safety is concerned.

This study found that a design-related air accident produces a drop of about 4 percent in the share values of the offending manufacturer. A powerful incentive for airline safety. Meanwhile, insurance brokers impose high premium costs on firms that incur many accidents or have poor safety records. Both these results suggest that airline deregulation in Canada is likely to produce an improvement rather than a deterioration in airline safety. Not the usual image. *M.W.*

ANTI-COMBINES LEGISLATION

Canadian anti-combines legislation is based on an untenable and outmoded theory that economic concentration and competition are inconsistent. This theme runs throughout the legislative codes, and can be expected to be found as the basis of any legislation that emerges in the future.

The truth is almost the exact opposite of that theme. Competition and concentration of achievement, in fact, go hand-in-hand in most human endeavours. Given that talents and abilities are unequally spread around among the population, and given that full and rigorous competition takes place, it should occasion no surprise that there are only a few winners, survivors, or eminent persons associated with each activity. This is true in sports, politics, the arts, and business as well, but it is only in business that unequal results are seen as evidence of non-competitiveness.

The winners in the highly competitive and democratic Canadian political arena are also highly concentrated. The Social Credit Party of Alberta enjoyed an uninterrupted reign of 36 years, from 1935 to 1971; and the Progressive Conservative Party has almost completely dominated Alberta provincial politics since 1971. Ontario had been ruled by one party, the Progressive Conservatives, for 38 years in a row. The national Liberals have been all but frozen out of the four Western provinces in the past decade, while until the 1984 election they managed a virtual monopoly over the national Progressive Conservative and New Democratic parties in Quebec.

The attack on business concentration, therefore, comes with particular ill grace from the political sphere, which is as highly concentrated as any institution in society. In focusing its attention on the red herring of concentration, our law is actually, if unknowingly, ignoring the real threat to competitiveness of the Canadian economy.

There is all the difference in the world between a company that attains a (temporary) monopoly position through service to the consumer (new product, lower price, better service, and the like) and one that attains a permanent monopoly position through the coercive power of the state. The pre-eminent example in the latter category is Canada Post. It owes its monopoly not to its superior competitive activity but to the law of the land which threatens those who would deliver mail privately with stiff fines and even jail sentences.

Present law is also curiously silent about the monopolistic practices of labour unions. Not only does organized labour have a high concentration ratio in many industries but, ever so much more important, it engages in entry restrictions and even prevention of job opportunities to non-unionized workers.

Imagine the hue and cry were business firms to engage in such practices. If corporations followed the example of organized labour, not only would they "fail to supply," but they would physically prevent their customers from patronizing other establishments (which is *exactly* what a union of employees does when it goes out on strike).

Labour organizations have traditionally been exempt from anti-trust legislation in the U.S. and from anti-combines edicts in this country. But there is no justification for making such an exception. Labour unions, especially unions of public employees, have a power to disrupt an entire economy in a way incomparably greater than business, even "monopoly" business. If there is no case for including labour unions under the restrictions imposed by an amended Combines Act, there is even less case for including business enterprise. *W.B.*

ARTS POLICY

People may think that the market system is good at securing economic performance but that it doesn't do much to preserve human dignity, maintain the quality of life, or preserve beauty and the arts. Even leading business people, while expressing strong support for free market institutions, express doubt about the ability of the unfettered free market to operate on these more ethereal and perhaps more essentially human aspects of the world in which we live. It's a question worth pursuing.

Let us ask which of the world's societies most respect human dignity, better provide a quality of life worth having, preserve freedom, beauty and the arts. Is it the totalitarian, interventionist regimes of the world that provide this or those nation states which espouse, at least in principle, the pursuit of something like a free market?

A more compelling argument is to be found by consideration of the alternatives to a system of private markets, even in principle. In that sense, one can think of a continuum of alternatives. One extreme involves no governments whatsoever, and the other extreme provides a wholly governmental determination of human action. In financial terms, the counterparts of those polar extremes provide a situation in which all individuals can spend every dollar they earn and at the other extreme one where no one could spend anything they earn directly but rather could only spend what was remitted to them by the state.

Quite apart from the practical difficulties associated with these two extreme views, it seems obvious that in the case where the state absorbs all of an individual's income there is little opportunity left for freedom, little possibility for an independent assessment of what constitutes beauty and, certainly, no consideration of individual human dignity since the function of the individual would be completely subsumed in the pursuit of the state's interest.

If all of these assertions are true, in what way could an individual assert his individuality, pursue his own peculiar concept of beauty, and encourage his own conception of art in a practical way? These are not idle questions. It is essentially in the choices of how people spend their incomes that they express their individuality. That is also how they influence culture and express their opinions about art. In our view, a system superior to the market has not yet been found for permitting people maximum expression in these matters. *M.W.*

ARTS POLICY AND FREE TRADE

The issue of arts policy is inextricably intertwined with foreign trade. It is agreed on all sides that a policy of free trade to sell to a market of 250 million people instead of a mere 25 million—the opportunities to enhance the continental division of labour and to specialize in the things we do best, while trading with the Americans for products which embody their particular excellences—guarantees an economic improvement for this country. All this is so blatantly obvious that even opponents of reduced trade barriers concede that Canada has to pay a price, a real price, to maintain the status quo.

But Canadian nationalists have an arrow in their quiver that is even more powerful than a fine calculation of dollars and cents advantages and disadvantages. They claim that closer commercial ties would put at risk our cherished political sovereignty. It is as if, along with the cheap goods and services which will come flooding into Canada, there would be hidden platoons of U.S. soldiers ready to pounce on the RCMP and take over the country. But when the argument is stated in this nuts and bolts manner, it is easy to see the nonsense it embodies. The United States does not need free trade to take over Canada militarily. If it wanted to do so (a ludicrous proposition), that nation surely has the means at its disposal under the present regime of trade barriers.

With this argument in tatters, the nationalists have a second one to fall back on. Free trade may not mean an actual loss of political sovereignty, but it may lead to a loss of the Canadian soul. And what is the Canadian soul, you may well ask? As expressed by no less than the arts community of this country, the Canadian soul is to be found in the unique Canadian spirit and character.

This, too, is questionable. Apart from a few hundred Canadian visual and performing artists who make it on their own without subsidies from government, there are no artists in this country. The several thousand people who line up at the Canada Council, Canadian Film Board, CBC and numerous other public troughs for grants are only welfare recipients whose "salaries" are a means of disguising the true reality. No doubt, some of these people could prosper in a free artistic marketplace, but we'll never know for sure until the welter of government arts grants is ended.

Who says that only homegrown art can express the culture of a nation? The U.S. is self-assured enough not to "protect" itself against foreign films, books, magazines, orchestras, and ballet companies. Canada will never attain any comparable level of artistic maturity and self-confidence if it continues to hide behind a system of subsidies for domestic artists and restrictions on the import of the products of those living abroad.

The way to save the national soul is to allow our artists to compete with foreigners for the allegiance of the Canadian public. Free trade, full free trade, can only hasten the coming of this glorious day. It is to be applauded on both pocketbook and artistic grounds. *W.B.*

AS MUCH AS THE MARKET WILL BEAR

How often have we used or heard others use the phrase "as much as the market will bear" when describing the price of a particular product? Usually, we mean the product is being sold at the highest possible price, as much as the seller can get away with, as much as the buyers will tolerate. While of course that is true, there is also the implicit understanding that the result is actually high prices.

In turn, this understanding leads well-meaning people to the conclusion that we cannot permit the forces of the market to determine prices. Instead, they say, we need government regulation of prices for essential things like dairy products, eggs, chicken, rent, fuel, water, electricity, communications, television and transportation, not to mention the real essentials, like alcohol and tobacco. Like many good intentions, this one isn't quite realized when put into practice.

A publication by Statistics Canada provides some revealing information about government regulation or approval of prices and how that affects the cost of living. In 1982, Statistics Canada began to measure the rate of price increases on goods and services approved or regulated by government and to compare those to the price increases on products that don't have the benefit of government regulation or approval. The comparison is quite revealing.

The figures show that from April 1973 until the end of 1986 government approved or regulated prices have increased 240 percent, whereas prices based on what the market will bear have increased only 167 percent. In other words, the unmistakable message from the Statistics Canada figures is that at least for that 13-year period, Canadians got a better deal price-wise on those products whose prices were determined by "whatever the market will bear."

The reason for this is not hard to see. Approved or regulated prices are usually prices that are produced under monopoly or special licence from government. For example, eggs, milk, chicken, and airline travel as well as telephone calls have in common the fact that those who produce them enjoy a form of government-sponsored monopoly. The monopoly, in turn, is regulated by government. The theory is that by removing the product or service from the marketplace and permitting a monopoly, government will ensure there is no duplication of facilities (e.g., telephone networks) and no oversupply (e.g., eggs and milk). By regulating the price, government also attempts to ensure that "the price is right."

However, in determining the price they will allow, regulators often have to rely on information from the industry to determine the costs of production and the reasonable profit that is added. What is lacking is the pressure of entrepreneurs who want to lure away their competitors' customers. In the end, what the market will bear is determined by customers and businesses looking out for the best deal. That is why what the market will bear serves the interests of consumers better than the well-meaning regulations of government. *M.W.*

B

BACK-TO-WORK LEGISLATION

Provincial governments often indicate an intention to legislate a settlement in long-standing industrial disputes if there is no movement toward compromise on the part of the participants. That is particularly true when a public sector employer is involved or when government revenues are heavily dependent on the industry involved. Not surprisingly, given the large political component of those negotiations and the desire of both parties to appear to have won, government's threat is usually followed by the necessity of having to act on it.

While having a certain measure of sympathy for the government's concern about disruption and the loss of revenue, we cannot in any way support back-to-work legislation. In a free country people should have the right to work or not to work, and governments should not be in the business of legislating them back to work. Employers should have the right to hire or not to hire and should not be told by governments when and under what conditions to operate.

The role of government in labour negotiations, as in other areas, is to establish a framework within which individual, private actions can be conducted to mutual advantage and without violent side effects on the rest of society. Back-to-work legislation would not be necessary if employers (public and private) were encouraged or at least effectively permitted to hire replacement workers. *M.W.*

BAILOUTS

Whenever economic circumstances take a turn for the worse, many businesses in Canada experience difficulty. Under such circumstances, one often hears cries for government aid to save jobs in those threatened industries. Better to subsidize an industry and keep people working than to let it fail and have to pay unemployment insurance—or so the story goes. On the face of it, this is a very plausible approach to this age-old problem. However, once we scratch below the surface, we find that things are neither as simple nor as attractive as they seem.

To begin with, we must clearly establish the fact that there is no such thing as government aid to industry. Governments have no capital of their own with which to provide aid to industry. What governments do have is the coercive power to extract taxes from the citizens of the country and redistribute this revenue to businesses and other people. The state also has the power to extract taxes from future generations in the form of bonds which they issue and which future generations will have to redeem. So, to get our thinking straight on government aid to industry, we must first acknowledge that it is taxpayer aid to industry. In many instances, those taxpayers will be the same consumers who refused to give direct support to particular industries by buying the products which those industries produce.

The other thing that becomes clear once we scratch beneath the surface is the fact that many of the taxpayers who will be providing this aid to industry have incomes below those of the beneficiaries. For example, the aid which was paid to Chrysler, Massey Ferguson, Consolidated Computer, or Maislin Trucking by the federal government was, for the most part, going to very highly paid industrial workers, on the one hand and/or to the shareholders of those corporations on the other. In both instances, the individuals benefiting from the aid had higher incomes than the average taxpayer.

Now this is a truly novel twist on the old Sherwood Forest ethic. Here we have Robin Hood working for the Sheriff of Nottingham and ripping off Friar Tuck and Maid Marion. Of course, it will always be said that it isn't as simple as that. But nobody can deny that aid to industry is nothing more than thinly disguised redistribution of income from one group in society to another group in society. It is also true that the recipients on average have higher incomes than the donors.

A final thing that becomes obvious once we sweep back the veil of rhetoric is the fact that most of these subsidies are not in aid of saving jobs but in aid of saving capital. A few years ago the Department of Industry, Trade and Commerce did a little-publicized study called Project Trace, which followed the lives of textile workers displaced when textile plants in the Province of Quebec closed down. What they discovered was that most of these individuals quickly found new jobs—in many instances better paying and more economically secure jobs. That is not surprising because typical worker skills can be adapted to a new environment very readily.

But the "poor" shareholders of some of these troubled firms, for example Massey Ferguson, found themselves in an entirely different circumstance. Their capital had been employed to purchase die-making equipment, to set up assembly lines, and to provide parts specifically for Massey Ferguson tractors. It will be very difficult for this capital equipment to be adapted for use in other circumstances and in other industries. As a consequence, unlike the workers at Massey Ferguson, the shareholders of Massey Ferguson can look forward to an almost total loss if that firm goes under.

There is little doubt that if these facts about "government aid" were more widely understood there would be quite a bit less enthusiasm for pursuing it. *M.W.*

BALANCED BUDGET

Whether you believe in the effectiveness of government spending or not, the clear lesson from economic experience is that you should be in favour of balancing the federal budget during normal economic times. Those who believe that government expenditure is not effective in achieving economic and social objectives are in favour of balancing the budget because it is simply a good thing to do.

Since a government can only finance its expenditures by printing money or levying taxes, a deficit amounts to the deferral of either of these two primary methods of finance. Running deficits which are financed ultimately by taxation implies that the government is not creating new economic activity but only determining the proportion of economic activity which occurs in the public and private sector. A tax with an associated expenditure serves only to transfer spending power from the latter to the former. No net new economic activity is thereby generated. To the extent that government defers the levying of taxation by issuing bonds, it merely substitutes public expenditure for the private expenditure which savings would otherwise have financed. This is true even under those circumstances, which are often noted, where private spenders seem unwilling to borrow funds for investment because of a lack of confidence. If the government did not borrow, interest rates would be lower and private spending would ultimately be stimulated.

If the deficit is financed by printing money, the end consequence is inflation. And, since inflation is ultimately reflected in higher interest rates, a long-standing deficit financed by the printing of money, although providing some temporary relief, could provide severe long-term economic difficulties.

Even those who believe that government spending is an effective bulwark against the forces of recession should also be in favour of balancing the budget during normal times. The reason for this is that the failure to run a balanced budget normally means an inability to run a deficit during times of economic reverse.

The recessionary episode of the early 1980s is a case in point. In Canada the federal government budget began to go into deficit in 1975. The deficit grew ever larger during the relatively strong growth in the ensuing years, until by 1978 the deficit had reached the $10 billion level. Accordingly, before the full brunt of the recession hit in 1982, the federal government was already deeply in deficit as a consequence of its previous spending and taxing programmes.

There have been attempts to show that this deficit is of no importance because it reflects, for the most part, the effect of inflation on government interest payments. Some analysts, including the Federal Department of Finance, have provided statistical analysis to show that because inflation reduces the size of the public debt in real terms the government has been in surplus rather than in deficit during much of this latter period. However, there are many flaws in this analysis. Not the least of which is the fact that it ignores the impact of inflation on the rest of the liabilities of the federal government—in particular the gigantic, unfunded pension liabilities.

Entering a recession with a hefty deficit means that as the demands of Canadians upon the social welfare system increase, as they predictably do, the financial wherewithal to respond to these needs simply is not available. It is generally conceded that the expenditure programmes government has been able to mount in the past have been trivial relative to the economic problems the country faces. The fact that the government had a high deficit level before the recession hit meant that there was no fiscal capacity to respond.

But the issue here is a broader one than simply the deficit itself. Evidently, if a government was spending 90 percent of the GNP—either directly or in the form of transfers—then its capacity to do anything in difficult times would be correspondingly minimized. And, of course, it is true that at the time of this writing the Canadian government is involved directly and indirectly in more than half of the economic activity which occurs. By comparison with 1926, for example, government determines how 50 percent of the total Canadian income is expended; in 1926, 80 percent of earned income was controlled by the original recipient of that income.

Some commentators pretend that those who disagree with a further extension of the deficit are without concern for the human aspect of economic recession. But the reason there is no fiscal capacity in some programmes to help those in need is because so many are helped who are not in need. For example, a study by the Economic Council of Canada some years ago showed that more than half the recipients of unemployment insurance had incomes above the national average. *M.W.*

BANKRUPTCY (see Culture, Government Support for)

Francis Ford Coppola, following a series of box office triumphs in the form of *The Godfather* series and *Apocalypse Now*, had backed a couple of dramatic dogs and found himself without the necessary wherewithal to cover his mistakes. As a result, he went bankrupt.

We are bound to feel a certain sympathy for such a man who has provided tremendous entertainment to his audiences for the past decade or so. On the other hand, one must recognize that his fate is a result of the fact that he has simply gotten out of touch with his potential audience. His success depended on the support of individuals choosing to patronize his productions and shunning the productions and blandishments of other potential sources of entertainment.

The sordid details are that Coppola borrowed $8.1 million from the Security Pacific Bank in Los Angeles and sank that, together with proceeds from earlier triumphs, into the purchase of the old Hollywood General Studios. He then poured in even more money to update the sound stages with new state-of-the-art equipment. Had he continued to produce films of the ilk of *Apocalypse Now* and *The Godfather*, presumably it would have been seen in retrospect as a wise investment. Unfortunately, Zoetrope proceeded to disgorge two major box office disasters: *Hammet*, based on the life of mystery writer Daschiel Hammet, and *One From the Heart*, a story about romance in Las Vegas which cost $23 million to make and grossed a paltry $1 million. Too bad for Francis Ford Coppola!

There is a lesson in this which needs to be learned. In competitive arenas such as the motion picture industry, it is the public that calls the tune. The public sent Francis Ford Coppola a message that they didn't like his two latest major film efforts. In consequence, it will be some time before Mr. Coppola will be given the opportunity to spend another $25 million of "society's" resources on the production of another film. By their individual decisions not to patronize the films, in effect, the North American viewing public has for the moment anyway consigned Coppola's talents to a back burner in favour of other rising talents whose works are more appreciated.

It is interesting to consider what might have been his fate had he lived in Canada. It is quite conceivable that he would have found himself eligible for a grant from the Canada Arts Council or some other state-funded organization designed to shape the cultural outpourings to which Canadians are exposed. If that had been the case, Mr. Coppola would have indirectly received consumers' money via government, although he was incapable of attracting consumers' dollars directly through his movies. The resultant movie production, of course, would reflect the tastes and interests of the bureaucrats controlling the outpouring of money from the Canada Council rather than the average North American viewer.

This is why we must oppose government control of grants to cultural activities. The only way people should be able to get money for cultural—or any other such—activities is by attracting the general public directly to spend their money on it. Who better to judge what the public wants than the public itself? *M.W.*

BISHOPS PASTORAL LETTER ON THE ECONOMY

The Canadian Conference of Catholic Bishops (Episcopal Commission for Social Affairs) is to be congratulated for its report, *Ethical Reflections on the Economic Crisis*. When 1.5 million people out of a labour force of slightly less than 12 million cannot find a job, in large part because of the economic policies pursued by government, this is not only an economic problem but a moral one as well.

The bishops' report is grounded on and begins with a "fundamental gospel principle" called the preferential option for the poor, the afflicted, and the oppressed. It is indeed rare in the annals of political economy that such a concern should even be mentioned let alone used as a foundation for the entire analysis. The bishops are, therefore, to be congratulated for this expression. However, it is one thing to identify with the oppressed emotionally but quite a different matter to fashion programmes which will actually help them. One of the major shortcomings of the bishops' statement is that despite its avowed concern for those at the bottom of the economic pyramid, it urges policies which will have the diametrically opposite effect of the results sought and expected.

For example, the bishops advocate an industrial strategy of low technology and high labour intensity. Motivated by the best intentions, they nevertheless fall victim to the specious argument that there is only so much work to be done and, if machines do more of it, less will remain for people to do.

On these grounds, the logical conclusion would be to end modern technology. The entire earth's population, to say nothing of a mere 1.5 million Canadians, could be employed in carrying by hand (in 100-pound parcels) all freight now transported between Vancouver and Halifax. But this Luddite vision and the low productivity associated with it would consign most of the world's peoples to death by starvation and those few who remained to living a life of poverty known last in the Stone Age.

The bishops call for greater emphasis on financial support for the poor and the unemployed. On humanitarian grounds, emergency economic aid of this sort can surely be justified. But once passed a certain threshold, it can threaten to promote continued unemployment.

In Canada, a family of four with one breadwinner can actually receive more money from welfare payments than in the form of after tax income from low wage employment. At the time of the bishops' writing, in British Columbia, for example, the minimum wage level was $3.65 per hour. At 40 hours per week, this translated into a monthly after tax, take-home pay of $562.52.

But the same family was entitled to $415 in support allowances, plus anywhere up to $455 in the form of shelter allowances, adding up to a relatively hefty $870 per month at maximum.

True, such a family could apply to the B.C. Ministry of Human Resources to make up the difference between actual earnings and welfare entitlements, so it would not actually lose out by engaging in paid labour. But it is the rare individual who would willingly give up his full-time leisure for the dubious prospects of low wage employment. Such a system is truly generous—but generous to a fault. It should be curtailed—in the interests of employment.

Next, the bishops single out labour unions to play a more decisive role in curing unemployment. Of course, the view of unions held by most Canadians is that of a long-suffering underdog, struggling valiantly against overwhelming odds to improve the wages and working conditions of all employees. But we must realize that the poor, the afflicted, the oppressed, those at the very bottom of the economic pyramid, are not found on union rolls in any great numbers. As well, unions have strongly supported legislation which impacts heavily, and negatively, on those at the bottom of the economic pyramid—textile tariffs, the minimum wage law, and opposition to prison labour all come to mind.

Bailouts for large corporations, subsidies to the arts, to sport, protective tariffs which make it impossible to import cheap products from abroad, marketing boards which artificially raise the prices of items such as eggs and milk, subsidies to export companies to allow them to sell more cheaply in foreign markets, foreign aid (which goes mainly to wealthy leaders of impoverished countries), these and more are all ways in which monies are forcibly transferred from the poor and given to the rich. One looks in vain to the bishops for any condemnation of practices such as these.

The bishops themselves, and the pundits as well, have interpreted their statement as a critique of capitalism. But whatever it is, the bishops' report is not and cannot be a critique of laissez faire capitalism, for it dealt with the Canadian economy of 1982-83, an economy which has many facets of public ownership and involvement. Therefore, in objecting to the unemployment which characterized the Canadian economy at that time, the bishops can and must be interpreted as objecting to the operation of our modern mixed economy. This is an economy in which government production of goods and services and government regulation and taxation account for nearly 50 percent of all economic activity.

Had the bishops concentrated on this needless, inefficient, and counter-productive government intervention, and on a swollen, burgeoning public sector, they would have much more nearly focused attention on the real cause of poverty in Canada—and in the rest of the world as well. *W.B.*

BRITISH COLUMBIA RESOURCES INVESTMENT CORPORATION (BCRIC)

The British Columbia Resources Investment Corporation was privatized in 1979 by the Social Credit government as an example of "people's capitalism." About 10 million common shares were distributed free of charge to the people of British Columbia and approximately 80 million more were voluntarily purchased by the public at $6 per share, making BCRIC the most widely held stock issue in Canada.

At the time, this giveaway was hailed as a success. It was widely credited with shoring up the political fortunes of the Social Credit Party. For the first time in the history of Crown corporations, the average citizen really owned "public property." He or she had a share of stock to prove it. This certificate provided direct income, and could be turned in for cash whenever other opportunities seemed more worthwhile.

But then the bubble seemed to burst. The share price plummeted from a high of more than $9 and began to hover at the $3 level. (At the time of the present writing, BCRIC shares are worth approximately $1.00.)

Bullish stock analysts became bearish about the future prospects of BCRIC. The whines and complaints of numerous small stockholders—who never before owned corporate shares—were widely publicized. And pundits and commentators who had all along opposed the privatization experiment for ideological reasons had, at long last, an easy target. It was agreed on all sides that BCRIC was a failure.

In our view, however, the BCRIC privatization was a success regardless of its share price. BCRIC would still be a success even if the company ultimately went bankrupt. Those who think otherwise do not understand the function and purpose of privatization.

The purpose of privatization is to transfer resources from the public to the private sector, not to guarantee that these transferred resources shall always and forever retain their market values at issue. On this basis, the BCRIC giveaway must be considered a success (although some important vestiges of government involvement such as the prohibition of concentrated ownership, still remain). A Crown corporation, previously protected from the vicissitudes of competition, was cast off from the public trough and left to sink or swim under its own power. For the first time, all citizens of B.C. were no longer forced to bear the risk and responsibility for "owning BCRIC shares." Now, only those who wished to bear this risk could do so—by taking stock ownership upon themselves.

Secondly, our economy needs a way of diverting investment funds away from "lemons" and toward productive enterprises. Why sink more and more money into a declining horse-and-buggy type industry (even though feather bedding jobs can be saved there) when the money can be better spent in the expanding sectors of the economy where better and more productive employment can be created?

Unless business is allowed to survive on its own merits, investment funds cannot be automatically allocated to their highest and most valued uses. This is why even a bankrupt private BCRIC would be preferable to a "viable" B.C. Crown corporation. If the resource options owned by BCRIC were scheduled to decline in importance anyway, far better that this be allowed to occur as it would in the private option (assuming no Chrysler-type bailouts). The alternative is to continually throw good money after bad, which occurs when a Crown-owned commercial enterprise is allowed access to the public trough.

In any case, the resources of a bankrupt private corporation do not simply disappear into the thin air. On the contrary, under corporate reorganization they tend to fall, ultimately, into the hands of those who value them the most—the highest bidders. True, the stockholders will take a financial beating, but that is the downside risk the capitalist always bears, complaints of unsophisticated first-time investors unused to taking capital losses notwithstanding.

Thirdly, it is difficult to tell whether BCRICs acquisition of Kaiser Resources, and subsequent consulting contract with Edgar Kaiser, was responsible for its financial doldrums. This is a chapter of economic history that has yet to be fully written. Whatever the facts, let us assume for the sake of argument that this decision was a serious blunder on the part of BCRIC management. Privatization is still justified. First of all, who is to say that had BCRIC remained under Crown ownership, management would not have made even worse choices? Secondly, and more importantly, society is better off with most of its resources under private management, because there is a universal tendency for public sector managers to be less efficient. Private managers have a unique advantage over their public sector counterparts, the profit and loss system.

Just as a relatively weak team sometimes makes it to the Grey Cup, it sometimes happens that a poor manager is given control of private resources and survives in this role for a time. And examples of super-efficient public sector management sometimes occur as well, despite the lack of a profit and loss weeding out system. But these are exceptions to the rule. Under the hypothetical assumptions we are making (BCRIC mismanagement), BCRIC might well be such an exception. The principle of privatization, however, still holds true. Over the long haul, and for the preponderance of cases, more reliance may be placed on the efficiency of private rather than public managers because of the incentives they face.

There are now several hundred Crown corporations in Canada, federal and provincial. When the various government bureaus and departments are added to this total, we find public enterprise pervading literally every nook and cranny of the Canadian economy. As the state clasps more and more business to its bosom, it substitutes planning by fiat and edict for the price and wage signals which are an integral part of the market process. And when prices are not based on the knowledgeable and freely made decisions of millions of individual economic actors, it is impossible for the price system to play its co-ordinating role.

Privatization is the last best hope for returning these tasks to the (almost always) more efficient private sector. The BCRIC episode was a trailblazer in this regard. It was a complete success in transferring control from the public to the private sector. It must be emulated again and again if the Canadian economy is to prosper in the coming years. *W.B.*

BRITISH DISEASE

The Ontario Labour Relations Board in a majority decision has ruled that political campaigning by trade unions in the workplace is not protected under Ontario provincial law. In other words, employers will be able to prevent union members from canvassing for political purposes in the workplace. This is a major block to a canvassing plan launched by the Canadian Labour Congress as one of the key elements in the trade union campaign to support the New Democratic Party.

Whatever one's politics, one must regard this as a fortuitous and beneficial development. The history of the involvement of the labour movement with politics has not been a good one. It will serve neither the interests of the labour movement nor the development of effective political institutions in this country.

The principal evidence on this score arises from the British scene where the Trade Union Congress and the Labour Party have been intertwined for many years. The consequence of this inter-marriage has often been unfortunate, and one of the offspring is undoubtedly the British disease. However they may characterize their position in society, unions do not represent the total interests of the citizens of a country and, as a consequence, will often be in favour of policies which are opposed to the public interest.

As Lady Barbara Wootton, a Labour Peer in the U.K. House of Lords, put it some years ago, "it is the business of a union to be anti-social, the members would have a just grievance if their officials and committees ceased to put sectional interests first." In other words, it is the business of unions to serve the specific interests of their members and not to serve the public interest.

A particularly glaring example of the conflict between the public interest and the union interest is to be found in the Labour Party's support for many years of inflationary fiscal policy to underwrite the effects of labour's attempts to raise the wages of guild workers or union members. Excessive wage demands which cannot be fulfilled are underwritten by an inflationary monetary policy to the general detriment of society, whereas union members benefit in the short term from such a policy.

Similarly, legislation which serves to exacerbate the workplace monopoly enjoyed by unions has often been enacted by labour governments under pressure from trade union supporters and to the detriment of workers in general.

It is entirely understandable that the Canadian Labour Congress wishes to become more actively involved in politics. It would enhance their power and their ability to use general legislation to seek the specific and narrow interests of the labour movement. However, it is not a development which Canadians should welcome and, therefore, we should rejoice at this stopgap in the union movement's attempt to become officially engaged in political action.

In the words of the Ontario Labour Relations Board Chairman George Adams, "a trade union should not be able to use its certified bargaining agent status to capture an audience for its political canvassing activities." *M.W.*

BROADCAST REGULATION

The Canadian Radio-Television and Telecommunications Commission has been holding hearings to determine whether or not religious organizations should be allowed to have broadcasting licences of their own. This is a crucially important issue. But why should this small group of CRTC commissioners be dictating such a choice at all?

The weakness in the present system of deciding such questions is easily seen. Suppose religious institutions were not allowed to publish newspapers, magazines, and journals without government permission. Suppose, that is, that the top circulation Canadian religious publications had to first convince a "Canadian Newspaper, Magazine and Journal Commission" of the worthiness of their endeavours, of the public interest inherent in their periodicals, and of the desire of millions of people that they be in existence—just to mention a few of the arguments put before the CRTC.

"But, but, sputter, sputter," say the opponents of a competitive enterprise in broadcast journalism, "a free market cannot function for the airwaves. People cannot be allowed the freedom to bid for broadcasting rights." For the following reasons.

First, the electromagnetic spectrum is not the sort of thing that can be privately owned, as can newspapers, magazines, and journals. It is a public good, and must of necessity be administered by the public authorities.

This argument is bolstered by early experience in radio. In the late 1920s, when radio was in its infancy, different stations would actually encroach on each other's frequencies, bringing disorganization and chaos to the entire enterprise. This was the result of the failure to set proper boundaries on the spectrum between the frequencies of neighbouring broadcasters and to ensure broadcast property rights to those who had first "homesteaded" the airwaves. Without clearly defined and protected property rights, no industry can function properly. All that was needed in the 1920s was to bring lawfulness to this industry. The government did finally set frequency boundaries, but also accorded to itself all broadcast rights—doling them out on a temporary and periodic basis in the form of licences.

Luckily for our free society, government did not seize similar power in the print industry, but the argument is very similar. If government can demand control over radio and TV on the grounds that chaos will ensue without clearly defined and protected property rights, it can do so in the print (or any other) industry with equal logic. Surely, newspapers and magazines could not be published if they were free to grab each other's scarce and valuable paper, ink, printing presses, and other factors of production.

Secondly, there aren't enough radio and TV frequencies to go around to satisfy everyone who wants one.

Welcome to the real world—one of economic scarcity. This is precisely the definition of any economic good or service: something which people want more of—at a zero price—than is available. The answer to this problem—when it arises in the case of limited ships and sealing wax, snails and puppy dogs—is to allow a price to be charged so that the scarce supply can be rationed among the more numerous demanders. It is a basic axiom of economics that there exists an equilibrium price, at which point the amount demanded will equal the amount supplied. This holds true for every other good or service and would obtain as well in the market for broadcasting rights. If such a market were allowed, no individual, group, or firm that could afford a radio or TV station would have to do without.

The identical problem, moreover, has been solved in the print journalism field. There is not enough newsprint, paper, ink, typographical equipment—to say nothing of the highly skilled labour necessary to gather the news, work the machinery, and the talent necessary to co-ordinate the whole enterprise—to give a periodical to everyone who wants one.

Scarce goods are rationed to the highest bidder in the absence of a newspaper commission to oversee the whole process. There is no earthly reason this market system could not work for the electronic spectrum as well—without CRTC interference.

The above analysis holds true for AM and FM radio and for VHF television. But the situation is vastly different on the UHF television band. There, according to informed sources in the industry, only two percent of all available Canadian bands are in use. This means that any religious broadcaster who wanted one could, at least theoretically, have a UHF band assigned to him—without displacing anyone else.

Of course other special interest groups will also seek broadcasting outlets. And why ever should they not? Special interests—including groups representing every stripe of opinion in politics, economics, philosophy, psychology, and religion—have attained their own print outlets. There are newspapers, magazines, journals, and other periodicals in glorious profusion which give vent to their views with no obvious harm to our society. Why should it be any different for our electronic media?

Thirdly, the needs of a modern pluralistic society can be best met under the guidance of the CRTC, which will ensure that all programming be balanced and in the public interest; that no one group can own an entire station to do with it what it will.

But why should the very disparate views of a modern pluralistic society be forced to pass muster before a small group of commissioners? This is not at all consistent with true pluralism, and has not been found necessary in the print media. Imagine this "balance" doctrine applied to the churches themselves. It would mean that each denomination would have to "balance" its programme to include representation of all other denominations and even all other religions. After all, is it "fair" that the Anglicans feature only Anglican programmes at their services? Shouldn't they be forced to give "equal time" to Jews, Hindus, Catholics, and Lutherans?

This doctrine is dangerous for and ultimately destructive to all our free institutions. Any of the organs of society—factories, schools, sports arenas, hospitals, recreational facilities, as well as churches, are open to the charge of specializing in one or a few things, and of being "unbalanced." Must we insist on a bland sameness in all our conduct? Hardly. Our interests in diversity may best be served by means of free competition in ideas, by allowing a veritable tower of babel of different voices—not by insisting that each and every person or institution soberly "balance" its views to represent an amalgam of all possible shades of opinion on every issue.

True "balance" may best be served by allowing people to set up their own electronic soap boxes to put forth their own views, a sort of Hyde Park Corner of the airwaves.

The case for continuing the CRTC as the ultimate authority of the nation's airwaves is extremely weak. It is an affront to the religious people of the nation who seek to purchase broadcasting stations and to all those who hold dear the rights of free speech. *W.B.*

BUILT-IN OBSOLESCENCE

Toronto Alderwoman June Rowlands is leading a campaign to stamp out injustice. The focus of her attentions is not, as you might expect, the plight of the unemployed, the difficulties faced by low income Torontonians, or even the scandalous condition of the animals in the Toronto Zoo. No, Rowlands' cause célèbre is the lowly pantyhose. According to Rowlands, the women of Canada are being used by hosiery manufacturers who produce a product which doesn't stand up, which constantly runs, and which is much less than they would be capable of producing if they had the true interests of consumers at heart.

Rowlands' campaign, therefore, is to have manufacturers produce a truly durable nylon stocking so the women of Canada will no longer have to pay $12 to $15 per month to purchase new hosiery. Ms. Rowlands is not even above citing the "good old days" when nylon stockings really did the job and very much less of a working person's income had to be expended to purchase this necessary item. Moreover, she maintains, nylon can be produced in a form literally as tough as nails, and there is no reason why manufacturers could not make a nylon stocking which would last forever.

What is interesting about this campaign, this pandemonium in a pantyhose, is that it reflects an underlying current which often is exhibited by consumer advocates, that is, the notion of built-in obsolescence. The argument is that manufacturers consciously design products which will wear out quickly so the poor consumer will have to buy more. Since it is the well-known ambition of every producer to make as much profit as he or she can, the built-in obsolescence argument has a certain plausibility. However, since there are usually several competing capitalists anxious to get their hands on the consumer's dollar, why is it that at least one of them doesn't take this sure route to the consumer's heart and produce a truly durable pantyhose?

Of course, the answer is that there indeed is built-in obsolescence but it is designed not by manufactures but by consumers. With many competing manufacturers of pantyhose or automobiles or refrigerators or whatever the product is, the one that will make the most profit is the one that provides consumers with the product they want. Maybe it is the case that consumers do want a $25 pair of pantyhose that would be virtually indestructible and that could be used, in addition, to strain spaghetti and snare rabbits. However, it is at least conceivable that the reason pantyhose manufacturers produce cheap, easily run pantyhose is because that is precisely what consumers want. Consumers are not flocking to purchase more expensive, sturdier hose but in fact are shunning them in favour of the easy to buy, cheap, disposable variety. The same, of course, is true of automobiles. The stainless steel DeLorean automobile which would be virtually impervious to Canada's salty winters did not prove to be an overwhelming commercial success because people were not willing to pay the relatively high price that automobile carried.

So, when we reflect upon the "good old days" when products were made to last and ask ourselves why it is that products aren't built to last today, the answer isn't that there is a conspiracy amongst producers. It is, rather, that not too durable products are a fundamental reflection of modern day consumers' attitudes. If June Rowlands really believes the public has been yearning for a durable, high-priced nylon stocking, why doesn't she start a firm to produce one? If what she says is true, she would make a handsome profit. *M.W.*

B B B B B B B B B B B B B B B B B B B B B B

BUY LOCAL

As a gesture of good corporate citizenship, Suncor Inc. of Toronto has instituted a "buy Canadian" policy. According to the terms of this order, Suncor suppliers will automatically award contracts to Canadian bidders unless their offer is more than 5 percent or $5,000 higher than the lowest bid received. Even in this case, company officials may still approve the high Canadian bid.

The company brags that so far $92 million worth of contracts have been let on the expansion of its Sarnia Ontario refinery—all of them to Canadian companies. This includes 217 orders to Canadian producers, of which 180 have gone to Ontario concerns. According to Wayne Wright, the Vice President of Suncor in charge of the refinery project, the company was originally aiming at 85 percent Canadian content but will in all likelihood achieve 90 percent.

Is this a gesture of good corporate citizenship? No. One doesn't know what goal Suncor is trying to achieve, but it is certainly not the economic well-being of the Canadian public. This is such a mistaken policy it could only be undertaken by a corporation shielded from the winds of competition, as is Suncor, ever since the Government of Ontario bought 25 percent of its shares for $650 million in 1981.

The interests of the Canadian people will best be served by the lowest possible prices for consumer items. But low prices cannot be achieved under a policy which purposely accepts high bids. Were any fully private company to undertake such an irresponsible course of action, it would soon achieve the bankruptcy status it so richly deserves and bother us no more. But when a publicly supported company like Suncor does this, it can long persist, thanks to the heavily suffering Canadian taxpayer.

But what of Canadian employment? Surely this policy will create jobs in the country? Yes, of course it will. But the employment opportunities will arise in areas where Canadians are inefficient—otherwise there would have been no need for a buy Canadian policy in the first place.

We Canadians could, if we so desired, create tens of thousands of jobs here in banana production. All we need do is spend millions of dollars on gigantic hothouses, and millions more on the energy needed to coddle these tropical fruits in our northern climate. Although it is not an extreme case, the Suncor buy Canadian experiment operates under the same ridiculous principle. If we are to have any hope for an improved standard of living, the Suncor policy must stop at once! *W.B.*

C

CANADA POST

Canada Post ought to be privatized. As a Crown corporation, it is a dismal failure. On poor postal service, everyone has their own favourite horror stories. But any list must include the Jesuit Priest in Toronto who in 1979 received a postcard mailed to him in 1947, and the Kitchener Post Office which lost 500 bulletins from a local golf club—for the second year in a row—certainly deserves honourable mention.

Regarding surliness, we can each relate our own tales of woe, but these take place on an individual, private basis, unknown to anyone else. Not so are the public statements by then Prime Minister Pierre Elliot Trudeau, who mused that the post office might do away with home delivery of mail altogether (it's such a bother) on the spurious ground that postal service is a privilege, not a right. (Can you picture the milkman, the druggist, or the department store owner threatening to end home delivery for this reason?) The public statement of then Postmaster-General André Ouellet, surely deserves first prize in the surliness sweepstakes. Said this worthy to businessmen complaining of shoddy unreliable service, "I can't accept that businessmen have to rely on the post office to make a living. If they do, they had better find other ways."

As for insensitivity, everything else palls into insignificance compared to the initial refusal of the post office to issue a Terry

Fox stamp while that Canadian hero was still alive. Such behaviour, of course, is only to be expected from an organization protected by a government grant of monopoly privilege. It can ignore the wishes of its paying customers, secure in the knowledge that no competitor is standing in the wings waiting to take over any lost business.

Instead of considering any superficial innovations to Canada Post, let us get to the crux of the matter and consider a completely different alternative: the introduction of the bracing and invigorating winds of competition into the mail service industry—the ending, that is, of all legal prohibitions against private mail delivery.

How would a private postal system in Canada work? Simple. Government could announce that henceforth the rules prohibiting competition with the post office were null and void. Then, anyone who wanted to could set up his or her own mail delivery firm, in competition with Canada Post. Private companies would be allowed to compete with government enterprise, as now occurs in such diverse fields as publishing, energy, airlines, mining, and ground transportation. The result we could expect would be lower prices, more efficiency, better service, and a greater consideration for the sensibilities of the Canadian public.

Such a proposal is in keeping with the philosophy which presumably underlies the present Combines Investigation Act; it is to render the Canadian economy more competitive. It would be hypocritical and inconsistent to push for more competition in the private sector under combines legislation while continuing to allow a post office Crown corporation to hide from competition behind government skirts.

There are of course several objections to competitive mail delivery. Let us consider them. First, it has never been done before. In many ways, we are slaves to the tyranny of the status quo. Competing private post offices are not within the actual experiences of any living person, so we conclude that such a scheme is wild-eyed and cannot work. It is a mistake, however, to think that just because a thing has never been done, it therefore cannot be done.

Had the government always been in the business of manufacturing shoes and someone asserted that private enterprise could probably accomplish this task as well, he would probably be laughed out of court. People would ask derisively, how many private shoe manufacturers would there be? Who would determine the length of shoe laces? The styles? The colors? And most telling of all, how would poor children ever be able to afford to buy shoes? Yet, in our present economy, all of these "problems" are solved without fuss or fanfare. Indeed, these questions never even arise.

So, even had there never been a working example of private delivery in operation, this would not prove the idea impracticable. Fortunately for the literal-minded, however, history is replete with such cases. Wells-Fargo, Pony Express, and the American Letter Mail companies were all private concerns that functioned and prospered during the last century—until driven out of business by laws instituting a government monopoly post office.

In the present era, independent courier and delivery services include D-Line, Speedy, Loomis, BCD, Purolator and Canpar. There was also a husband-and-wife postal company in Rochester, N.Y., which successfully competed with the U.S. postal service for first-class mail delivery—until forced out of business by post office monopoly laws.

The second objection is that private mail delivery services would "skim off the cream" by concentrating on the lucrative urban centres (where even the present post office can operate in the black) and ignoring the unprofitable rural and outlying areas.

This, however, is an argument for competition in mail delivery, not against it. Under the present system, the government charges far less than the full costs for rural postal service and makes up for this by highly overcharging cheap-to-deliver urban mail. This is unwise and uneconomic. It artificially stifles the growth and development of Canadian business located in cities by, in effect, imposing an extra tax on mail communication.

True, the mail subsidy in remote areas of our country encourages settlement there. But this is yet another argument for, not against, competition. The reason is simple. There is no public policy benefit whatever to be obtained by artificially encouraging the over-settlement of Canadians in outlying districts.

The economic reason for migrating to a wilderness or tundra location is the additional wealth to be obtained there. If so, then the economic (or psychic) surplus should be sufficient to defray the extra costs of importing mail service. The price of food, entertainment, fuel, and other items reflects additional transportation costs to the northern climes. Why not mail?

Newspapers, periodicals, and junk mail also receive a postal subsidy. (This is perhaps an important explanation for the popularity of the present system throughout large segments of the media and the business community.) But the same analysis applies here as well. There is simply no public policy justification for this sector of the economy not pulling its full weight. Resources cannot be optimally allocated and consumer sovereignty assured unless all goods and services are worth more to buyers then the full costs necessary to produce them. The third class mail subsidy, moreover, is a regressive tax on the poor who are under-represented in the ranks of its beneficiaries.

A third objection is that with private competing post office companies, there would be great confusion as to prices, reliability, quality of service, extras, and so on. Welcome to the real world. This is what competition is all about—continual struggle on the part of each firm to lower prices, improve product offers, and increase reliability and service.

Naturally, under such conditions, there will be a certain amount of "confusion." This is a necessary symptom of progress, and usually a sign of economic health. Witness the continually changing state-of-the-art regarding business office equipment, telecommunications, computers, satellite dishes, video discs and tapes. If electronic mail is to be effectively introduced, it will certainly not be done by a moribund monopoly Crown corporation post office.

Those who relish continuity, stolidity, and old ways of doing things can be served by the marketplace as well. All that needs to be done is to continue to patronize Canada Post (the Crown corporation). There is nothing to fear from the private sector. If enough people simply ignore private postal firms, they will go away soon enough.

A final objection to competitive mail delivery is that labour relations would be exacerbated. On the contrary, there is every reason to expect a labour relations improvement from competition in the postal industry. It is difficult to imagine how labour relations could possibly worsen under competition. The record of the Canadian postal service is truly unenviable. Under the present monopoly, when any of the postal unions walk off the job, Canadian postal service is stopped dead in its tracks. But with both potential and actual competing private firms, it would be far more difficult to end service entirely. Any such occurrence would immediately encourage the expansion of already existing firms and the creation of new ones.

We must conclude that the case for competition in mail delivery is a compelling one. It will help consumers, business people, and the entire Canadian economy. These changes are long overdue. *W.B.*

CANADIAN BROADCASTING CORPORATION (CBC)

Employees of the CBC were informed that the cutbacks in the corporation's budget would imply a loss of jobs for some of those employed in operations across the country. While the loss experienced by these employees is unfortunate, it must be recognized that the basic move to curtail subsidies to the CBC is a move in the right direction. Unfortunately, the government has not gone far enough and, in our view, has missed a sterling opportunity to do something truly constructive.

In observing the CBC budget cuts, the average Canadian could be forgiven for not placing them in the context of the saga which is the doleful tale of the CBCs recent past. However, such perspective is essential in helping evaluate the torrent of abuse which has fallen on the head of the government.

A few excerpts from a 1978 Fraser Institute study calling for the privatization of CBC station operations indicate what we mean. The first relates to the corporation's role in fostering national unity—a much referred to critical function. "The CBC, as everyone knows, operates an English and a French network. It decided to centralize production and programming in Toronto for the English network and in Montreal for the French network—a classic example of operationalizing the concept of the 'two solitudes.' There is minimal co-operation and interchange between the networks—a sort of cultural apartheid." This situation prompted Mr. H.J. Boyle (then Chairman of the CRTC) to write to Prime Minister Trudeau: "the CBC has thereby, in the Commission's view, failed in its very important responsibility to 'contribute to the development of national unity'."

Notwithstanding the current tide of opinion to the effect that the CBC plays an important part in the cultural affairs of the nation, the 1970s report of the Committee of Inquiry into National Broadcasting Service issued a damning indictment of the CBCs role. But the most problematic aspect of the CBCs operations is the fact that it is essentially beyond anyone's control.

In 1977, the CRTC reported that "certain anomalies in the setting up of the CBC have made it basically accountable to nobody, and, as a bureaucratic reflex action, it consistently rejects all efforts to make it accountable. This was evident in the CBCs response to this inquiry, in its refusal to permit detailed examination, below the management level, of the way in which practices, policies, and controls are carried out." This stands, of course, in sharp contrast to the extent to which private broadcasters are subject to supervision and inquisition by emissaries of the CRTC.

Of course, the CBC delivers a wonderful service to many Canadians. It also delivers a lot of material of questionable value but which is beyond the control of Parliament or the tastes of the Canadian radio and television consumer. The way to make it accountable in the way that other broadcasters are and sensitive to the needs of the Canadian consumers of public affairs, news, and cultural programming is to make the CBC a private broadcasting service similar to the PBS system in the United States.

Quite apart from the other advantages of doing so, privatization would empower local CBC managers to separately raise the revenues they require to retain their staffs — a freedom not available under the system which now exists.

To those who believe the Canadian public would not choose to support a privatized public broadcasting system with voluntary contributions, one can only reply that if Canadians don't voluntarily support the system, why does it exist?

There are other reasons for concern about CBCs operations. For years, those of us who are called conservatives, neo-conservatives, capitalists, or free market supporters, have been concerned about the tendency of the Canadian Broadcasting Corporation, which some call State Radio, to give undue attention to the views of those with a leftist perspective. As sometime decorative items on that network, we have often marvelled at the unabashed way productions are slanted to provide systematic exposure of what could be called a left of centre philosophy. We never say much about this sort of thing because, of course, one's perceptions can be influenced by one's own views.

Now, evidence has been assembled by three university professors from two different parts of the country which seems to confirm widespread perceptions. According to Professor Barry Cooper, Lydia Miljan, and Maria Vigilante, left-wing opinion outweighs right-wing opinion three to one on public affairs programming. This result emerged from a study of some 1,400 stories during a four-month period and is no casual passing impression. In an interview with the *Globe and Mail*, Margaret Lyons, CBCs Vice President of English Language radio service, noted that "CBC radio follows a very firm journalistic policy of fairness and balance and every program is reviewed constantly to see that it meets these standards." One might well ask, who is it that surveys the network to see that balance is obtained? In the words of these three researchers, "when important political points of view are involved and criticism of government is expressed, the CBC adopts a left-wing ideological perspective."

As well, CBC stations costs 233 percent more to operate than do their private counterparts. Converting them to private operation would save between $108 million and $134 million on an annual basis, plus providing a one-time increase in revenues when these stations were sold off.

Why, therefore, be so tentative? Why not, instead of merely controlling the CBCs budget, eliminate it entirely and turn it over to private enterprise? Where is the case for giving a radio and TV network to Big Brother for his very own? The traditional media role is as a watchdog over all aspects of society—business, religion, sports, education—but especially government. CBC, as presently constituted, is destructive of these ends. It is an incestuous relationship, more in keeping with the UNs New World Information Order with government at the helm of communications than it is in keeping with our traditions of separation of government and media. *M.W.*

CAPITAL SPENDING

The headline read "Capital Spending Rise Aids Recovery," and the story on the front page of the business section of one of our most highly respected Canadian newspapers went on to outline the details. Just like they teach in journalism, it gave the what, where, why, when, and how. It painted in glowing terms the quantity of new capital spending, it quoted the prominent investors, it marshalled the statistics on overall investment in the economy, and it confidently looked forward to rising prosperity as a result of all this economic activity.

There was only one thing wrong with this exercise in business journalism—it forgot about common sense. Careful consideration leads us to question the notion that capital spending necessarily enhances economic recovery, as claimed in this story and in virtually every other such story written by the financial press in Canada.

In order to better dispel this myth, let us consider a case where investment does not help the living standards of the people involved. Exhibit A in any such study must surely be the pyramids of Egypt. Now here was investment on a grand scale. Can't you just see the business journalists of the day waxing eloquent about what a shot in the arm these pyramids will be for the Egyptian economy? Why, they could babble on about the number of new jobs it created and the thousands of gigantic stone blocks used in the construction. They could quote the Egyptian Princes to the effect that this investment will promote economic growth.

Actually, of course, this investment was a complete loss from the point of view of the average ancient Egyptian worker. He needed these pyramids like he needed a second nose on the back of his head. This massive capital expenditure had tremendous alternative costs—all the goods and services which would actually have improved his life style but which could not be produced because of pyramid construction.

It is the same thing in the modern day. Take, for example, a multi-billion dollar investment in arctic oil exploration. If oil is discovered, well and good. But if the expedition fails to locate sufficient oil to make the venture profitable, the entire operation is a drain on the economy, not an expansion.

If the Swiss Family Robinson invests lumber, hundreds of person-hours, and part of their precious stock of nails in a rowboat which sinks in a storm the next day, did this investment help the family economy or hurt it? Obviously, this investment was an economic detriment, not a benefit.

The point is, not every investment is good for the economy. This is the idea which escapes most business journalists. One cannot assume, merely because an investment takes place, that it will aid, increase, or enhance economic recovery. It may well have the very opposite result.

Investments can fail for many reasons. In the case of the pyramids or the Edsel automobile or many Broadway plays, the investment fails because consumer demand for the product simply is not there. In the case of oil drilling or many resource explorations, the investment fails because there really isn't any gold in them thar hills, at least not in sufficient quantities to be commercially exploitable. In the case of the Swiss Family Robinson rowboat or the tragic loss of the Ocean Ranger, the investment fails because of poor planning, poor management, or poor construction coupled with a natural disaster.

But investment can fail for many other reasons: because the market is satiated; because, by the time it takes to bring the new product on stream, people have long since changed their minds; because, while all the investment is taking place, a new invention or innovation comes along which obviates the need for the product; because complementary factors of production—land, labour, capital, transportation—are not available, at least at the prices predicted; because of changes in weather, consumer preferences, or styles; because of strikes; or because of government nationalizations, regulations, or subsidies to competitors. The list goes on and on.

And what of the businessman who succeeds in making a profitable investment, overcomes all these pitfalls, and enhances the economic well-being of consumers? We ought to hold ticker tape parades for these people. We ought to carry them around town on our shoulders. We ought to pour champagne on their heads like we do for sports victors. We ought to realize that they are economic heroes to whom we owe our comfortable standards of living.

The correct understanding of investment's relationship to economic growth is further clouded by the fact that there will often be a direct relationship between decisions to make capital investments and economic growth. The reason is that most capital investments are made by firms which anticipate growth in their businesses. To the extent that that is a widespread expectation, successful investment decisions will always coincide to some degree with economic growth.

Let us return to our original headline: "Capital Spending Rise Aids Recovery." We can now see the error in this way of looking at things. When next we see this sort of thing in the business pages of our newspapers, hear it on the radio, or see it on TV, we can recognize it for the economic fallacy it is. *W.B.*

CENSUS—THE ECONOMICS OF COLLECTING STATISTICS

What is the case for government census-taking over and above mere head counts which are necessary for the determination of political representation? The usual economic argument in favour of such endeavours is that private enterprise will not undertake a modern-type census because it simply would not pay. Even though the information gathered will doubtless prove valuable, business firms will not undertake the arduous process, because they will not be able to collect. In technical economic jargon, there is a spillover problem; external economies are said to prevail where private census-takers will not be able to capture the full benefits of their efforts. But there are problems with this view.

The main beneficiaries of government census-taking are empirically-oriented economists who use this material in their economic regression equations. This argument is a self-serving attempt to pull the wool over the eyes of the general public, if ever there was one. (By the way, the Fraser Institute, an empirically-oriented economic research think tank, is also a free-rider on tax financed public sector censuses. Nevertheless, this is certainly no argument for continuing this raid on the public trough.)

Although beloved of many economists, we must reject this argument. Contrary to their views, there is an entire information industry in the private sector. It consists of computer firms, the media, public opinion polling, market research, consumer reports, and measures of business confidence. Of course there are spillovers. Private firms are never able to perfectly capture all the benefits of their operations, but they are still able to operate despite these externalities.

If statisticians, econometricians, and mathematical economists want this data collected, let them, or their employers, pay for it. Census Canada should limit itself to head counts. If there is enough support for an all-encompassing statistical census on the part of private individuals and firms, then the marketplace will provide it—at a price which reflects the full costs. *W.B.*

CAESAR CHAVEZ EFFECT

A number of years ago Caesar Chavez sprang to the headlines across North America as a leader of the downtrodden. He virtually singlehandedly was successful in mobilizing farmworkers in California to form unions and subsequently press for a "fairer" wage. Canadian residents were involved in that struggle because they were asked on a widespread basis to boycott grapes and lettuce which were being shipped from California by employers who were the target of unionization attempts. The growers, although harassed by the activities of Mr. Chavez and his United Farm Workers, were managing to ship quite a volume of grapes to their normal markets.

Ultimately, the campaign of boycott and harassment was successful in that Mr. Chavez succeeded in unionizing some 50,000 workers—including grapepickers—in California. And, of course, working conditions and wages earned by the grapepickers improved dramatically under the strike threat and other paraphernalia of organized labour.

Thus far the story is not that different from that which many industries have faced; however, this particular story does not have a happy ending for the grapepickers involved.

Recently we had the good fortune to tour Napa Valley, one of the most famous grape and wine producing regions of California. During the course of our tour, as economists are wont to do, we began discussing the economics of the industry with various people with whom we came in contact. Needless to say, we studiously avoided asking any pointed questions about the recent difficulties with Mr. Chavez and the development of the union presence in the grape and wine industry.

It was pointed out to us, without prompting, that one of the prospective developments in the industry was research into new strains of grapes. These new grapes, it was said, would be more limited in variety than the existing grape stocks and potentially less interesting from the point of view of wine consumers. Why was it that such developments would occur? The reason was the increasing adoption of mechanical grapepickers in the vineyards. This, in turn, was a consequence of the fact that the cost of hiring grapepickers had gotten to the point where some mechanical solution to the harvesting problem had to be found.

The consequences of the mechanical grapepicker in the vineyards of California can be inferred from the earlier experience with tomato and vegetable harvesters. In the case of California tomatoes, a tomato harvester displaces roughly 91 man-hours per acre of tomatoes harvested or roughly 20 million man-hours of harvest labour eliminated per year of operation of the harvesters. The reduction per acre is from 163 man-hours to 72 man-hours, a development which can be expected to continue to some extent as current methods are refined and developed. Similar job displacement effects have been seen in vegetable harvesting.

Assuming that the grape harvesters have the same sort of effect, it is clear that one of the consequences of unionization of the industry will be a dramatic decline of employment in the industry and, indeed, that has already begun to occur in California. Current membership in the United Farm Workers Union is down to 30,000 from the apex of 50,000 and less than 10 percent of table grapes are now picked by union workers.

Mr. Chavez has not limited his activities to California. As well, he paid a visit to Canada for a morale boosting junket to shore up the waning spirits of agricultural workers in British Columbia who are in the process of attempting to organize for better wages.

One does not have to be a bleeding heart to acknowledge that ofttimes the working conditions of agricultural harvesting workers are far from ideal. In fact, the conditions which are most frequently depicted in press accounts of the plight of these workers can only be described as disastrous. And, of course, it is these living and working conditions that attract the attention of media and provide the raw material for the support which the general public usually lavishes on the conditions of such workers. That was certainly the case in the grape boycott and has certainly been the case in the recent attempts of Canadian agricultural workers to organize.

However, in analysing the situation of these workers and their future prospects, one must be somewhat less emotionally motivated and look at the harsh realities that these individuals face. In the first place, it must be recognized that the individuals involved in harvesting have very few alternative employment opportunities. In the Canadian case, they are almost entirely newly-arrived immigrants who have few language skills and little in the way of job training or other attributes that would recommend them to prospective employers. While the jobs they find in the agricultural industry may not be ideal employment, it is nevertheless employment. And, as menial labour has for millions of new Canadians, it may provide many newcomers to the country with the stepping-stone they need to find a more normal employment status in the community. It mustn't be forgotten that in many instances, while these agricultural workers are paid modest wages, their work is not worth more in the sense that they are being paid the value of their marginal contribution to the farm's output. Of course, the bottom line from the point of view of the employer is that they continue to be a better source of work effort than the mechanical devices which could replace them under some circumstances, due to cost of labour versus the cost of the machine.

Whether or not grapepickers will be entirely replaced by machines or whether Canadian farmworkers will find themselves displaced by the vegetable harvesters which have become so prevalent in California remains to be seen. However, the threat is clearly present and to the extent it is realized those workers who are displaced will have nothing for which to thank Caesar Chavez.

There will be some beneficiaries of Mr. Chavez's movement, however. These are the workers who continue to be employed in spite of the adoption of machinery. Obviously, even in the presence of mechanical harvesters there will be a requirement for some farmworkers and, as a result of the activities of unions, these workers will be more highly paid than otherwise.

The moral of the story, however, is that workers who are employed at the higher wage will not benefit at the expense of the employer. Mr. Chavez will not have achieved a victory over the "greedy" farmers or "greedy" winegrowers but rather over the unfortunate workers who have been displaced directly by the harvesters but indirectly by the activities of Mr. Chavez and his well-meaning movement. *M.W.*

CHEQUE CASHING FIRMS

Young aspiring MBA graduates do not look forward to careers with cheque cashing firms. These companies cash cheques for the poor, for welfare recipients, and for the unemployed. They do so with no identification required, but they charge a hefty fee—up to 10 percent of the total value of the cheque. They work behind bullet-proof windows, fingerprint their customers, and equip their stores with electronically locking doors to trap customers inside—in order to guard against the ever-present dangers of theft. Hardly your top-drawer, mainline, gilt-edged banking establishment. But they are open seven days a week, twelve hours a day, for easy convenience and people have been flocking to their doors.

The cheque cashing industry, however, is not without its critics, and they are legion, angry, and vociferous. The main accusation is that these firms take advantage of the poor. Says one self-styled poverty activist, "businesses that are basically leeches pop up during bad times to take advantage of people." And according to another, "they are a rip-off of the poor because they charge for cheque cashing while banks do it for free."

Vancouver City Council takes these charges seriously, and is so concerned that welfare and unemployment insurance recipients are being victimized that it is considering a proposed by-law that would set strict guidelines for the cheque cashers.

Who would benefit from such a law? Let's reflect a little more carefully on the actual function of this business. First of all, while it is true that the cheque cashers charge for their services and banks do it for free as an accommodation to their customers, the banks require at least two pieces of identification, and the cheque cashers do not. This may not be a stringent roadblock for the middle and upper classes who are simply awash in credit cards, automobile licences, and other evidences of the good life, but it is a requirement with which many poor people are unable to comply. What good does the bank's offer of free service do the poor person who cannot, in any case, take advantage of it?

Secondly, the cheque cashers offer immediate service and are open to the public for many more hours than are banks. In addition to the greater flexibility, their storefront ambience is far more comfortable to their clients than are the more traditional banking offices.

The cheque cashing industry provides a valued service to the general public, as attested to by their continued existence. If customers refused to patronize them, they could not long survive. True, in the view of many people the cheque cashing industry is a scruffy, inherently exploitative enterprise. But in the eyes of the paying customers, it is a benefit and a blessing. *W.B.*

COLLECTIVE FARMS

Eastern bloc food production difficulties are perennially in the news. A typical story indicates that Poland and Russia itself are scrambling to make up the shortfall between their production levels and their required consumption during the coming year. While, of course, the human misery which is implicitly associated with their difficulties is something that should concern us all, there is also a lesson in it for Canadians which is too often not drawn.

Many people remember Nikita Krushchev pounding his shoe on the table at the United Nations, threatening that Russia would bury the free world. But few will remember or even have heard his comments to the 22nd Congress of the Soviet Communist Party in October 1961 in which he confidently predicted, "by 1980 our country will have caught up with and decisively surpassed the United States in per capita agricultural and industrial production." The objective for feed grain production contained in Krushchev's 20-year plan was to increase grain output from 131 million tons to more than 300 million tons by 1980. In fact, there was a drastic shortfall of over 100 million tons, and there were similar shortfalls in hydro-electric generation, industrial output, and so on.

The lesson to be learned from the Russian experience is that central planning and direction of food production is not the answer to any of the problems which face Canadian agriculture. On the contrary, in the Soviet Union itself collectivized farms account for some 97 percent of the arable land but produce only 75 percent of the foodstuffs. But on the 3 percent of the land which is under private ownership—in the form of small plots surrounding the homes of the farmworkers—fully 25 percent of the agricultural product is grown.

It will always be argued, of course, that the Soviet example is an extreme case and is not relevant for Canadian circumstances. But, the fact is that the Soviets have pursued the idea of central direction of agriculture to its logical extreme, and we would be silly not to learn from their disastrous experience.

The U.S. agricultural production system has, of course, greatly outstripped the Russian system during the same period of time. It is largely because the American system has been so productive that there is not more widespread starvation within the Soviet bloc.

But why, it may well be asked, is it that private farms are vastly more productive than state-collectivized ones? This may be readily seen by facing the basic question: who stays up all night with the proverbial sick cow? In the case of private enterprise, this is easy to answer. It is the farmer (or his employee or his veterinarian). The owner of the enterprise has an incentive to save the life of the cow if he possibly can. If he doesn't, he loses money. And if this happens once too often, he goes broke.

In contrast, the pay of the serf on the collectivized farm in the Soviet Union does not depend upon taking the extra and above-the-call-of-duty efforts to stay up with the sick cow. As a result, it is less likely that the cow will be saved or that expensive farm equipment will be sheltered from the rain so that it does not rust.

It may be argued, however, that great productivity is garnered on the Hutterite colonies in Western Canada, even though this institution is thoroughly collectivized. But there is a great difference between this case and the forced collectivized farms in the Soviet Union or Ethiopia or Cuba or Tanzania. The kibbutz and the Hutterite colony are strictly voluntary. No one is forced to go there in the first place, and anyone can leave at any time. This, of course, has strong effects on the incentives in operation.

We must conclude that it is not collectivization *per se* that leads to inefficiency and ultimately to starvation, it is collectivization coupled with coercion that leads to this end. *W.B.*

COMPARABLE WORTH (see Discrimination)

Comparable worth legislation would require employers to pay the same wage to those doing different though comparable work. In principle, each job is analysed according to its component parts such as skill, responsibility, effort, and working conditions. Jobs requiring comparable components should be paid on a comparable basis.

This sounds like a good plan. But consider the latest book by Len Deighton, a British author of spy thrillers to whom the public has long been addicted. Suppose we were to spend the same amount of time and effort in writing a spy thriller. Should we be paid comparably for it on the basis determined by Len Deighton's compensation?

Why, of course, the idea is simply silly. Len Deighton is paid as an author not on the basis of the time, skill, effort, and imagination he puts into his books but rather on the basis of how much we addicts in the community value his output. The same, in a variety of indirect ways, is true of most of the jobs which are done in the community. It is not the work, skill, effort, responsibility, and so on which go into a job which determines its value but rather the collective expression of the community's valuation of the output relative to the number of people who want to and are capable of producing that output.

In our own case, for example, while we are very willing to supply spy novels, they seem to lack a certain indefinable something. It is that "certain indefinable something" which differentiates our spy novels from Len Deighton's spy novels. This also determines what, as spy thriller writers, we are comparably worth. *M.W.*

COMPETITION

According to an untenable and outmoded economic theory, economic concentration (only a few firms accounting for a large fraction of output) and competition are inconsistent.

But the truth is almost the exact opposite. Competition and concentration of achievement go hand in hand in most human endeavours. This is the rule, not the exception. Given that talents and abilities are unequally spread round among the population, and given that full and rigorous competition takes place, it should occasion no surprise that there should be only a few "winners," "survivors," or eminent persons associated with each activity. This is true in all areas of human endeavour, sports, politics, the arts—and business as well. But it is only in business that unequal results are seen as evidence of non-competitiveness. Far from an indication of lack of competition, inequality of retrospective results is perfectly compatible with rivalrous struggle.

In focusing its attention on the red herring of concentration and its statistical manifestations, this theory ignores the real threat to economic competitiveness. It is literally impossible to overestimate the importance to the free operation of the marketplace that entry not be barred by the government. There is all the difference in the world between a company that attains a (temporary) monopoly position through service to the consumer (new product, lower price, better service) and one that attains a permanent monopoly position through the coercive power of the state. The pre-eminent example in the latter category is the post office. It owes its monopoly not to its superior competitive activity but to the law of the land which threatens with stiff fines and even jail sentences those who would deliver mail privately.

Industrial concentration is rather imperfectly related to competition. In contrast, legal barriers to entry are the absolutely essential key to understanding how competition is undermined. Industries where government reduces competition in this regard include professional occupations, railroads, trucking, taxicabs, airlines, and agricultural products. In each of these cases, governments have reduced economic competition by setting up barriers protecting incumbent firms and practitioners at the expense of new entrants—and the public.

If government truly had the interests of the public at heart and wanted to promote competition, instead of pressing this largely spurious connection between concentration and competition it would rescind its complex welter of regulations which discourage new entry. *W.B.*

CONFLICT OF INTEREST

The newspapers are continually filled to the brim with stories about conflicts of interest suffered by politicians. Indeed, this is a perennial issue in Ottawa and in the provinces. According to a typical proposal, ministers and senior mandarins should be forced to either put their assets in a blind trust or make a "full and complete disclosure" of their investments. If the momentum from these political shenanigans continues apace, the day is not far off when all MLAs and MPs, whether in power or not, and all senior bureaucrats with executive responsibility will have to make similar disclosures.

There are, however, numerous drawbacks to such a scenario. Openly acknowledging one's investment portfolio is no guarantee that the elected official or civil servant will not be able to use his public position for private gain. It may make things more difficult, but a person who is so minded may still be able to mix his public and private life in this manner. Nor is a blind trust a necessary impediment to such activity. The public figure may rely on the fact that portfolios need not be changed, even when in blind trust, and may act so as to increase the value of his holdings on the day they were given over to the administrator.

Such a policy may not maximize his private wealth, but it may well enhance the value of his property, especially if the portfolio has not been radically altered. In any case, the fact that this is a possibility may divert those in public office from discharging their duties as they would had they no potential conflict of interest to contend with.

But this is only the tip of the iceberg. There is also the siren song of nepotism to deflect our public servants from their steely determination to "act in the public interest." For example, the resignation of one federal minister was prompted not because of any charges made against him personally but because of loans on very favourable terms made to his wife.

This problem is easier to point to than it is to solve. First of all, if the activities of the wife of a government official must be scrutinized lest they cast doubt on the propriety of his own position, what about his children or his parents? What about his uncles, aunts, cousins, in-laws, and grandchildren? The difficulty is that there is no non-arbitrary way to draw the line. No matter where it is drawn, there will always be some (perhaps distant) relative whose business relations may cast aspersions on the legitimacy of the politician in question.

Secondly, what about the rights of the relatives of politicians or leading civil servants? Must they be prohibited by law from engaging in commercial transactions? If they are, this is a clear breach of their own rights. If not, there is always the possibility that someone may treat them advantageously in hopes of currying favour with the principal.

Nor have we even yet completely catalogued the difficulties of conflicts of interest for public functionaries. So far, we have concentrated solely on monetary gains. But this does not go far enough by half. So far all attempts to come to grips with potential conflict of interest problems have been limited to dilemmas about money. But money, as we all know, is only one of the many things sought by human beings. In fact, this insight is so well-entrenched in the social sciences that economists have even developed jargon to express it. We commonly distinguish between money income, on the one hand, and psychic income, on the other. Psychic income denotes all non-pecuniary benefits, such as the gratification of sex, power, notoriety, fame, or the satisfaction of seeing one's fervently held ideology implemented.

This concentration on money income in attempted resolutions of conflicts of interest actually discriminates against those who wish to benefit themselves financially. What about those who wish to benefit in these other ways? We can hardly attempt to make people place their psychic sources of income in a blind trust or force them to make "full disclosure."

These difficulties are basic, not superficial. They transcend political affiliation, jurisdiction, even national boundaries, and apply to *all* office holders and government officials. They do not apply, however, to private enterprise. For if a corporate officer engages in a bit of nest feathering, it is in the interests of the firm to ferret out this behaviour. Business concerns may best be understood as competing not only with regard to providing their primary product but also as regards their ability to stop employees from acting against the interests of their principals.)

Conflicts of interest plague the public sector at present, and are likely to do so for the foreseeable future, or for at least as long as human nature remains the way it now is. What, then, may be done about this ubiquitous problem? The answer is simple. If there is no airtight way to avoid conflicts of interest amongst public servants, let us at least resolve to reduce their numbers as much as possible. Thus, the best way to eliminate virtually all conflicts of interests amongst civil servants and public officials is to decrease the number of these positions to an irreducible minimum. There are many other good and sufficient reasons for cutting back on the public sector, but extirpating conflicts of interest is certainly one of them. *W.B.*

CONSUMER SOVEREIGNTY

While the level of government activity and the extent of its involvement in the Canadian economy has increased quite dramatically in recent times, it has done so in the context of a rapidly expanding general affluence. As a consequence, except in rare circumstance, the average Canadian simply is not being confronted by developments in the size and extent of government. In a world where everything is growing and moving very quickly, the fact that government has been taking an increasing piece of the economic action has largely gone unnoticed.

Let's face it. Canadians by and large have done very well in the last decade. So what if we had to pay 30, 40 or 50 cents tax out of every dollar earned? We still did very well. Certainly, it is true that for most of us government didn't cramp our style very much, largely because we have learned to frame our plans in after tax income terms. We have taken government in our stride. We have, as a result, become quite apathetic.

Lately, however, Canadians and North Americans in general have been increasingly sensitive to the tax take of various levels of government. In the United States this produced the Proposition 13 phenomenon. No similar movement is evident in Canada, although there are some encouraging signs. Politicians at every level find it convenient or expedient to campaign on the basis of less expansive and less expensive government. But the average Canadian doesn't really have a feel for these developments—what they imply, what they are intended to achieve, or indeed a very strong feeling about them in any event. The current move to restrain government expenditures may be no more than the latest fad in the market for votes.

As Canadians, we all participate in a great number of elections—some in the political sphere and some in the economic "dollar votes" sphere. We cast votes on a wide range of issues—some of them involving people's careers and some involving the income and employment prospects for whole segments of the population. During the Christmas buying spree, for example, some of us voted that the person who invented Pet Rocks, should have an income of $1,000,000 or more. By not voting, on the other hand, some of us will have helped determine a great number of other issues. For example, we may have helped decide that some struggling producer of Canadian films shall go bankrupt by our decision not to go to a Canadian film.

We continually make these decisions and cast these votes to buy or not to buy various products. In deciding to buy a particular good or service, we cast a vote in favour of the production of that good or service. In some cases, ours will have been a minority vote. When we go back to buy more of the goods or services previously purchased, we will find they don't exist, precisely because we were minority voters. For example, perhaps you regularly go to a particular barbershop or wallpaper store. Over a period of time that store may cease to exist in your neighbourhood. Perhaps it has moved to another neighbourhood where it acquires more votes—a neighbourhood where people are more highly desirous of a wallpaper store or a barbershop. But in the majority of cases, you will find that you have been a majority voter. The good or service you habitually bought will continue to be available.

Aside from these various elections that you participate in directly, you have also been party to a whole range of other elections. These are the elections or casting of votes done on your behalf, collectively, by the various levels of government to whom you have relinquished some of your voting power. That is to say, government decided to buy or not to buy a good or a service on your behalf.

The strange thing about this second set of votes is that, in many cases, the votes cast on your behalf collectively through the governmental system were, in fact, cast in a different way than those which you personally cast. In fact, in a great number of instances, you might find that government used your dollar votes, in one way or another, to turn the majority vote against you.

For example, consider your decision not to vote for the success of a Canadian film by not patronizing it. It may well be the case that the government used some of the votes it taxed away from you to ensure that the Canadian film would continue to be shown. Undoubtedly, government would claim that it had taken this decision in your own best interests—to protect Canadian culture.

In addition to the votes you cast yourself and those government casts for you, a third set of votes cast during the past period of time were ultimately your votes also but weren't, of course, cast by you. These are the votes government took from you only to give to your neighbour. These are the so-called transfer payments—payments for welfare, unemployment insurance, old age pensions, and so on.

In other words, the total income generated in the economy amounts to the potential to make decisions—the potential to exercise a certain degree of power over the allocation of resources in the economy. All of this voting or deciding power is produced by the people in the economy. Some of the power to make decisions is taken away from the original producers of this allocative power by the process of taxation and given to government. Some of the votes taken away by the government are used to acquire control over goods and services: to build bridges and public buildings, to provide police service, defence, and so on. Government takes voting power from individuals and makes collective voting decisions about the allocation of resources.

These votes, once taken from individuals, are lost to the private sector. Ultimately, the decisions governments make about how to cast these collective votes are subject to the approval of the electorate when they cast their political votes, but it is reasonable to assume for all practical purposes that the collective voting process is, by and large, not controlled to any great level of precision by the private sector.

An important feature of this collective acquisition of goods and services is the fact that unless the voting process adequately reflects the desires of individual Canadians, no value is created when the goods and services are bought by the government sector. It is often said by people of a certain persuasion, "how can it be argued that expenditures made by the government sector on such obvious amenities as parks and swimming pools and provision of health services in rural districts, are not productive?"

How can it be said that these decisions may or may not involve the creation of wealth, whereas the purchase of a Pet Rock or a hula hoop or some other such indispensible item, in fact, does create wealth, and therefore creates value? This conclusion is reached for a very simple reason—value is not an objective reality. Value exists because people place a value on something. They do so by freely giving up some of their voting power (some of their money) to acquire the object of interest. A freely made decision to exchange creates wealth and therefore has value. If the members of the community would rather spend their leisure time watching movies, sitting in a tavern drinking beer, or at a bowling alley, and the government builds a swimming pool because, in its collective wisdom, a swimming pool is better for the people, then the creation of that swimming pool does not create wealth or value for that community—irrespective of what the objective assessment may suggest. The people in that community see value in other activities than swimming.

To the extent that the collective voting process does not reflect how individuals, left to their own devices, would allocate their voting power, the use of that voting power by the public sector drives a wedge between the potential for creating value or wealth in the economy and the amount that is actually created. Moreover, the size of this wedge is virtually impossible to determine.

When Statistics Canada produces quarterly numbers on the total production of goods and services in Canada, it includes the production of goods and services in the government sector—at cost, not at value. In other words, if the government spends $5.00 to pay somebody to work for one hour making mudpies, then that $5.00 is included in the national accounts as an increase in the production of goods and services during that period. But, of course, the production of mudpies adds nothing to the national wealth. Less obvious is the fact that if there are any other goods and services included in government expenditures which individuals would not freely support and not freely choose, these too do not involve the production of value, or the production of wealth. Nevertheless, they are included as such in our national accounts.

One reason to worry about the size of government is because the governmental process of collective voting may represent monumental waste in terms of what the actual needs and desires of Canadians are. This loss can be more than a material loss, as for example when a pro-lifer's money and voting power are taken from him and used to subsidize an abortion clinic or that of a pacifist is used to subsidize the production of napalm. That these sorts of activities lead to a loss for the individual cannot be seriously questioned.

The issue here is not whether abortion clinics or just or unjust wars or any other activity is inherently worthy or unworthy. The issue is whether or not the individuals who provide the wherewithal for these activities find them worthwhile. In the case of collective voting decisions made by government to support these kinds of activities, they only create value to the extent that they represent the wishes of the individuals who have given up their voting power in order that these activities be subsidized. *M.W.*

CRIME

One of the principal explanations for a decline in the crime rate is that there are fewer crime-prone teenagers in the 1980s than there were in the 1970s. Undoubtedly, at least part of the drop in the crime rate is traceable to that cause. However, the increase in the crime rate during the 1970s and the current decline have been much larger than the swings in the composition of the population.

Luckily, there is another perfectly obvious explanation for this phenomenon: the cost of crime is going up. Studies by the U.S. Department of Justice show that whereas 6.6 percent of reported criminals were jailed in the 1970s, by 1982 the imprisonment rate had swollen to 8.4 percent. This 30 percent increase in the cost of crime, as it were, is continuing to be reflected in crime rates in the U.S. During 1985 the number of crimes committed in the U.S. fell to the lowest level since the Justice Department began keeping the records in 1973. The peak of criminal activity was 41.5 million crimes in 1981. Total crime has fallen 16 percent from that level. In other words, there is evidently a predictable connection between the cost of crime and the likelihood that it will occur.

Economists are constantly pointing out to people that as the cost of something goes up, less of it will be used. If the cost goes down, more of it will be used. It turns out that crime is very much the same. These recent investigations by criminologists in the United States show that the cost of crime—in the sense of the chance of being discovered, apprehended, and sentenced—fell steadily from 1960 until the end of the 1970s at which time it began to increase. There may be something in all of this for Canada's judiciary to examine, at least if they are interested in curbing the country's crime rate. *M.W.*

CROWN CORPORATIONS

There are over 300 Crown corporations, all just quivering in anticipation of a return to the private sector and greater economic efficiency. The comparative advantage of the marketplace derives not from better managers and a more highly motivated force—many Crown corporations can match their private counterparts in these regards—but from the necessity to meet the businessman's requirement to make profits and avoid losses. This process continually weeds out the inefficient and encourages the successful, to the betterment of all enterprises in general.

Consider what the actual position of a manager in a Crown corporation is relative to his private sector counterpart. The imperative of the manager of a private corporation is quite clear—maximize profits. To enable him to accomplish this goal, the private sector manager has a profit and loss statement and a balance sheet which are similar in aeronautical terms to the climb and glide and turn and bank indicators used by a pilot to enable him to orient himself in an environment where the normal senses are not always a good guide, particularly if travelling at any speed. But, the most important function of the pilot's instruments, just like the balance sheet in the profit and loss statement, is to help the firm get re-oriented in the event that something should drive them off course or turn them head-over-heels.

The unfortunate manager in the public sector has instruments which are somewhat similar to the balance sheet and the profit and loss statement, but in most instances they aren't relevant for the firm's operation. The main reason is that the instruments as used in the Crown corporations are subject to constant override by management's desire to please his political masters.

It is politics which determines the rate structure charged by our megalithic public power corporations. It is politics which influences the choice of the management which will determine which tunes the CBC plays. Undoubtedly, it was politics which influenced the disastrous financial choices made by the management of Canadair. In other words, although all Crown corporations have potential access to efficiency maximizing tools, they are precluded from using them by the interests of their political masters. As a result, the very best thing that could happen to Crown corporations is that they be privatized.

But who, then, will look after the public interest? In the first place, there is no such thing as the public interest. There are only individual interests. Those who pretend to pursue the public interest are very often pursuing a very special interest. Like, for example, those who intervene at public utility hearings, allegedly in support of the public interest in environmental protection, but who are personally paid thousands and thousands of dollars for their trouble. A neat dovetailing of the public and private interest, one is bound to remark.

One of the most important defects of the notion of the public interest is that it is often used to defend or justify policies which involve serious interference with the abilities of individuals to seek their own interest. And, since the public interest—to the extent it exists at all—is a summation of the private interests of individuals, it is simply nonsense to pretend to pursue the public interest while denying private interests.

That Crown corporations pretend to pursue the public interest is particularly ludicrous in those instances like Canadair, where the operations of the firm involve an ongoing transfer of subsidies from one group of Canadians to another and from one region to another. Most of the jobs "created" in Canadair are paid much above the Canadian average. Meanwhile, the subsidies which are used to support the corporation are derived from general tax revenues which are raised by taxing all Canadians including those with low incomes. In effect, the subsidies to Canadair involve, to some extent, a transfer from low income Canadians to high income Canadians.

Nevertheless, some economists, even those otherwise receptive to the case for the competitive system, have accepted the argument that government enterprise ought to be allowed to compete in the marketplace. In this view, there are no "natural limits" to direct government involvement in the economy whatever. It is only a historical accident that government has never entered the business of running mom and pop grocery stores, newspaper and shoeshine stands, boutiques, babysitting agencies, restaurants, massage parlours, and flower shops. Should government one day decide to take on these tasks in addition to its already multitudinous Crown corporation functions, there is no economic principle at all which could be adduced in opposition.

To be sure, these economists insist that the competition be "fair." That is, the public enterprise—whether local, provincial, or federal level; government department or bureau—should not enjoy any special privileges denied to private enterprise. No grants of monopoly privilege can be conferred as are presently enjoyed by the Canadian post office. (It is now illegal in Canada for private citizens to offer to deliver mail for a fee in competition with Canada Post.) No automatic underwriting of extra budget expenditures can be undertaken based on general government revenues. No exceptions from tax obligations can be given. All firms, private as well as public, must pay taxes; and the tax rates should be invariant regarding the two sectors of the economy. This principle would be consistently applied even up to and including bankruptcy. According to the view we are considering, if the costs of a government-run Crown corporation were not offset by earned revenues, it would be dissolved under bankruptcy procedures, just as in the case of the failure of a private firm.

Naturally, this regime could not feasibly bc applied to "natural money losers," such as welfare, and to programmes which are thinly disguised income transfer schemes such as health care and unemployment insurance. But advocates of this philosophy are anxious to apply it to most "traditional" government-run business enterprises which produce real goods or services, such as Crown corporations.

There is no doubt that such a scheme would be a vast improvement over present institutional arrangements—at least as far as already existing corporations are concerned. No longer would they have an automatic free ride. No longer would their very existence be guaranteed, regardless of whether they pulled their weight or not. This plan, moreover, would allow for a certain flexibility and hence efficiency. If a public corporation were allowed to go bankrupt, private concerns could purchase the resources, capital goods and equipment, and manage them competitively.

One difficulty with this philosophy, however, is that if government were allowed to enter any industry, public enterprise would be unleashed upon many different, small, and petty tasks. Even the communist regimes allow scope for some private initiative. Nor is it even possible to reply that government business would eventually fail in these new endeavours, thus paving the way for the re-entry of private firms. For with enough initial capitalization, they could be immune for long periods of time from the vicissitudes of the marketplace.

Which brings us to the crucial point—initial capitalization. In the free enterprise system, the start-up investment for new firms must also be strictly voluntary. It may be based on individual contributions, stock flotations, or bond purchases, since each of these methods involves funds invested through free choice. If "putting government enterprise on a business footing" meant raising the initial capitalization in such a voluntary way (plus an adherence to all other "fair" competition provisos discussed), then government could truly take its rightful place alongside all other private enterprises.

But in what way would they be a public institution at all? It would be indistinguishable in all respects from a private firm, and thus could not properly be identified with the public sector.

And if public enterprise contrived to raise its initial funding not from voluntary payments but out of tax revenues, it would still retain a crucially important unfair advantage over private concerns, thus denying the "government as competitor" thesis. *W.B. & M.W.*

CULTURE, GOVERNMENT SUPPORT FOR (see Bankruptcy)

The culture industry is upset with regard to government funding for two reasons. First, because they allege that the government is cutting back on total funding for the arts and for cultural activities in Canada. A second and inconsistent charge is that the government is not so much cutting back on funding for culture as transferring control of such funding from groups like the Canada Council to the direct control of the Minister of Communications. This, they allege, will lead to a peculiar variety of nepotism and to the despoiling of the fine heritage which Canada has of funding only the brightest and the best in an unbiased fashion through the Council.

There are two questions that deserve comment. First of all, the appropriateness of government funding for the arts, and secondly, the issue of who should control the purse strings. If there is to be government support for the arts, the only condition under which it should be offered is if the elected representatives of the people who pay, namely the taxpayers, have direct control over how the money is spent, an opinion shared by painter Alex Colville who was courageous enough at an artists conference held in Halifax to be the only senior member of the artistic community to speak against what the arts community calls the "arm's length policy." That is the notion that government funds ought to be laundered through a body like the Canada Council which is allegedly independent from politicians. The unanswered question is why should Canadians wish to abandon control over how cultural enhancement funds are spent?

An even more basic question, of course, is should there be government support for the arts at all? One response is that governments are the modern day equivalent to the princes of old who supported and were responsible for much of what today passes for culture. So governments have to fund the arts to keep up the aristocratic tradition. But the aristocracy and the princes were a manifestation of subjugation and totalitarianism, and we should not be seeking to perpetuate that aspect of more primitive times in our current institutions.

Populist capitalism, and the individual rights that made it possible, have overturned all of the economic and social institutions that characterized the world up until the last 200 years. The fact that individuals control their incomes also means that individuals, through the marketplace, can have an impact on their own culture. They do so by expressing their preference for Bryan Adams over Beethoven and Johnny Cash over Johann Sebastian Bach and video tape players over symphonies and operas. Whether classics fans like it or not, the expression of the popular cultural urge is reflected in the marketplace.

The activities of government allegedly in support of culture are nothing so much as an attempt to subvert the choices consumers have already made about what they want in the way of culture. The reality pokes through the charade when we realize that the elaborate sound and light shows quite standard at a modern rock concert and which make even the most elaborate opera seem puny by comparison require no subsidy but reap a substantial profit for the performers. *M.W.*

CULTURAL NATIONALISM

Nothing drives a wedge between the ranks of those who claim to be supporters of competitive enterprise like a discussion of government subsidies for the arts. Those in favour say there are "public good" features about art and culture that make it unlikely that enough will be produced if they are left to the market process. Once a poem is written, all enjoy without depleting the available enjoyment, and it is difficult to exclude free riders. These are classic instances of where the market is not supposed to work.

Other culture subsidizers point instead to the manifest benefits that are generated. National pride is enhanced because there is a stock of Canadian poetry or drama. There are educational benefits. Why teach music appreciation if there is no music to enjoy? Why teach Shakespeare if there are no performances of Shakespearean plays? If it makes sense to subsidize the education, then why not the performance? There are even economic spinoffs associated with the performing arts in the form of associated consumption—the night on the town frequently includes dinner as well as a play.

Some supporters of government aid for the arts are more direct. Richard Musgrave, author of the most famous college text on public finance states that, "situations may arise, within the context of a democratic community, where an informed group is justified in imposing its decisions upon others." His focus was education, but this idea of "merit goods," is now generally applied to the arts.

Many, however, oppose subsidies to the arts largely because of this authoritarian, elitist implication. A more important reason is the concern that subsidies to the arts may be no more than thinly disguised redistributions of income to higher income folks. Evidence suggests that four out of five subsidized theatre-goers have incomes above the median and nearly 70 percent are college graduates.

As a result, we have always found the activities of cultural nationalists to be somewhat irritating. First, because the expression of cultural nationalism most often finds its outlet in the form of restrictions on the choices Canadians can make, whether in the kind of television they wish to watch, the kinds of songs they wish to hear on the radio, or the kinds of magazines that would be available to them. It is also mildly irritating that Canadian governments ladle out a lot of public funds to support the activities of self-styled artists, writers, and poets whose main characteristic is that their work doesn't reflect the Canadian psyche well enough that Canadians will voluntarily support their efforts by purchasing their works.

But this cultural nationalism has recently taken an ugly and sinister turn, and that has to do with the publication of school books. Currently, two missionaries from Federal Communications Minister Marcel Masse are gadding about the country urging provincial governments to buy only school books published in Canada. Such a policy is to rescue the Canadian textbook market from its domination by U.S. producers of textbooks.

Departments of education ought to select the very best textbooks available for our children. They should not be limited to those created under the auspices of Canadian publishers, who may or may not reflect the most current research and the latest developments in the particular subject covered by the textbook. It's one thing to subsidize the relatively harmless renderings of a poet or even to buy the art of a Canadian artist who might otherwise be up to more significant mischief, it is quite another matter to tamper with the kinds of material our children have access to in school. *M.W.*

D

DEFENCE IDEOLOGY

Most people believe there is a connection between the form of political institutions adopted in a country and the attitudes which that country espouses and exhibits towards matters military. There is a widespread presumption that those of more conservative ideology are more inclined to be hawks on the issue of defence and more militaristic in their outlook than those on the left.

This is as true in political commentary and discourse as it is in popular diversions such as movies and literature. The image of a semi-crazed, fascist Dr. Strangelove prepared to visit his self-destructive urges on the world is etched into the psyche of North America. It is the image that many would like to convey as the archetype of the capitalist world. And, of course, we are all too familiar with the threatening image of the military-industrial megalith which is alleged to be essential to the prosperity of Western civilization, driven, as it is, by a dependence on unstable capitalist urges.

So it is that when we come to discuss matters of this kind, the agenda has been pre-empted to a considerable extent by preconception and foregone conclusions. The reality is that there is no such connection between militarism and the ideology which informs the political institutions of a country. This is very clear in the data compiled yearly by the British Institute for Strategic

Studies and the U.S. Arms Control and Disarmament Agency. Each prepare very similar figures on the extent of militarization of populations in different countries. The militarization ratio—the number of active, full-time military personnel per 1,000 population—for a large number of countries is displayed in the following table.

MILITARISM AND IDEOLOGY

Selected Non-Marxist Countries

	Militarism Ratio	Wealth-Adjusted Militarism Ratio
Western Hemisphere		
United States	9.1	4.6
Canada	3.3	- 0.9
Mexico	2.0	0.4
Guatemala	2.3	2.8
Honduras	3.9	5.7
El Salvador	5.4	6.8
Costa Rica	1.5	2.6
Colombia	2.6	2.6
Venezuela	3.2	1.1
Brazil	3.6	2.7
Argentina	6.0	3.9
Chile	10.3	9.2
Europe		
United Kingdom	5.8	2.0
France	8.9	4.7
West Germany	7.8	3.6
Sweden	8.4	3.7
Switzerland	3.6	-1.3
Austria	5.3	1.5
Italy	6.9	3.8
Mid-East		
Israel	46.2	43.4
Turkey	13.3	13.5
Jordan	19.7	19.8
Eypt	10.0	11.7
Saudi Arabia	5.4	0.5
Iran	11.4	11.0
Libya	16.7	19.8
Africa		
South Africa	2.3	0.9
Nigeria	1.6	2.5

	Militarism Ratio	Wealth-Adjusted Militarism Ratio
Ghana	1.0	0.3
Zaire	0.9	5.3
Liberia	3.5	5.8
Sudan	3.3	5.3
Asia		
Japan	2.0	-2.0
India	1.6	5.3
Indonesia	1.7	3.7
Thailand	4.8	6.1
Taiwan	27.2	25.9
Australia	4.8	0.5
Philippines	3.0	4.3
Marxist Countries		
Albania	18.9	19.6
Angola	6.4	7.1
Algeria	6.0	5.2
Benin	0.8	4.1
Bulgaria	19.7	17.6
Burma	4.9	9.3
Cape Verde	10.0	12.9
China (Mainland)	4.3	5.9
Congo	10.0	10.4
Cuba	23.5	22.7
Czechoslovakia	13.8	10.0
Ethiopia	8.2	12.9
Germany (East)	14.0	10.0
Guinea	3.2	6.4
Guinea-Bissau	5.0	9.4
Hungary	10.5	7.5
Iraq	32.1	31.7
Korea (North)	38.0	39.1
Laos	15.8	21.6
Madagascar	2.2	5.3
Mongolia	21.2	21.6
Mozambique	1.6	4.4
Nicaragua	27.8	28.7
Poland	11.3	9.3
Romania	10.5	8.1
Somalia	8.9	12.0
Soviet Union	16.3	13.3
Syria	30.9	30.4

	Militarism Ratio	Wealth-Adjusted Militarism Ratio
Tanzania	2.7	6.1
Vietnam	21.5	25.3
Yemen (South)	12.5	14.8
Yugoslavia	10.9	9.3
Mean		
32 Marxist countries	**13.3**	**14.1**
39 Non-Marxist countries	**7.2**	**6.2**

The militarism ratio is the number of active, full-time military personnel per 1,000 population (data are for 1982). The wealth adjusted militarism ratio is based on the relationship between national wealth and the militarism ratio. Each country's figure represents the deviation of its actual militarism ratio from the militarism ratio it would be expected to have given its level of wealth.

———

Source: *World Military Expenditures and Arms Transfers, 1972-1982*, U.S. Arms Control and Disarmament Agency, (Washington, D.C., 1984). As compiled by James Payne for the Reason Foundation.

As can be plainly seen, those countries wherein the governmental ideology is Marxist tend to have a militarization ratio nearly twice as large as those countries which are not so influenced.

This is, of course, a very crude measure of the relationship between ideology and attitudes on militarism. But refinements or objections would not modify the numbers enough to account for the fact that there are nearly double the number of full-time personnel per 1,000 population in Marxist countries as compared to non-Marxist countries. The reality is that in Marxist countries, on average, there are 13.3 full-time military personnel per 1,000 population whereas in the non-Marxist world there are only 7.18 military persons per 1,000 population.

It is thus quite incorrect to assume that preoccupation with the military or the maintenance of large military forces is a characteristic of people who might generally be described as on the right of the political spectrum. This fact comes out most clearly in examining the extremes of the political spectrum. Compare, for example, Chile, a totalitarian government on the right with countries like Cuba or Nicaragua—two dictatorships of the left. Each of the latter has more than double the number of people under arms per 1,000 population than maintained by Chile. (Moreover, the data also reject the argument that might be mounted to the effect that Cuba and Nicaragua both have higher militarization because of the threat from internal or external sources. This is clear by comparison with El Salvador, for example, whose militarization rate is less than a fifth that of Nicaragua even though El Salvador is similarly beset from their point of view by internal and external threat.)

And so, while it may please some members of the public to imbue discussions of Canada's military options with an ideological overtone, at the very least the facts of current military deployment in the world ought to convince us that such connections are not easily made. Moreover, the data suggest if any inferences are appropriate, they are to the effect that militarism is essentially a preoccupation of Marxist governments. It behooves those who think Marxism is compatible with established Canadian political ideals to take due notice.

More particularly, the regularity of the association of Marxist governments with high militarization ratios must make us ponder carefully the sympathies and intentions which motivate the central actors in issues like arms control and strategic defence initiatives. We can all be forgiven our skepticism and confusion in unravelling what may be implied by the number of ICBMs, warheads, and satellites employed respectively by the Soviet Union and the U.S. There is less room for ambiguity in deciding why a country like Mongolia, safely nestled in a surrounding of like-minded Marxist regimes, nevertheless mounts an armed force 6.4 times that maintained by Canada. The residents of Mongolia know, as the citizens of Nicaragua are discovering, that governments that seek to impose a single-minded conception of the "just society" require a large apparatus of force to ensure conformity. *M.W.*

D D D D D D D D D D D D D D D D D D D D D D

DEFENCE STRATEGY IN A NUCLEAR ENVIRONMENT

From the point of view of an economist, the central role of government is to maintain an umbrella of security from both internal and external threats to the social order. In fact, as is well known, many in the profession would maintain that this maintenance of the legal framework and a system of defence is the only function which government ought, in an ideal world, to assume.

In this limited state view of the world there is, of course, no room for interventionist militarism or expansionist militarism of the kind that involved aggression against non-aggressors. Maintenance of a defensive force is required because, while Canada has no history of or interest in aggressive expansionism, this certainly cannot be said for other countries in the world. It would take the most innocent disregard for reality to suppose that there is no substantive justification for Canada maintaining a defensive military force. Even if that were not the case, Canada's historical role as a sensible and sensitive peacekeeper and as a non-threatening member of the Western alliance would suggest the maintenance of a reliable and well-trained military apparatus.

It is important to recognize that, from an economic point of view, defence is one of those goods commonly referred to as a "public good." As such, it would not be reliably provided by the market nor are there clear market mechanisms by which Canadians can effectively signal the extent of their desire for investment in military apparatus. In other words, the extent of military establishment and the amount of defence which Canadians wish the state to purchase is a classic case where the political mechanism must be the principal source of information.

Given this basic protective role which government is supposed to provide, how does it relate to the nuclear environment in which current military decisions must be made? Only the most naive idealist would assume that Canada's largest cities are not the targets of Soviet missiles. As cohabitant of the North American continent with the Americans, whether or not we have strong military ties with that country we must be regarded by the Russians as a potential ally of the United States and, in the event of any all-out confrontation, as a willing or un-willing accomplice in the American war effort. Whatever our posture, we must assume that from the Russian point of view our population centres are targets for nuclear attack.

From the point of view of discharging its responsibility to maintain at least a minimum defence of Canadian lives and property, the Government of Canada ought to have some strategy for dealing with this threat. Not, of course, that we can defend ourselves from an all-out nuclear war between the United States and the U.S.S.R. Such protection is, at least at the present time, impossible. If there is an all-out nuclear war, the consequences would be devastating to Canadian society, whatever defensive posture we may adopt. But between the "we can't do anything anyway so why bother" position and the total commitment to a strategic defence programme, there are a great number of options, some of which have a good deal to recommend them.

The most important, pressing, and sensible of these alternatives is to recognize that in practical terms the most significant danger that arises from the fact that Canada is targeted by Soviet missiles is the possibility that one may be unleashed by accident. This, indeed, is the threat which most heavily rests on the minds of many Canadians who find it impossible to confront the possibility of total nuclear annihilation. There is also, of course, the possibility of the use, by some terrorist organization, of a nuclear missile to intimidate this or other countries.

At the moment, Canada has no protection whatsoever against such an eventuality. Given the relatively large amount of the gross national product spent every year on military preparedness, we are entitled to ask, "why is there no such protection?" It is, first of all, well within the reach of current technology. It would represent a purely defensive posture on Canada's part. It could not possibly be construed as aggressive or threatening. Moreover, it is a strategy which has already been pursued by the Soviet Union itself to protect Moscow. (It is important to note, however, that the Soviet defensive system itself involves the use of nuclear missiles. What is being proposed here does not.)

We should reciprocally see to our own narrow interest and begin at once to incorporate this technology into our defence capability to protect against this unspeakable, accidental destruction of life and property. Unlike the Soviet defence system, Canada's defence system could be non-nuclear in nature because of recent technological developments which permit the non-nuclear destruction of incoming missiles. As all are aware, such conventional missile defence systems do not involve lasers or particle beams but employ off-the-shelf technology.

It may be that from a technical point of view this defence is better conducted on a continent-wide basis in collaboration with the United States. If so, then we should hasten to persuade our North American allies to co-operate in this venture and proceed with due haste to deploy such defences. At the moment, as is well known, the United States has committed only to research the possibility of such systems.

There is an economic aspect to strategic defence matters. If the incremental cost of defensive weapons is less than the cost of offensive weapons, a strategic defence initiative will ultimately overwhelm any other option irrespective of whether we decide this is a good idea or not. As we have observed with regard to the idea of totally annihilating offensive weapons (to wit, the atomic and hydrogen bombs), once an idea of this sort has been let out of the bottle, it is very difficult to get back in. Having turned attention to the possibility that strategic defence may be cheaper than strategic offense, it seems that mankind may be on the verge of a defensive arms race—one that is much to be preferred to the current offensive posture. *M.W.*

DEFENCE: ECONOMIC IMPACT OF GOVERNMENTAL EXPENDITURES

One of the aspects of defence expenditure that frequently arises is consideration of the economy-wide impact expenditures of this sort may have. There is a view that if a government can be encouraged to spend more on defence, this will somehow provide a boost to the economy, to employment, and to production. This is the notion that an additional benefit of defence spending is its economic side effects.

That position is untenable. Except under very rare and unusual circumstance, an increase in expenditures by government has no effect on the aggregate level of employment or the aggregate amount of production. It has "no positive effect" because the overall process of government spending actually has a deleterious effect on the level of both those magnitudes. The reason, quite simply, is that government expenditures must be financed. There isn't a "widow's cruse" from which governments can draw financial oil with which to grease the gears of the economy.

All money spent by the government emerges, in the first instance, from the private sector. The wherewithal government uses to finance its expenditures has to come from the pocket of some Canadian who would otherwise have spent or invested the funds in some other form. So, while there may be many reasons to endorse expenditures for defence purposes, one of those is *not* that it would have a positive effect on the aggregate level of employment and production in Canada.

Rather than being a boost to the economy in any real sense, defence expenditures are a kind of redistribution of spending power from the private to the public sector. The process of that redistribution can have real economic effects, however, because of the regional incidence of the withdrawal of spending power from the private sector and its redeployment in the public sector. For example, a drawdown of private spending power in the form of taxation from the Western regions in order to facilitate defence expenditures in Quebec or Nova Scotia would have the effect of reducing economic activity in the West and increasing economic activity in those locales. And, of course, if the pattern of spending were reversed, the economic consequences would also be reversed.

The fact that defence spending is regionally redistributive may alter the judgement that it is neutral in its employment and income-generating effects. For example, if the net effect of the redistribution is to take spending power from regions of the country with above-average levels of unemployment and idle capacity and to expend the purchasing power in other regions of the country which have average or below-average levels of unemployment and excess capacity, then part of the economic effect of the defence expenditures will be dissipated in bidding up the regional prices of those relatively scarce resources. This strongly suggests that if neutral economic effects of defence expenditures are to be achieved, care must be exercised in the distribution of those expenditures. This consideration is one that would happily fit with the federal government's alleged interest in regional economic development as well.

In sum, it must be said that military expenditure should be regarded as a cost rather than as a benefit to Canadian society. While those costs might be willingly borne to support a defence apparatus, we should in no way justify the level of military expenditure on the grounds that they have positive economic side effects. *M.W.*

DEFICIT (see Balanced Budget)

The government deficit is the difference between the total spending and the total income of the government in a single year. In Canada, both the federal and provincial governments may have deficits—usually, municipal governments may not. The notion of the deficit must be distinguished from the national debt, which is the accumulation of deficits and surpluses since the formation of the nation or province.

While it is usual to say that governments engage in deficit finance, deficits do not finance spending. They simply defer the cost of the spending to a future time. If a government runs a deficit, that deficit must be financed by the issue of bonds or the printing of money, a form of government debt which does not bear interest. Each dollar of deficit represents a dollar of spending power that the government requires but has not acquired from the electorate by taxation. By issuing bonds, the government borrows a dollar of purchasing power which it must repay in the future by taxing members of a future electorate who had no voice in the decisions about the spending that the borrowing financed.

Deficits during the slump matched by surpluses at the peak of the business cycle do not, in principle, pose any problem for economic management. Under those conditions the budget would be balanced over the economic cycle. Problems emerge because it is politically easier to run deficits than surpluses. Thus, through peak and trough, Canada's federal government has produced deficits in each year since 1975. Now there is concern that the very structure of government spending and taxation is such that there is a 'structural deficit' and therefore little prospect of ever eliminating it.

In recent years, the federal government has not permitted spending to rise as rapidly as tax and other revenues and as a consequence the deficit is declining both in dollar terms and relative to the national income. The national debt, however, will continue to grow as long as there is any deficit level. Currently, the federal deficit is about $26 billion and the federal debt is about $300 billion. *M.W.*

DISCRIMINATION (see Affirmative Action/ Comparable Worth)

Canada is now in the process of implementing a spate of legislation to promote "equality in employment" as called for most notably by Judge Rosalie Abella. The main finding of the Abella Royal Commission is that the female-male wage ratio of 63.9 percent in 1982 is largely due to sexual discrimination on the part of the nation's employers, both public and private. Its chief recommendation is that a new affirmative action policy of "employment equity" be implemented which would require business and Crown corporations to change their hiring and promotion practices until balanced job representation and equal pay have been much more nearly attained.

This is the wrong solution to a non-existent problem. The income gap between genders is not due to employer discrimination but rather to differences in productivity. There is no determination, here, that these differences are inherent or based on genetics. Rather, one major factor is the asymmetrical effect of marriage on earnings. It raises the earnings of the husband,

and reduces those of the wife. This, in turn, is because of unequal child care and house management responsibilities, and different psychic attachments to the labour force versus home and hearth. The proof? Women who have never been touched by the institution of marriage, and who thus can be presumed to have productivity levels similar to those of men, do not suffer from lower incomes than their male counterparts.

The statistics are revealing. In 1981, the last census year for which such data is available, the female-male ratio of earnings for Canadians who never married was 83.1 percent. But even this is an underestimate of the true relationship, because the statistics have not been corrected for labour force experience, age, education, and unionization. When just one of these corrections is made, for example, and we compare female-to-male income ratios for never marrieds with a university degree, the figure rises to 91.3 percent. (For 1971, such university-educated never married females actually earned 9.8 percent more than their equally accomplished male counterparts!)

When we consider only males and females who have never been touched by the productivity-differentiating institution of marriage—men and women who are likely to have similar market productivities—we find no statistically significant differences in their earnings. Nor are these findings a statistical aberration limited to the most recent figures. An intensive study of the data collected over the last five censuses (1941-1981) shows that the female-male ratio for the never married has not fallen below 80 percent, and has not risen above 47 percent, for those never married.

The recommendations of the Abella Royal Commission Report, predicated as they are on the role of employer discrimination as the cause of the income gap, will not solve the basic problem. Instead, they will cause considerable mischief. If the reason women are receiving roughly $6.50 for every $10.00 of male earnings is lower average productivity, it is easy to see the effect of legislation which requires they be paid on an "equitable" basis. Females will be priced out of the labour market and become unemployed.

The tragedy of the matter is that in the market, discrimination on the basis of sex or race is simply not viable. Were equally productive male and female employees paid widely varying salaries, strong profit incentives would tend to wipe out the differential. Entrepreneurs would seek to hire the underpaid women and fire the overpaid men. Suppose you, as an employer, were faced with two job applicants, each with a productivity level of $10.00 per hour. Assume that the male had to be paid $10.00, while the woman, thanks to the magic of "discrimination," need only be paid $6.50. Who would you choose? Unless you were an extreme sexist, you would hire the woman because you could make an additional profit of $3.50 per hour from her labour. If you were an extreme sexist and hired the man instead, you would soon enough go broke as your competitors, with cheaper female labour, could underprice you. *W.B.*

DOCTOR SURPLUS

Two interesting stories in the press have not been linked but together they convey a very interesting message indeed. First was a story indicating that a tentative agreement had been reached between the B.C. Medical Association and the B.C. government that doctors would forgo an increase in their fees.

The second story was a *Globe and Mail* report on a federal provincial task force study showing that Canada has a surplus of doctors. In fact, if Canada's medical schools continue to graduate as many doctors as they do now, we will face a surplus of 6,000 physicians by the end of the century. In 1980, according to the study, Canada already had 822 doctors too many.

This comes as no real surprise to British Columbians, as the Government of British Columbia has already acted to control the supply of doctors in populated areas by limiting the issuance of Medicare numbers. If doctors are to be paid by the medical insurance plan in British Columbia, they must have a number. New numbers are only being given to doctors moving to areas which are deemed under-supplied. Without putting these two stories together, one may have regarded the news that B.C. physicians were taking a hold-the-line stance on their fees as a public-spirited and praise-worthy action. But, once combined, these two stories produce a kind of preposterous result.

Let's imagine that we're talking about apples instead of doctors. Suppose that during the summer there is a bumper apple crop. Farmer Brown, interviewed by the media, indicates that he and the supermarkets have agreed there will be no increase in the price of apples this summer. You might object that that is nonsense. If there is a surplus of apples, the price should fall in order to boost apple consumption and eliminate the surplus. Of course, in the case of the supply of doctors and medical services, no such flexibility is possible.

An even more stupendous aspect is the task force prediction that as a result of the bumper crop of doctors thc costs of medical care will actually increase. This increased supply of doctors will have to be paid incomes to which doctors have been accustomed out of the present medical care programmes. As the number of doctors increases, the slice of the medical care income pie going to each won't decrease in size. Rather, the size of the medical care income pie will simply have to increase. *M.W.*

DOLLAR VOTE

Economics as a subject is a set of ideas describing human behaviour towards scarcity. We human beings have to make choices amongst the limited number of things that we can do. In that sense, the marketplace is a set of coping skills to resolve the conflicts that inevitably arise as we try to do all the things our imagination tells us we should do as against the list of things that are actually possible to do in the world with the limited resources we have.

Perhaps we can best see what the market is by comparing it with other ways humankind has evolved to resolve conflicts over scarcity. In Central Australia, the bushmen have very simple coping skills to solve the problems of scarcity and the conflict between their needs and wants and their actual abilities. They use tradition. When the harvest of grubs came in, how many you got depended on your status within the tribal network—whether you were a number one or a number six or whatever.

Another way to go about solving the problem of scarcity, of economic production, is by command. One person or one group of people decide what everybody else will do.

Then there is the market, which is an on-going series of elections by individuals casting dollar votes to determine how they individually would like to see this conflict resolved. For example, should there be a barbershop on the corner of 114th and 82nd Streets? Who knows? How could we decide whether there should be one there or not? One way is to say there has always been one there—that's the traditional solution. In the command system somebody would say that we'll put one there because it makes sense in terms of our overall city plan. But the market allows individuals to try to make a dollar by setting up a barbershop. If they can in fact attract enough dollar votes from the public in the area to sustain them in business, then they can continue. In allocating their own basket of dollar votes, individuals make choices across a wide range of objectives from the food they eat to the entertainment they purchase.

Let us now consider the objection to dollar votes, that is, that the wealthy make the determinations in the marketplace. As a matter of fact, 85 percent of the dollar votes (i.e., income) in Canada are owned—originally, at least, before the government taxes them away—by people whose incomes are less than $50,000. So, in Canada we have a system of coping, of making decisions about what we ought to do economically—whether we produce blue cars or red cars, whether to have three different coloured pencils or 25, or whether we should have six kinds of chewing gum or 18—by a process of dollar voting which depends not mainly on the rich but on the low and middle income class.

One benefit of dollar voting is that it is based on contract, a voluntary relationship between individuals. This is opposed to coerced relationships between individuals—a feature of tradition or command. Status is less important in our society now than in the historic past. We have evolved away from the kind of society in which the Australian bushman lives, in which we all lived at one time, wherein what you got depended on your status in the society. Of course, the economic system in Canada is only predominantly a market society. It has large elements of command and tradition: market outcomes are attenuated, economic actors are in fact coerced by government policy, and people do receive consideration on the basis of status.

Another advantage of dollar voting is that consumers have more control over businessmen than voters do over politicians. The former vote every day; the latter only at four-year intervals. The consumer may focus his vote on a particular good or service; the citizen's choice is limited to a package deal concerning *all* public enterprises.

Consider, in this regard, the following. On April 6, 1981, Eaton's department store unveiled a display of doctors' gowns featuring a mock operating room scene. A larger-than-life female patient doll was placed on an operating table with her legs spread apart, while a male doctor doll stood between her legs. This "doctor" held a giant power drill pointing at her abdomen, while a nurse doll, wearing frilly pink underwear, stood by. For a month afterwards, the Vancouver store received no complaints against this display alleging "sexploitation," "violence against women," or anything else. On May 7 and 8, 1981, several newspaper articles appeared which were critical of the display. One was written by a female Vancouver columnist who urged women customers to take their business elsewhere. This prompted an outraged response from several dozen people, who complained to Eaton's management. The display was removed on May 11, 1981.

The shocking thing about this occurrence was *not* the offensiveness to women. Much worse has been alleged to have occurred in the past, and in any case, a second female journalist vehemently *defended* Eaton's against sexploitation charges in her own newspaper column. Nor is it amazing that Eaton's management should have mistakenly assessed public reaction. Business people have made mistakes before, and will again. To err, after all, is only human. No. The remarkable thing is the extreme quickness with which Eaton's changed its initial response to the furor and acceded to the public will.

At the outset, general merchandise manager Bill McCourt is reported to have said: "Violent? It's funny. It's meant to be good fun, just a funny operating room. We have strict rules about displays. Nothing that resembles violence of any kind is permitted." And yet a scant four days later, the display was dismantled with profuse apologies.

The reason for this extremely quick responsiveness to public opinion is of course the fact that all private businesses are completely dependent for their very financial lives on the good will of the customer. ("The customer is always right" is almost the motto of the private sector.) A mention of returning an Eaton's credit card in 10 pieces, a letter to the editor announcing intent to shop at another department store, a few dozen complaints to management, and the job is done. (Other examples of similar private sector accountability include the immediate dropping of the Edsel automobile and the hyper-sensitivity of the networks to TV ratings.)

Eaton's extreme responsiveness to public opinion is in sharp contrast to several other sectors of our society. Our politicians, for example, have proven very reluctant to satisfy public demands in several areas. Most Canadians favour the death penalty in certain circumstances, oppose sex education classes in the high schools as causes of venereal disease and youthful pregnancy, and favour prayer in the public schools. Yet these widely held and deeply felt desires are ofttimes dismissed as mere public clamour and uninformed mob demands.

Public opinion polls have shown an overwhelming opposition to Ottawa's stand on the unilateral repatriation of the Constitution, public sector strikes such as those by the air traffic controllers, post office employees, and bus drivers, RCMP illegal activities, and high taxes. Yet these continue unabated, since politicians are insulated from public feedback through the electoral process which need take place no more than once every few years. This compares rather unfavourably to the dollar vote which reigns in the business sector. It occurs each and every day, day in and day out.

More people wanted a Terry Fox stamp, while he was still alive, that is, and wanted this passionately, than there were who ever heard of the Eaton's display, let alone protested it. Yet Postmaster-General André Ouellet remained obdurate in his refusal to comply. (In the end, he agreed to a stamp commemorating the Marathon of Hope but not Terry Fox himself.)

Ouellet was insulated from public feedback, and thus unaccountable to the "paying customer." Can anyone imagine the management of Eaton's thumbing its nose at the public in such a manner—and getting away with it? *W.B.*

DRUG PATENTS

It has been fascinating to observe the brouhaha about drug patents. The government is being savaged for having given in to pressure from lobbyists and exposing Canadians to higher drug prices. Unfortunately, most of the comments completely miss the central point at issue—whether or not Canada will have a national policy involving systematic theft and whether the real interests of Canadians is served by such a policy.

Critics have been roasting the government because the result of the proposed drug legislation would be higher prices for drugs. Note that the drugs currently available would be more expensive; the levels of those prices will continue to reflect the same forces that determine them at the present. However, new drugs brought to the market in the future will sell for higher prices than they would have under the old rules.

The government, in the person of Minister for Consumer and Corporate Affairs Harvie Andre, has responded by denying the rising price claims of critics. But that is a mistake. First of all, it is undoubtedly true that drug prices will be higher under the provisions of the new law than they would have been under the old. For the government to deny that prices will rise causes legitimate concern for either its understanding or its integrity. Instead, paradoxically, we should congratulate ourselves on higher drug prices! Rather than complaining, we should be happy that drug prices are going to increase under new legislation. Higher prices actually signal an improved situation for consumers.

The mechanics of current drug practices reveal why that is so. At the moment, if a new drug is introduced to the Canadian market, the inventor must in due course give the right to use the new formula to a Canadian manufacturer in return for a 4 percent fee. That licensee, who has incurred none of the costs of developing the drug, can sell it at the cost of simply putting together the ingredients. The difference between the cost of the resulting "generic" drug and the cost of the original is the value of the inventor's investment. In effect, the reason generic drugs are cheaper is because the law in Canada permits, and indeed is designed to encourage, Canadians to steal most of the value of the inventor's idea. Of course, we don't call it theft because it is done under the aegis of government.

Instead of the current arrangements, suppose our government passed a law which made legal the use of industrial espionage. Canadians could then pay spies in foreign corporations to sell industrial secrets, like drug patents, and our government would protect its nationals from prosecution for their efforts. Under such a scheme, the prices of the products whose designs were stolen would undoubtedly be lower, but it would certainly involve theft. It would still involve theft if the government ruled that the company from whom the patent had been stolen be sent a regular, small payment—call it a licencing fee if you wish—in recognition of the theft of its ideas.

Higher drug prices are a sign that we have stopped such practices, and we shall all be better off for it. The higher prices we will pay for drugs in the future is a direct reflection of our decision to reject theft as the basis for government policy regarding drugs. It marks a recognition of the value of ideas and inventions and hopefully paves the way for a broader policy regarding the protection of intellectual property in general. That is a most important building block for an economic future which will be increasingly determined by the investment in and protection of knowledge capital.

Those who have little patience for this line of argument and long for a more "pragmatic" approach to such policy issues—one less hide-bound by old fashioned principles and notions like property and theft—ought to reflect long and hard on the experience to which we were subjected by the last such major spasm in Canadian public policy, the National Energy Program with its retroactive expropriation (theft) of the property of American and Canadian investors. Don't forget that the slogans of that programme were "made in Canada" and "lower oil prices," goals which proved to be elusive and the pursuit of which was one of the most destructive policy adventures of modern times. Whether of oil or inventions, theft is neither a sound moral nor economic basis for public policy. We should applaud the government's stance in the face of the considerable opposition. *M.W.*

DUMPING

During the great potato war in British Columbia, the complaint was that U.S. farmers were "dumping" potatoes—selling them at below U.S. prices—on the Vancouver market. According to the B.C. Coast Vegetable Co-operative Association, Vancouver wholesalers can buy U.S. potatoes at $7.35 per 100 pound sack, while this costs $7.80 when purchased from B.C. producers.

As can be expected, this concatenation of prices has had adverse effects on B.C. potato growers, who have been pushed down from a 70 percent share of the Vancouver market, to a 49 percent share. This loss of sales, it is feared, may be the straw that breaks the back of many a B.C. potato farmer.

True, this flood of U.S. potatoes will benefit the Canadian consumer, but this is only in the short run. For in the long run, when most or all B.C. growers have been driven to the wall, it is contended that the large scale corporate farms in the Columbia Valley of Washington will be able to charge whatever they wish. The protectionist's answer to the problem was to slap an extra duty on U.S.-grown potatoes so B.C. farmers could compete more effectively against their southern rivals.

U.S.-Canada trade is very important to both nations and could be harmed by such a move. The balance of trade between the two nations is usually in our favour in any case. Moreover, such additional primitive duties would be reciprocated by a U.S. tariff boost on Eastern Canadian potatoes exported to the U.S. As well, there is always the danger of retaliation by U.S. timber interests against alleged B.C. dumping of lumber south of the border.

However, this alleged dumping is not really dumping at all. If U.S. producers can bring 100 pounds of potatoes to the Vancouver market for $7.35 and it costs B.C. farmers $7.80 to create an equal amount, this shows only that the large-scale U.S. farms are more efficient. For dumping to be proven, it is not enough to show that farmers south of the border can produce potatoes more cheaply than their Canadian counterparts; it must be shown that these farmers sell in Vancouver markets at prices below those charged in the U.S. or at prices below actual costs. This has not even been claimed, let alone proven.

But let us suppose, just for the sake of argument, that this was indeed a bona fide case of dumping so we can analyse the impact of such a provision. The very phrase "dumping" is a misnomer and misleading. The word evokes a picture of U.S. farmers flying a fleet of B52s filled with potatoes 50,000 feet in the air and dumping them on hapless Vancouverites scurrying around seeking a fall-out shelter. Nothing could be further from the truth. Far from bombing B.C. residents with potatoes or forcing this vegetable down the unwilling throats of the Vancouver citizenry, U.S. farmers, in this scenario, would be offering Canadian consumers "a deal they can't refuse." It is a voluntary trade which benefits both parties, otherwise it would not—it could not—take place.

As to the claim that Washington farmers are hoping to drive B.C. potato producers out of business so as to raise prices through the roof, this is a scare tactic—a basic fallacy in economics used only by demagogues. Large successful businesses do not retain dominant market shares by raising prices. They are achieved in the first place by price cutting, and this is how they are retained. A high price, in contrast, is like a bleeding fish in the ocean:

predators come to attack, lured by the spectre of high profits. When (and if) the Columbia Valley farmers make inroads in the B.C. market, the last thing they will do is arbitrarily raise prices. This would only encourage the competition of other Washington growers, Idaho potato producers, and others from farther afield. As well, the most efficient cost-conscious B.C. potato farmers would still remain in operation in such a scenario. Protected by low transport costs, they would be able to pick off their higher priced Columbia Valley opponent, and begin to raise their market shares once again.

If consumers fear that present low prices will lead to vastly higher ones later on, they or their agents, the wholesalers, can buy potato futures and thereby protect themselves against such an eventuality. They don't need the protectionists to ride to their rescue—armed to the teeth with the coercive power of the state. They can see readily enough that this argument only protects the interests of the potato growers in B.C. (But even here, they are remiss in their duty. If they really wanted to help local farmers, they would press for an end to the agricultural land reserve which compels them to use their property uneconomically. Potato farmers would be far better off if their land could be re-allocated toward more precious uses such as industry and housing.)

There is an even more basic economic point at issue here. If the Columbia Valley farmers were really selling at below cost prices or for less than they could receive elsewhere in the U.S., they would be presenting a gift to the inhabitants of Vancouver. The amount of the gift would be equivalent to the difference between the actual sale price and the greater amount that could have been attained elsewhere (or the difference between the price sold to the Vancouverite and the supposedly higher cost of production.) Why the greedy capitalist pigs in Washington had so suddenly been overcome with charitable instincts would still be a puzzle, but we could concentrate our attention on the old farm adage—"don't look a gift horse in the mouth!" and apply it to a "gift potato" as well. *W.B.*

ECONOMIC CALCULATION

Recently, the City of Victoria was considering the installation of a garbage burner. This would solve the disposal problem associated with garbage to some extent and, as a by-product, produce energy which in turn could be used for electrical generation. From the point of view of the City of Victoria, the question is whether that makes any economic sense. It does make economic sense, apparently, largely because in doing their calculations the City of Victoria is able to put a zero cost on the electrical generation facility. The reason is that the capital cost for the electrical generation facility will be provided from Ottawa.

Now, from the point of view of Victoria, it makes great sense to undertake such a project given that the cost of the electrical generation capability is, for all practical purposes, zero. But what about Canada as a whole? If every local municipality engages in the same kind of economic calculus and puts a zero cost on the capital installation required to make electricity from garbage, then we will install many electrical generation units in Canada which may not be economically efficient.

From the point of view of the country as a whole, the cost of the capital to install such electrical generation capability is not at all zero. And, in fact, the costs must be weighed in terms of other capital projects which cannot take place because the capital is being used to put in an electrical generation facility. For example, if a facility were to be built by a hydro corporation such as B.C. Hydro, they would at least have to ask the question of whether or not electricity generation from garbage was less or more efficient than hydro generation or geothermal generation or coal generation such as in the Hat Creek project.

As it stands, the existence of these capital cost grants from Ottawa means that for one whole aspect of our national strategy of developing electricity generation capacity there will be no economic calculus applied. This is yet another aspect of the difficulties which arise when the natural forces of the marketplace are suspended by a government which undoubtedly means to do good but can in the process do considerable mischief. *M.W.*

ECONOMIC JUSTICE

Should a single female parent with three children have a right to expect economic support from the state? Most people would have considerable sympathy toward that view. It seems to be a statement of an inalienable personal right. However, that is because we ignore one side of the personal relationship involved. By saying that she has a right to expect support from the state, we ignore the fact that the state is comprised of other people.

If we reduce the state to a neighbourhood setting, then the woman's claim is seen to be that she has every right to expect her neighbours to support her, irrespective of the economic conditions in which her neighbours might find themselves. In this form, the single parent's assertion is not one that all of us can readily accept. Indeed, it is not one which we would accept without much qualification.

While entitlements are always expressed positively, such as, "she has a right to support from the state," the truth of the relationship is quite different. In fact, the only way somebody can be delivered the right to support is if some other person is denied access to the resources they have earned. In the most prosaic terms, for every person who receives a dollar they didn't earn, somebody else earns a dollar they don't receive. The question of economic justice in this circumstance is clearly less straightforward than is often supposed. *M.W.*

ECONOMIC NATIONALISM

Economic nationalists claim that soon after a free trade deal is struck, corporations will pressure government to reduce their support for medicare to ease the corporate tax load and increase competitiveness. Medicare and free trade are not compatible in this view, because the Americans don't have medicare and if we are going to compete with them medicare will have to go.

So much for the mythology. The fact is that at the moment the U.S. spends more per capita and a much higher fraction of its GNP on medical care than we in Canada do. They have a superior health care system utilizing more advanced technology and providing more extensive access to life-saving procedures such as organ transplant. American firms face higher costs of medical care provision in the form of the premiums they must pay. As every school child knows, the pressure on American firms to reduce the costs of medical care is one of their most significant challenges. Some will move to Canada as a result.

The economic nationalist protectionists represent the view that Canada is better to go it alone and strongly resist pressure for closer relationships with any other country and in particular the United States. They press aggressively against a free trade deal with the United States because, they say, such a free trade treaty would inevitably lead to a common market, and then to political integration of the two countries. As well, many Canadians see trade relations with the U.S. as implying an inevitable political connection.

While in some visceral sense one can understand this point of view, it is difficult on the strength of the evidence to support it. One need only look at Ireland and England, two countries which couldn't be more politically and culturally sovereign and independent but who have had free trade for many years, or the Norwegians and the Swedes. And what about the French and the Germans, co-existing members of the European Economic Community (EEC) along with Italy and Britain. It would be difficult to discover six countries more jealously independent than these, notwithstanding the existence of the European Parliament. There is no necessary connection between free trade and national independence, and we shouldn't make one. *M.W.*

ECONOMIC RIGHTS

All rights involve equal and opposite obligations. If you have a right to property, you have an obligation to refrain from stealing it or trespassing upon it. If you have an inviolable right in your person, everyone else has an obligation to leave you unmolested. These are *negative rights*. They make it incumbent upon people to refrain, to cease and desist, to avoid certain aggressive behaviour, but they impose no positive obligations whatsoever. Rights such as these, the rights to person and property, have been acknowledged since time immemorial. They are at the core of the Magna Carta and the constitutions and actual practice of all Western democracies. They are the backbone of Western civilization.

Of late, however, some new types of rights have arisen. Widely trumpeted, these include a claim to everything from a "decent" level of clothing, food, housing, and medical care, to rock music, sexual orgasms, and meaningful relationships. If this were only an emphasis of everyone's right to seek happiness in whatever manner chosen provided no one else's rights were infringed in the process, it would be unobjectionable. Indeed, this is the essence of the right to person and property. But something quite different is meant by those who hold that "housing is a basic human right."

What is claimed is not the right to be left alone, free to build, buy, or rent whatever shelter one can afford, but a right to housing which implies an obligation on the part of other people—to provide it. This claim involves the so-called *positive* rights, not the negative rights of classical origin.

What is actually at stake here, however, has nothing to do with rights at all. On the contrary, it is a disguised and therefore quite insidious demand for wealth. In the case of rights proper, all that is required of outsiders is non-interference. But in this fraudulent case, a myriad of material goods and services is at stake.

To see how radical a departure are the new positive rights, consider this. Mankind could, at one fell swoop—if it were so minded—completely banish all violations of negative rights. All that need be done is that each and every one of us resolve not to initiate physical violence or fraud, and then act on this basis. But all the agreement in the world would not be sufficient to provide the level of wealth necessary to fulfil our so-called positive rights to health and happiness, certainly not at the levels sought by the advocates of positive rights.

There are other grave problems with this contention. If housing is a basic right imposing ethical imperatives upon strangers, each of us is immoral—not only if any of our countrymen are without decent housing, but as long as anyone in the world is so lacking. Rights know no national boundaries. If it is morally incumbent on anyone to supply a good or service without his contractual agreement, then this applies to everyone. Another logical implication is even more insidious. For rights, by their very nature, are egalitarian. It is clear that all of us, rich or poor, old or young, have equal negative rights. We are all equal in that, for example, murder committed on any innocent person is wrong, and to the identical degree. The mass murderer is guilty of the same immorality in each of the specific acts he perpetrates.

If positive claims are also rights, then people must not only have a right to decent shelter but an absolutely equal share of the world's housing. Since there is no logical stopping place for positive rights, the claim of basic human needs as rights really amounts to a demand for absolute income equality.

And the situation gets even worse, for there is nothing in the logic of the argument to prevent the demand for equal intelligence, equal beauty, equal athletic and sexual prowess, and even equal happiness, if these things could somehow be contrived. We must reject this claim and with it the moral swamp it necessarily involves us in. *W.B.*

E E E E E E E E E E E E E E E E E E E E E E E

ELECTRICAL UTILITIES

The special deal enjoyed by public electrical utilities in Canada has led to behaviours which are costing the country something over $4 billion a year. Public utilities in Canada have two special concessions which are not given to private enterprises. In the first place, they are exempt from federal income taxes as are all provincial government enterprises under the old principle that "the Crown can't tax the Crown." But the second and more important feature is that when such public utilities borrow from capital markets, their loans are guaranteed by provincial governments.

In consequence, the utilities borrow at below market rates because the interest they pay does not have to compensate lenders for the risk of default. Such protection is important for utilities which have no equity and are completely debt financed. And, of course, utilities are also instructed by their provincial government owners to sell electricity at bargain basement prices, sufficient only to cover their financial costs.

The net effect of these provisions is that electricity is overused and inadvertent subsidies are provided. The end result is a loss every year amounting to approximately one cent out of every dollar earned in the country. The public policy implications are clear. Put this industry on the same footing as all others, take away its special privileges, and leave it free to compete. In that way, the allocation of resources can be improved and with it the economic welfare of Canadians. *M.W.*

EQUAL PAY FOR WORK OF EQUAL VALUE (see Comparable Worth)

The real issue here is whether the wage a person is paid can be objectively compared to the wage another person receives if the two are doing different jobs. Can there be an intrinsic value attached to secretarial work and truck driving skills? How does a librarian compare to a registered nurse?

Equal pay for work of equal value laws would force employers to somehow relate the wages for such jobs without reference to the supply and demand of workers. But, it isn't clear that even people who do the same work ought to be paid the same. For example, the law would compel male and female aerobic instructors to be paid the same wage. Even if female instructors were in short supply, higher wages could not be paid to encourage more to train unless the same wage were paid to the males. Males who teach weight lifting could not be paid more than females. As Jane Fonda pointed out when she was sued for wage discrimination, "we pay men more because they are more productive—they put more people per hour through the exercise machine."

The fascinating aspect of all this is that equal pay for equal work laws are called pay equity laws. They are, of course, nothing of the sort. They are arbitrary interference with the wage mechanism which is attempting to reflect a wide range of elements like productivity—as Jane Fonda pointed out—and supply and demand. Calling them pay equity laws completely distorts the issue—but, you can see why the term is used. After all, who can be against pay equity? *M.W.*

EQUAL PAY LEGISLATION (see Affirmative Action)

The starting point for calls for equal pay legislation is that women are allegedly paid one-third less than males. One explanation for this gap is that it reflects nothing more than the discrimination of employers. But the alternative (and correct!) explanation is that the wage gap is the result of the asymmetrical effects of marriage on earnings. Marriage raises the earnings of the husband and reduces those of the wife, largely because of the unequal sharing of child care, house management, and marketable economic activities. In 1984, never married females aged 45-54 actually earned 13.4 percent more than similarly aged never married males. If we correct the figures for differences in education and compare, for example, the female to male income ratios for never marrieds with a university degree, the figure rises further. In 1971, such university-educated, never married females earned 9.8 percent more than their equally accomplished male counterparts. By contrast, university-educated females who have either been married, widowed, divorced or separated earn only 43.9

percent that of males with such marital status. Clearly, it is marriage which explains most of the wage gap, and no amount of equal pay legislation is going to affect that. *M.W.*

EQUAL PAY FOR EQUAL WORK

Companies which failed to adopt a policy of equal pay would no longer be eligible for federal government contracts if its advocates have their way. It is astonishing that such proposals are not met by more critical comment. Can it be that the concept of equal pay, although largely unchallenged as yet in Canada, has come to be taken for granted? If so, it is a black day for Canadian workers and, particularly, a black day for Canadian women.

The case for equal pay for work of equal value is based on two beliefs. The first is that women are doomed to spend their days in certain jobs because of sex discrimination on the part of employers. The second belief is that pay in those jobs is depressed simply because the jobs are typically held by women. The implication of these two beliefs is that if truck drivers were predominantly female and secretaries were predominantly male, secretarial work would pay higher wages than truck driving. That these beliefs are widely held cannot be denied. But if we are actually to advance the cause of women in the workplace, we must take into account the operation of immutable economic laws which will determine the success or failure of legislative measures.

Why will an equal pay for work of equal value policy actually have a deleterious effect on women? In the past, women were encouraged by a variety of cultural pressures to seek employment in traditional women's jobs. However, as the number of females enrolled in professional and technical courses in universities and colleges attest, that day is rapidly passing. But, there are some developments which would impede that progress.

A reversion to the customs and beliefs of the 1950s, is one example. Another is the development of incentives for women to remain in traditional roles, such as a large increase in the relative pay available in those jobs. One reason both women and men undertake the additional training necessary to practice law, accountancy and the other professions is to earn the relatively higher incomes they provide. Suddenly imposing a higher wage scale on so-called traditional female occupations will be a signal to young women that they don't need to practice a profession to earn high incomes.

However we may denigrate them, the forces of supply and demand continue to work. The imposition of higher wages for clerical, secretarial, and other positions will reinforce the job stereotypes of the past. An unintended side effect will be to reduce the number of such (now high priced) jobs available. This would imply more unemployment for women.

Consider in this regard the very puzzling fact that equal pay for equal work was a policy supported by the white racist unions in South Africa. Given that this policy had such boosters, could it really be the sort of thing that progressive-minded individuals should support? Unions in South Africa support equal pay for equal work legislation as a replacement for the currently existing white-only job restrictions. Under these restrictions, some jobs may only be done by whites. Black workers are explicitly prevented from occupying these positions. Under great pressure from the more progressive elements in South Africa, the unions have begun to suggest that they would be willing to give up the white-only restrictions currently framed by law provided that they are replaced by equal pay for equal work legislation. Of course, what they realize is that equal pay for equal work would have the same effect in South Africa as white-only restrictions.

Why is that? The reason is that the equal pay for equal work will effectively prevent blacks from breaking into job situations which are currently dominated by whites. Under existing circumstances, blacks are not allowed to take the white-only positions and, as a consequence, have acquired no skills or history of employment in these sorts of jobs. Consequently, an employer faced with the prospect of hiring either a black or a white for a job currently restricted for whites only will find a preponderance of white people qualified for the job and very few black people qualified. If the white employer must pay the black worker the same wage he must pay a white worker, given the greater productivity of the former, the employer will always select a white over a black.

We can imagine another situation, one where the white-only job restrictions in South Africa were removed and equal pay for equal work legislation was not imposed. Under these circumstances, an employer considering blacks and whites for a particular position will be able to say to the black, "I would like to hire you, but I am not confident that you can do the work." The black is then placed in the position of saying, "I'll work for less than the white just to show you that I am capable of doing the work, that I can acquire the skills in a very short period of time and, once I have acquired those skills, you can pay me what I'm worth rather than what you now feel that I am worth."

In other words, in South Africa, as everywhere else, it is the ability to offer services for a slightly lower wage than the competitors that enables workers to overcome prejudice, discrimination, or the lack of appropriate training in competing for jobs. Equal pay for equal work removes this ability of workers to use the most potent weapon they have in overcoming these barriers to their employment.

In a modern Canadian setting, of course, the most often considered "minority" group is women, and it is in connection with the wages paid to women that equal pay for equal work is most often raised. However, it must be recognized that women attempting to break into a labour force situation which has typically excluded them may find that the ability to offer themselves at lower wages is their single most powerful tool to break down barriers imposed by tradition and by narrow-minded or discriminatory employers.

At the very least, women's groups which so vociferously support equal pay for equal work ought to well consider the company they keep in the economic propositions which they support. They should ask themselves whether they should find themselves fellow travellers with racist unions of South Africa. *M.W.*

EQUALITY

What does economic equality mean? Why do we worry about equality anyway? The usual meaning of the term in everyday language is "exactly the same." Two things, two people, two situations are equal if in all essential respects they are the same.

This literal meaning notwithstanding, the term equal is most often used to denote a state of justice, and we are interested in equality because of what it implies about justice. For example, two children are typically required to drink a glass of milk at each meal. Sometimes they don't want to drink their milk and, on these occasions, one or the other almost invariably will note that the rule is not being equally applied because they have more milk in their glass than the other has. "That's not fair." Inequality arouses a natural sense of injustice. In this case, the notion of justice creeps in because there is a rule and, in the eyes of one child, the rule is not being uniformly applied. Moreover, it is objectively clear that the rule is not being uniformly applied. In this case, inequality and injustice go hand-in-hand.

Consider another case of equality. A research director of the Atlantic Provinces Economic Council receives a salary which is probably twice as high as the average wage earned in the Atlantic provinces. Applying the simple glass of milk sense of equality and justice, that situation is unjust. But is it really unjust? In what sense is it unjust? In assessing incomes, don't we have to recognize the fact that this person has invested time in learning—going to graduate school? Does justice really imply equality? The simple rule—justice is equality—doesn't seem to work.

Do we really want equality anyway? What does equality imply? Guy Lafleur is probably one of the best centre forwards the game of hockey has seen in its history. His talents are obvious and were so from an early age. The present authors on the other hand, were undoubtedly the worst centres ever to lace on a pair of skates. It's not fair that Guy Lafleur is so much better than we are. Guy Lafleur should be forced to wear sandbags, slippery-bottomed street shoes, and use a rubber hockey stick to make us all equal.

Imagine the Stanley Cup playoffs. Ken Dryden would have to play with a bigger net because he is so good as a goaltender. Bobby Clarke would be blindfolded, Darryl Sittler would be given only one skate, Scotty Bowman would have to wear a helmet which emitted sharp, shrill, mind-shattering noises every three minutes to prevent him from using his mind to form strategy, and Danny Gallivan would have to give the play-by-play broadcast with his mouth full of marbles and a clothespin on his nose. Everybody would be equal, every talent eradicated. Justice would, at long last, prevail in the NHL. Not only that, but those guys wouldn't be able to ask for those fancy salaries once we made them equal.

But the average person's sense of justice does not require that sort of equality. Some people do suggest, however, that while we shouldn't penalize or handicap talent, there is no reason to reward it either. In other words, even though Ken Dryden is one of the best goaltenders in history, he shouldn't get any more money for playing goal than any other goaltender. He wants to play hockey, so the story goes, and would probably play hockey regardless of what he were paid.In Ken Dryden's case, that poses a problem. He is also a lawyer, and the cost to him of playing hockey is the difference between what he would earn as a lawyer and what he earns as a hockey player. Perhaps the equality rule for hockey players would mean that only those people who had no other alternative would play hockey.

Well, the "solution" to that is to make sure that Ken Dryden couldn't make more money as a lawyer. Make all incomes the same, then we would have equality, justice and good hockey players. *M.W.*

EQUALIZATION PAYMENTS

We must be very careful to distinguish between equality of opportunity and equality of result. Everybody should be given equal opportunity in the sense of government not setting up obstacles but that does not mean that everybody will achieve equally. The attempt to accomplish equality after the fact may mean a very unjust system. To make everybody equal in economic terms after the fact may imply economic handicaps of the sort we discussed regarding the hockey players.

Unequal incomes between Eastern and Western Canada have nothing at all to do with equality of opportunity. They do have something to say about the size of the trees in British Columbia and New Brunswick, the fact that Vancouver handles much more freight than Halifax, that Alberta seems to have more hydrocarbon in usable form than Nova Scotia, that the world's largest deposits of potash are in Saskatchewan, and that you can't grow wheat in Newfoundland. That is what those numbers show.

They don't say that a person born in Newfoundland must stay in Newfoundland. They don't say that the riches of the West are reserved for a chosen few. They don't tell us anything about the fact that most people in British Columbia weren't born there, or that some of the people who earned low wages in the Maritimes in one year are earning high wages in Alberta in another. What the numbers show is that if people stay in the Atlantic region, they will probably earn a lower wage than they could earn if they went to Alberta.

Consider a young person making decisions about what to do with his life. Will he be an economist or a ski instructor, a mechanic or a philosopher? As he tries to make up his mind, he will undoubtedly consider a number of aspects of each job. How much will it pay? How hard will he have to work? Can he stay in his hometown, or will he have to go elsewhere? What are his talents? What combination will make him happy?

Some jobs pay more, but they require long hours. Others pay less, but are outdoors. Some promise high incomes, but require a long period of training or mean a move away from home to Toronto or Alberta where a house and a summer camp would be beyond reach. (We chose economics because it was clean work, indoors, with no heavy lifting.)

As people make their selection, they will doubtless come to realize that there is more to a job than the money it pays. Some jobs in some locations have a very large compliment of irksome characteristics, and the higher incomes associated with them are required to offset the bad aspects. Life in Cold Lake, Alberta, or at Goose Bay or Churchill, Manitoba, requires a certain kind of person or a relatively high income compensation. Life in Toronto is very different from life in Moncton, and is not everybody's cup of tea. Similarly, life in B.C., relatively isolated from the population centres of the country, doesn't suit every taste.

In short, higher average salaries in one occupation or one geographical area don't necessarily mean that people in other areas or in other occupations are necessarily worse off. That would be the case if there were people who wanted to move but were prevented, or people who wanted to be lawyers or teachers but were denied the opportunity. As long as people are given the opportunity to choose where they live and, given their talents, what they do with their lives, in what sense is a comparison of wages in the Atlantic and Western regions meaningful? What does it tell us about equality in the sense of justice? In our view, it tells us nothing at all.

But the matter goes deeper than that. Inequality in economic terms serves a real function in our society. Higher wages in Elliot Lake, Thompson, and Cold Lake attract people to go and develop the resources there. Low wages in Newfoundland make economic activity possible there that otherwise would not occur and, hence, provide jobs for those who, for non-economic reasons, want to stay there. About half the young people from Newfoundland choose to stay there. Many of them would be unable to do so if the government imposed strict minimum wages on all occupations—if manufacturers had to pay Toronto wages; if truckers had to pay the same wages as truckers pay in British Columbia; if, given the different size of the trees, and the ease of harvesting, woodland wages were the same in B.C. and Newfoundland.

Some think government should overcome income inequality. Industry in the Atlantic area should be subsidized to get it going. Jobs should be created to make it possible for more people to stay in the Atlantic region. That sounds great. It sounds like we can have our cake and eat it too. We can create more economic equality by regional economic development. But let's consider how that will happen in fact.

In order to finance economic development in the Atlantic region, the funds must come from elsewhere in the country. They must come from higher income taxes on people who moved to Elliot Lake or Toronto or Edmonton. They must come from penalizing economic activity in those areas. Subsidies do not come free. In order to make incomes more equal, we have to reduce the economic opportunity available elsewhere in the country. We have to sandbag the successful industries elsewhere in the country.

Why be a Canadian if we aren't going to get income equality? What is the point? The point is that Canada is one of the most favoured geographical areas on the face of the earth. Wherever people happen to be born in this country, their options are virtually unlimited. Their opportunities are profoundly greater than any generation in history has had. It would be unwise in the extreme to undermine that on the principle of sandbagging economic opportunity. *M.W.*

EXPORT SUBSIDIES

Consider the contract between the Quebec-based Bombardier Inc. and the New York City Metropolitan Transport Authority as an example of the species. According to the terms of this agreement, Bombardier sold 825 subway cars to New York City for a price of about $1 billion in Canadian funds. The clincher in the deal was an accompanying Canadian government (Export Development Corporation) subsidized 15-year loan of $563 million (U.S.) at a bargain basement interest rate. It was this subsidy—at a cost of $230 million U.S.—that enabled the Quebec manufacturing company to underbid competitors for the contract.

The Budd Company of Troy, Michigan (whose bid was higher than Bombardier's), petitioned the U.S. Commerce Department and the International Trade Commission for a tax that would offset the subsidy-loan on the grounds that such activity was "predatory and uncompetitive." And the AFL-CIO joined forces with the spurned Budd Company, demanding retaliation against these "unfair trade practices" under section 301 of the U.S. Trade Act.

It is easy to see why the AFL-CIO and the Budd Company might be more than just a bit perturbed with the Bombardier subsidy. The profits and the estimated 15,000 man-years of jobs necessary to manufacture 825 subway cars for New York City will be transferred from Michigan to Montreal. Likewise, it requires no great power of reflection to understand the enthusiasm of Bombardier or New York City for the project. Thanks to the largess of the Canadian government, a private company managed to sink its hooks into the taxpayers' hard-earned money, and each Big Apple transit commuter will be able to save a nickel a day as a result.

More difficult to discern are why the Canadian government should have entered into any such hare-brained giveaway scheme and why the U.S.—the recipient of this largess—should object. All this deal amounts to, in effect, is the granting of Canadian foreign aid to the U.S. with the condition that our southern neighbour then turn around and spend the largess in this country.

Are they so impoverished and we so wealthy that Canadians should be granting foreign aid to the U.S.? Hardly. Is the U.S. so rich that they can afford to spurn foreign aid from this country? Not bloody likely either?

Instead of giving the subsidy to New York City, on condition that it be spent in Canada, our government could have given the money back to the long-suffering taxpayers of this country (a rebate) in the confident expectation that it would have been spent here. (True, some of this money would have been spent on foreign goods, but these dollars would eventually come back to us and thereby stimulate our export industries.) In any case, an appreciable portion of the Bombardier work took place in Vermont and Pittsburgh, of all places, through sub-contractors).

As well, the American attitude is truly inexplicable. Not only are they looking a gift horse in the mouth, but their adherence to the free trade philosophy is thereby exposed as a sham. In threatening to raise tariffs on subway cars manufactured in Canada, they are endangering what little remains of the unimpeded movement of goods across national borders. Their complaint under GATT (General Agreement on Tariffs and Trade) rules is more of the same, and it is hypocritical. The U.S. has been "guilty" of the same practices. Last December, the U.S. Export-Import Bank floated a $550 million loan at 7.75 percent interest for Argentinean hydro-electric power generation. As well, the U.S. offer to Air Canada of an 8.7 percent interest 12-year loan of $1 billion in order to help flog Boeing 767 airplanes was an export subsidy.

We cannot control U.S. decision making. If they are intent on economic error, it is not within our power to stop them. However, we can put our own house in order by stopping this senseless use of taxpayers' money. *W.B.*

EXTRA BILLING

The government is continually engaged in a process intended to close some "loopholes" in the Canadian medicare system. Specifically, it is concerned with the increasingly popular practice of extra billing (doctors charging patients more than the price set by the medicare programme for a specific service) and user pay or user fees (hospitals receiving part of their compensation directly from the customer). Advocates of socialized medicine have been wailing and gnashing their teeth at these occurrences, and pundits have waxed apoplectic with outraged indignation.

Why all the fuss? Why shouldn't we be asked to pay our own way in health and hospital care? After all, we pay for our own clothes, food, books, movies, piano lessons, and virtually every other consumer item under the sun. Shouldn't individual citizens take responsibility for their own medical care, too?

The impression left by welfare state advocates is that hospital care and other such goodies come to us free, compliments of the government. Nothing could be further from the truth. The fact is that every penny given to us by Big Brother must first be taken from us in taxes (or inflation). If government would lower the tax burden, we could afford to pay not only user fees and extra billing but for our entire health and hospital care costs as well. And, by cutting out the wasteful Ottawa middleman, we would probably have money left over for ourselves.

In order to see this more clearly, let us leave off our discussion of the emotion-laden field of health care and consider instead an item not as likely to raise the decibel level: milk. Right now, we can safely assume there is no crisis concerning milk. There seems to be enough of it (although see Marketing Boards) but not too much. There is neither an over- or under-investment in the industry.

But suppose that our milk supply were put on the same economic footing as medical care. Under such a system, we would not have to buy milk at its given price. Thus, no longer would investment in this beverage be limited to the amount of money the public voluntarily paid for this product. Instead, under this modern, forward-looking and progressive scheme, all milk would be given out for free—courtesy of a benevolent government. Well, not exactly, for government isn't a magical milk-creating machine. All its resources must first be extracted from the citizens. So milk is not really given out for free under milk socialism. Rather, the public is (collectively) forced to pay for this item through taxes, and then each person can obtain all he wants for free—that is, without further payment.

Is there any doubt that under such a scheme the amount of milk demanded would skyrocket? At present, people do not spend their money frivolously in this regard. Each expense is carefully weighed to see if more satisfaction could be obtained by an alternate use of the given funds. But with free milk, why worry about expense? People would use milk for all sorts of frivolous purposes, for example milk baths, or children would have "milk gun" fights instead of "water gun" fights. True, we'll pay for it in the end, through taxes, but the tie to costs is completely broken *for each individual.* No one person has any real incentive to economize and, hence, few people would. More expensive and elaborate milk products would soon be demanded. This is the problem of "moral hazard"—allowing people to consume additional units at a zero price only encourages them to engage in "immoral" wastage.

Critics might claim that milk is a poor analogy to health care. However, they cannot argue that medical care is necessary for health but that milk is not. Further they allege that under socialized medicine, the level of care is determined by doctors, not patients, but this is untrue. We all know that our demand for health care depends at least in part on price—certainly for all but the most serious of illnesses. Secondly, it may be all well and good to rely on advice from doctor specialists—we do this for many purchases—the final decision should always remain with the ultimate consumer and not be determined by a government bureaucrat, expert or not.

And, now, suppose that under this ludicrous scheme of milk-socialism, the government were to allow extra billing for milk purchases. Should we the public rise up on our hind legs and demand our ancient heritage of free milk? Not a bit of it. For as we have seen, the moral hazard implicit in "milk-care" only encourages us to over-utilize this item. (This is why Canadians must wait so long for many surgical services, over-stimulated demand and limited government budgets.)

Indeed, the problem with merely keeping user fees is that this does not go far enough. What we need is a return to a system of individual responsibility. Instead of being forced to contribute to medical care and then being allowed to grab off as much service as we can for ourselves, let us keep our money and pay only for the care we deem more worthwhile than its costs (and/or patronize private insurance schemes).

It's true that our system of health care also transfers funds to poor people to enable them to purchase a service they could not otherwise afford. But this function can better be handled directly through the welfare system without artificially encouraging most people to utilize more health care than they really need.

After all, we don't have to set up a policy of "milk-socialism" in order to ensure that the poor have reasonable access to milk. *W.B.*

F

FAIR TRADE

What is the distinction between fair trade and free trade? Free trade means that citizens of Canada are able to trade with citizens of other countries on a completely unrestricted basis. For example, Canadians would be able to buy shirts, shoes, and other commodities manufactured in the Third World and not be forced by trade quotas or tariff barriers to purchase the Canadian variety.

Fair trade is a concept recently concocted in the United States by those attempting to defend declining smoke-stack industries in that country unable to compete with Third World producers of products ranging from steel to shoelaces. The notion is that it is unfair to expect domestic producers to compete with those in the Third World as long as the latter have the advantage of very low wage rates. It would be fair for the U.S. and Canada to trade in men's shirts, for example, since the wage rates here are only slightly higher than those south of the border. But it would be unfair to expect Canadian shirt producers to compete with those in Third World countries. In other words, First World countries should compete with First World countries, and Third World countries should compete with Third World countries.

Whatever the attractiveness of this proposition in a rhetorical sense, it is quite obvious that as a description of reality it is complete nonsense. It certainly would be disastrous to base our future economic policies in Canada and the United States on such a distinction. The effect would be to make Canadian and American industry increasingly uncompetitive in the global sphere and lead to an economic decline comparable to that experienced by Great Britain in the pre-Thatcher days.

From the consumer's point of view, fair trade means higher prices because it represents the attempt by industries to restrict their competitors to those countries which, like themselves, have high costs of production.

Now, of course, this claim for fair trade is only made in certain industries—those industries which are not particularly competitive in North America at the moment. The problem is that pursuing a so-called fair trade policy will, over a period of time, lead to a lengthening of the list of industries no longer competitive internationally. The reason is that protecting existing declining industries from low-cost competition also imposes costs on those industries which are at present competitive. Canadian industries which compete, for example, in high tech or other areas with Pacific Rim counterparts will be forced to use high-cost inputs while their Pacific Rim competitors use lowest-cost-possible inputs produced under free trade conditions.

While fair trade is a seductively attractive idea—everything should be fair, right?—we have to look for the unintended side effects. In this particular case, they would be disastrous. *M.W.*

FARM SUBSIDIES

"Early to bed, early to rise, makes a man healthy, wealthy, and wise." This might hold true in some times in some places, but certainly not for the small modern family farmer. Although he gets up at the crack of dawn, labours all the day long, sinks exhausted into his bed, and may be healthy and wise as a result—he certainly is not becoming wealthy. On the contrary, his reward, in many cases, is only insolvency, bankruptcy, and tears. On the Eastern seaboard, a bank foreclosed on the farm and prize-winning pure-bred Charolais cattle of a 48-year-old farmer. In response—and in an attempt to publicize his quest to save his farm—he dumped three dead cows in front of the Toronto offices of the foreclosing bank. He did this on the grounds that the bank's refusal to carry his debt was really responsible for the death of his livestock, since without further financial support he did not have enough money to feed his herd. A local newspaper headlined its front page coverage of this event: "Bank seizes cattle, land, of tearful farmer." (One wonders what the Society for the Prevention of Cruelty to Animals had to say about this!) This particular farm was seized because of a default on a loan. More generally, farmers are having difficult times because of high interest rates and tightening margins between feed, fertilizer, and other farm costs on the one hand and farm output prices on the other hand.

What public policy ought to be followed to deal with the crisis in the small family-owned farm? Not unnaturally, the response of some people might be that "the government should do something about the plight of the farmer." Suggestions range from farm subsidies, to price supports, to impeding banks from foreclosing on farms. But each of these policies has serious flaws.

Farm subsidies cannot be created out of thin air. They must come from somewhere, at a cost to at least some people. If the government merely prints up additional money and presents it to impoverished farmers, the inflationary fires are stoked up. If it does the same with the borrowed money, other bond sellers are crowded out of the loan market, and high interest rates—the issue that started us off on this quest in the first place and a problem for many other businesses as well—are increased even more. If government diverts tax money to farmers, it must either increase taxes, which the public opposes, or reduce other programmes.

Price supports for farm produce likewise have serious defects. They have a habit of raising food prices, a particularly vicious result in that the poor spend a far higher percentage of their household budgets on food than do the rich. Then, too, by interfering with the free play of the price mechanism, supports also reduce the accuracy of the information conveyed by the price system and make it harder for the numerous economic actors in the marketplace to co-ordinate their activities with one another.

Legislation which violates the right of lenders to foreclose on the property of loan defaulters will also have unforeseen and disturbing consequences. Banks are a popular target of demagogues because they usually have lots of money. But if financial institutions cannot collect the collateral put up for debts that turn bad, they will be less willing to make loans in the first place. This will reduce the incomes of savers, many of whom are people with little means. It will also increase the costs of future loans (the interest rates charged), and this will harm all future and potential borrowers.

Of course, it is unlikely that the small farmer will long endure, at least in his present state, without government aid. This, without a doubt, will be a tragedy for thousands of people who will be forced to enter other, now more productive fields. It is important to realize, however, that such a policy will be of great *benefit* to the remainder of the citizens. The present spate of bankruptcies is part of the long-term reduction of the proportion of the workforce on the farm.

In early colonial times, the proportion of the population on the farm was well over 90 percent. This fell regularly and precipitously over the 18th and 19th centuries, reaching a level of 44 percent in 1880, 35 percent in 1910, 25 percent in 1930, 15 percent in 1950, and 5 percent in 1970. This pattern was welcome, as it arose from great increases in farm productivity coupled with a far less than proportionate increase in the number of mouths to feed. To compare 1880 and 1970, for example, this trend freed up fully 39 percent of the labour force for other, now more important work. Imagine what would happen if these people had to go back to the farm so we could feed ourselves. This would be a disaster. We would have to do without the truly huge number of goods and services now provided by these people. So the long-term trend from farm to city is to be applauded, not denigrated and artificially halted.

Moreover, there is not a shred of evidence to support the much-vaunted claim that psychological, moral, and spiritual benefits spill over from the small family-owned farm to the remainder of society. Supposedly, the farm is the creator of honesty, independence, thriftiness, trustworthiness, and a whole host of other Boy Scout characteristics. There is no doubt that many people raised on farms exhibit these qualities, but this is hardly a rural monopoly. City folk, too, number amongst their offspring children with high moral qualities. So, if there are any geographical moral spillovers, and this has never been scientifically shown, they are likely to be in both directions, not just one.

We must conclude that the case for government initiatives to help the farmer is extremely weak. Based on the evidence, these initiatives are likely to add to the general rate of inflation or raise food prices or ruin loan markets. And, if these efforts are successful in stemming the tide from farm to city, they will reduce the rate of increase in our standard of living. *W.B.*

FEATHERBEDDING

Ultimately, what increases wages is higher productivity. Blood cannot be squeezed from a stone, nor can everyone have a better standard of living if the size of the pie is shrinking.

What is the effect of union-inspired featherbedding on productivity? Clearly, productivity decreases, or does not rise as fast as it otherwise would. When "firemen" are kept on diesel locomotives (when they are no longer needed to shovel coal into a now non-existent furnace), there is little doubt that the economic pie—the sum total of goods and services available in society—will be less than if these able-bodied men were freed up to do productive work.

Consider containerization. According to some pundits, retention of the container clause is a victory for organized labour. This allows longshoremen the right to unpack and then pack again those large freight containers which are travelling to local destinations. This might create more jobs in the short run at the local waterfront docks, but since it needlessly raises costs, this bit of featherbedding is an attack on the Canadian consumer, already suffering from high prices at the checkout counter. Nor will this head-in-the-sand policy even serve the long-run interests of longshoremen. With the reduced effectiveness of containerization, other ports will become more economical and competitive, and freight shipments will be diverted away. *W.B.*

FOOD BANK

Food banks are becoming a feature of the Canadian social landscape. Some regard their presence as a shocking and disgraceful comment on our society and the failure of government to discharge its responsibilities. They first rose to prominence in British Columbia in the aftermath of the steep recession touched of by the boom and bust in natural resource industries. Because the recession was accompanied by a stiff programme of governmental restraint, social critics were quick to point to the government as the prime culprit. Economic restraint caused the recession, the recession caused unemployment and social distress, and in the face of insufficient welfare payments the food lines have swelled and lengthened. Moreover, they continue to do so. While no thinking person today believes that the restraint programme caused B.C.'s unemployment problem, there is still a lingering belief that food banks are a barometer of economic malfunction and government miserliness.

We don't accept this connection. It is undoubtedly true that the people who use food banks are in need. However, it must be said that those who use food banks are also typically those who receive public assistance. Many of those people are public wards because they do not have the minimal skills to manage their own affairs. That their welfare money runs out is to some degree a barometer of that fact. But more importantly, whether they could stretch their welfare cheque or not, people who are habitually dependent on public charity will obviously take advantage of whatever free food and other benefits are offered. And, the more who do, the less the stigma and the more demand there will be.

While that's our view, it is not a popular one. Now, however, there is independent evidence in support of it. The evidence has been provided by the experience with food banks in Ontario. By way of background, the unemployment rate in Ontario is currently about 7.2 percent and has been steadily falling for the past two years. Hardly an indicator of economic distress. In fact, Ontario is faring almost as well as the United States under the scourge of Reaganomics. Even though the Ontario jobless rate is dropping, what do you think is happening to the demand for free food from food banks? Come on, guess? Why, it's positively exploding! Second Harvest, a well-meaning food bank organization operating in Toronto, has found that since its inception in April 1985 the demand for food has risen steadily. In January they distributed 22 tons of food; in February the total jumped to 33 tons—a 50 percent increase. Of course, that's not surprising. The food is free.

There's nothing wrong with food banks. They give food to low income people who are better off for it. The people who contribute also feel better. Food banks do no harm unless we misinterpret why the lines are so long, but some people have done precisely that. Because of their misunderstanding of the economics of the situation, spokespersons for the Vancouver Food Bank, the Richmond Food Bank, the First United Church, the New Westminster Unemployment Action Centre, and the Federated Anti-Poverty Groups of British Columbia have indicated that they believe giving food to the poor should really be a government enterprise. In a good society, in the view of these people, there would be little scope for private initiatives such as their own—the public sector should do the job.

The Reverend Alan Bush of St. Alban's Richmond Food Bank even went so far as to claim that the B.C. government in its restraint programme was taking advantage of the "kindly and loving people administering to the poor." According to Sylvia Russell of the Vancouver Food Bank, they have no intention of expanding their base of operations to take up the slack left by government. The Right Reverend Robert Smith, then Moderator of the United Church of Canada, held that all those who support private food banks are not really engaging in an act of Christian charity. Rather, they are "prolonging the agony" of the poor and "letting the government off the hook."

This is a rather peculiar view. Does it mean that when Christ performed the miracle of the loaves and fishes he was not really undertaking an act of Christian charity but was instead acting as a sort of shill for the Romans, the government of the day? The very idea is highly problematic. Yet, such a conclusion is the one forced on us by the logic of the Reverend Smith and other advocates of increased government action. *W.B.*

FORECASTING

It is customary for economists and others to provide their prognostications for the year ahead. Like many of the activities in which humankind engages, this has become a ritual with little actual consequence. We know of almost no one who places serious trust in the forecasts which are the result of the exercise and for very good reason. They tend only to be accurate under circumstances wherein the world is unfolding in a more or less regular fashion.

Economists, to the extent that they predict, are engaging in what must be one of the oldest, truly professional activities in the history of mankind. (The *I Ching*, for example, the Chinese book of changes, is reputedly the oldest book in civilization and it is effectively a kind of predictor.) The reason prediction has so preoccupied the human imagination is because the human psyche is dogged by anxiety about what the future may hold.

Everybody is intuitively aware that the future is a collective noun for ignorance and uncertainty, and anything upon which we can rely to pierce the veil of ignorance is grasped with amazing ferocity. Horoscopes are to daily living what computer models and economic research units are to governments and corporations. They are, in effect, repositories of faith and confidence about the future. Anybody making a long-term decision, whether about marriage or machinery or the money supply, wants some external assurance that the decision is a correct one, or at least some indication of the developments which will surround the decision.

The main reason we have reservations about providing predictions is because the thing to be predicted doesn't exist. The future is not something which exists out there and which, if we study long and hard and try our very best, we can come to know about and, therefore, predict. The future is not yet made. The future will be made from the raw materials which lie about us today—the ideas, the resources, the efforts, and imagination of the people. The fact that the future does not exist explains the wide divergence of views of seers of the future as to its likely outlines. The depressing tendency of "unforeseen" circumstances to crop up explains the divergence between even the average prediction made by seers and the actual turn of events.

Consider in this regard predictions made about the energy crisis. First, from an impeccable source, Sheik Yamani in the *New York Times,* we had the zinger: "irreversible physical shortfalls in supplies may take place as early as 1988. The result is likely to push market prices to levels three or four times the current one." Or, what about Lester Brown of the Worldwatch Institute in March 1980, who intoned solemnly, "it would be prudent for any American contemplating the purchase of a new car to assume that gas will cost $2.08 a gallon in a few years and $4.20 per gallon during the vehicle's lifetime." Finally, there was the *New York Times* of November 14, 1980, which said: "Ronald Reagan brushed aside energy issues during the campaign, insisting that shortages could be overcome by unleashing private enterprise. But not even his most fervent supporters in the energy business share that optimism." Ha!

Next, consider forecasting the future course of business. The first thing we always tell people when they come for advice about their investment strategies is that the scientific aspects of economics do not provide helpful guidance for precise predictions about variations in the prices of financial assets. This comment applies with particular force if a prospective investment involves divining information about the future. (Our Second Law of Forecasting is that *economists provide precise forecasts of economic variables only to show that they have a sense of humour.*)

Accordingly, our first piece of advice on financial management strategies is to beware of those who provide such information as though it had a scientific basis. Economics as a science provides very little assistance in this regard. For the serious, aggressive investor who seeks to make above-average returns on invested money, there is no substitute for intensive industry-by-industry or firm-by-firm analysis. While broad economic indicators such as the number of housing starts may be an important ingredient in the analysis, their influence should be regarded as the least predictable and, therefore, the least reliable aspect of it.

Another difficulty is establishing a connection between the macro variables, assuming they could be forecast with any degree of accuracy, and the particular investment decisions that have to be made. A perfect illustration of this problem in the case of British Columbia is the relationship between growth in the United States and the price and quantity of demand for British Columbia forest products. In the past, robust growth in the United States has normally meant a substantial demand for housing and a good market for British Columbia forest products. Strong growth in the U.S. should translate into expansionary development in British Columbia. However, this linkage has, in part, been broken. Growth has not translated into housing demand as it had in the past, and alternative supplies of forestry products have taken some of the market away from British Columbia. A combination of these two events has meant that notwithstanding good volumes, prices have been lackluster. Accordingly, an investment made on the assumption of strong growth in the United States would have turned out to have been incorrect—even though the economic variable had been correctly forecast. *M.W.*

FOREIGN AID

At first blush, aid to underdeveloped countries seems noble, humanitarian and serendipitous, and in our own national interest as well. After all, Canadian aid to less fortunate nations surely must save people from starvation, encourage the development of primitive economies, increase our exports, and enhance freedom by forestalling the spread of communism.

There is much evidence, however, showing aid programmes to be questionable means toward these worthy ends. Further, there are indications that private trade and investment, currently shackled and hampered by tariff and import barriers in the

Western industrial countries, may be more efficacious than intergovernmental transfers.

Food grants are a major part of foreign aid, and Canada is the world leader here, meeting about 30 percent of its bilateral commitments in this form. (Canada funnels 70 percent of its total donations bilaterally; 30 percent is given through multilateral channels such as the Organization for Economic Co-operation and Development.) Foodstuffs are obviously basic. Malnutrition unfortunately prevails in many less developed countries, and food provides one of the building blocks of economic betterment. But compelling humanitarian requirements in cases of actual famine aside, even this sort of aid is fraught with danger. Massive gifts can take the profit incentive out of local agriculture. With fewer farmers and less land under cultivation, this can paradoxically worsen, not improve, the long-term prospects of food production and safety from future starvation.

Capital grants are likewise destructive to long-term productivity. Although the ancient Egyptian pyramids were an extraordinary instance of capital accumulation, they resulted in no economic gain in the basic sense of contributing to the well-being of the great masses of people. Even more wasteful are the modern equivalents of such monument building made possible by foreign aid: steel mills in Egypt, modern chemical plants in India, tractors given to aboriginal peoples who cannot operate them, and automobile assembly plants scattered widely throughout the Third World (which are the result of protective tariffs on motor vehicle imports as well). These are wasteful because the products fabricated in this highly technological manner actually cost the underdeveloped countries more to manufacture themselves than they would have paid importing the finished product from more developed countries.

Many people deduce from the fact that the rich countries have much capital and the poor ones little that what is required is vast capital infusions. But this wet-sidewalks-causes-rain reasoning points to almost the exact opposite of what is really needed. Capital, in and of itself, does not create wealth. It is rather the *result* of a process of economic development that also includes, as complementary factors, such things as the willingness to work, the skill and education of the labour force, and relatively free and private markets protected by a stable code of laws. One indication of the importance of these other phenomena is the fact that a large proportion of the very limited capital generated in poor countries is actually invested in the more advanced nations where private property rights are far more secure.

Then there is foreign aid in the form of technological and other education. Canada ranks third among the donor nations in this category, behind only France and New Zealand, meeting just over 15 percent of its bilateral commitments to the underdeveloped world in this form. In the absence of such facilities as fully equipped laboratorics, libraries, computer centres, and without the mutual support of thousands of other similarly educated scientists and technologists, such aid cannot be efficiently utilized. The proof can be seen in the immigration patterns of the educated classes in the Third World, a "reverse brain drain" toward the more advanced countries.

Moreover, foreign aid of whatever variety—food, capital, technology or outright cash grants—sets up a welfare-like dependency status on the recipient country. In much the same manner as domestic welfare programmes sap the economic ambition, vitality and progress of their local clients, programmes on the international level have similar effects.

If foreign aid is unlikely to help the recipient, can it at least help the donor? (Note that the focus here is on economic aid, not military aid which must be justified on entirely different grounds.) Pragmatic considerations would seem to support this view. For one thing, the Canadian International Development Agency requires that about 80 percent of its bilateral disbursements be spent on Canadian goods and services. But behind the bookkeeping legerdemain, this amounts only to a free gift of goods and services from Canada to other countries with no offsetting returns. No one is foolish enough to suppose that West German reparations to Israel actually benefited the economic self-interest of West Germany—even though much of it took the form of exporting domestic items. Nor does the defendant in a civil case rejoice in his new-found wealth when he is forced by a court decision to compensate the plaintiff—even in the form of goods he himself produces.

Will Canadian aid to other countries at least make it more likely that they will choose the path of democracy and market institutions rather than fall into the communist and coercively collectivist ambit? Unfortunately, not only will Western foreign aid not attain this end—it is likely to undermine it and encourage forced socialism and totalitarianism in the Third World. First of all, Canadian aid is traditionally in the form of government-to-government grants. This strengthens the role of the public versus the private sector in the underdeveloped countries. It helps create the classic "three Ms" of foreign aid: monuments, Mercedes, and machine guns. But political freedom is a delicate and precious flower; it cannot live where the bulk of economic activity is carried on in the public sector. Secondly, Canadian foreign aid has been given to countries that have made explicitly socialist avowals in their centralized economic plans—our largess has in no small degree shielded them from the repercussions of such policies and allowed them to continue unchecked down this path. For example, we find in the five-year plan of India—a country which continues to receive strong Canadian support—the statement that "planning should take place with a view to the establishment of a socialistic pattern of society where the principal means of production are under social ownership or control."

Of far greater benefit to all nations is a policy of free trade and unregulated international flow of capital. This will greatly benefit the Canadian standard of living, as we can purchase many goods, such as clothing, from the less developed world for less than it costs to make them ourselves. But of far greater importance, such policies will truly lead to Third World economic development—and to tighter integration with our own economy.

How, then, to account for the hypocrisy of a nation whose leaders loudly proclaim their interest in economic development for the poor countries and yet remain steadfast in their determination to maintain protective tariffs, quotas, and other impediments to economic intercourse with the Third World? *W.B.*

F F F F F F F F F F F F F F F F F F F F F

FREE ENTERPRISE ZONES

It would be in the economic interest of Canada if the federal and provincial governments permit or actively encourage the establishment of free economic zones through the selective reduction or elimination of regulations, controls, and taxes. The following types of activity zones could be established by setting aside geographically defined areas of operation.

First, *free trade zones*, where firms can import free of duty goods for assembly, processing and distribution for either export or sale in Canada.

Second, *free retail zones*, where foreign tourists can purchase goods free from customs and excise taxes.

Third, *free enterprise zones*, where closed shops and other restrictive practices of unions are prohibited, contributions by employers and workers to the unemployment insurance and Canada pension plan programmes are voluntary, minimum wage legislation is inapplicable, other regulations and controls are minimal, and there are no local taxes, with all services needed in the zone paid for by users.

Fourth, *free medical zones*, where doctors and drug companies can make available drugs, surgical procedures, and therapies—even if they have not been approved by governmental or professional regulatory authorities of Canada.

Fifth, *free gambling zones*, where all forms of gambling are permitted without restrictions.

And finally, *free investment zones*, where securities and other assets can be sold, unrestricted by the existing government regulations governing such sales.

In addition, governments should free the following activities selectively through the elimination of controls and taxes on specific types of business or customers.

First, banking activities where banks can carry out business denominated in foreign currencies without the requirement to pay certain taxes levied on regular banking. And second, insurance activities where companies can underwrite hazards normally afflicting customers that do not require paternalistic protection by the government.

The proposed establishment of free economic zones can be expected to have several benefits for society. The economic activities freed from the costly burdens of regulation, control, and taxation will expand rapidly as they become competitive in world markets and in Canada. There will be favourable employment, productivity, and balance of payments implications from such expansion.

The rate of innovation of products, technology, and services in the free activity zones will be raised by the absence of controls and regulatory burdens which will lead to increased sales and productivity of capital and labour.

All members of society will enjoy the benefits of decreased paternalism. Consumers can choose products and services more freely; workers can elect to trade off the benefits of higher wages and occupational mobility for the absence of public retirement plans, unemployment benefits, and the right to strike; wealthholders and entrepreneurs can place their capital and talents in potentially high-profit ventures in return for additional risks they consider worth taking.

Free economic zones represent a form of partial deregulation that permits society to maintain regulation and control for the broad, general public and specific industries and consumers, while the benefits from free competition and unrestrained freedom of choice accrue to those not desiring government protection. Producers, consumers, and workers with a vested interest in existing regulation would continue to enjoy any benefits derived from it.

The success of free economic zones, in terms of greater efficiency and dynamic growth, may be considered an economic indicator that measures the costs associated with government regulation and control. The economic performance of free zones therefore can serve as a useful guide to the determination of the socially optimal degree of regulation and controls.

The major costs of free economic activity zones consist of two parts. To a certain extent, activities in the zones will not create new business but only divert business away from regulated and taxed areas within Canada. Such diversion can lead to locationally determined inefficiencies and to the loss of tax revenue. However, these costs are mitigated by the diversion of trade away from other countries and towards Canada. In fact, the establishment of such Canadian zones may be required in the near future simply as a defensive measure to prevent excessive diversion of trade to such zones in other countries. And secondly, the free economic zone activities lead to the appearance of economic and social costs that regulation and control were designed originally to reduce or eliminate. For example, it is argued that costs occur in the form of lower protection for import competing industries. However, these are more than offset by consumer gains in purchasing foreign products. Standards of morality are said to be lowered as a result of more gambling, but this is a very subjective charge and difficult to quantify. As well, there may be more deaths from medical treatment and more unemployed workers without insurance benefits. If so, however, this will be restricted to those who willingly and knowingly decided to bear the extra risks.

Whatever the costs—if any—of partial deregulation through free activity zones, they must be compared not with a situation in which regulation works perfectly and creates no costs of its own, but with real world conditions in which regulation is accompanied by great costs, the limitation of which represents the benefits of free activity zones noted above.

But the nature of the regulatory process and the incentive structure determining the behaviour of politicians, regulatory agencies, the regulated industries and their customers is itself strongly biased towards over-regulation. This is only one further indication of the need for free enterprise zone deregulation. *W.B.*

FREE TRADE: THE GENERAL CASE

Canadian barriers to foreign trade are among the highest in the Western industrialized bloc of countries. Furthermore, with regard to quotas and other non-tariff barriers, which are far more insidious and less quantifiable, Canada has increasingly been taking on a more protectionist stance in recent years.

Unfortunately, most Canadians are not aware of the economic harm created by the policy of squelching international trade. Self-imposed banishment from the benefits of specialization and the international division of labour is a serious mistake even for a large country which contains within its own borders a global scale market and many of the skills, raw materials and capital available in the entire world. For a small country such as Canada, this is folly indeed.

The very term "protectionism" is a vast misnomer. It implies that the citizens are being defended against economic exploitation somehow made even more sinister by its foreign genesis. In fact, nothing could be further from the truth.

In order to see this clearly, let us start not with a nation which refuses to trade with others but with an individual who sets up trade barriers between himself and all other people. Such a person, of course, will have to provide for all of his needs. He will have to grow his own food, make and mend his own clothing, build a house for himself, minister to himself when he falls ill, entertain himself, and so on. Not being able to specialize in any one thing, his productivity will not be able to attain livable levels. He will be a "jack of all trades, master of none." If everyone tried this path of economic solipsism, this fertile earth which today supports the lives of more than four billion people, might possibly be able to keep at most a few million snarling savages living on a miserable semi-starvation basis.

On a national level, one argument for protectionism is that a policy of free trade would mean the loss of jobs for Canadians. And this, it must be conceded, is true. If buyers are offered the choice between a made-in-Canada sweater for $50 and an identical one manufactured in Southeast Asia for $10, there is little doubt that virtually all consumers will choose to be thrifty and save 40 of their hard-earned dollars. The inevitable result will be the loss of Canadian jobs—in sweater production.

But let us not stop here, as do the free trade critics, for there are several more effects to be considered. What, pray tell, will the consumers do with the extra $40? They may spend it on other Canadian products, and if they do, some of the now unemployed sweater workers can find jobs in these other lines. They can save this money. Then the banks will be able to make loans on easier terms, thus creating additional jobs in construction, housebuilding, and heavy industry. Alternatively, they could purchase four additional foreign sweaters (or other imports from other countries) for the same amount.

What will the foreign suppliers do with the $10 (or $50) paid to them by Canadians? One possibility is to buy Canadian products, strengthening domestic industry. They might also spend the dollars in a third country, whose nationals can turn around and purchase Canadian goods, again giving our country a boost in employment.

But what if the foreigners, perhaps determined to wreck our economy, decide instead to merely sit on their newly acquired Canadian funds? What if they merely stuff this money into their mattresses? If they were so foolish, they would only succeed in giving us their sweaters for free! By this policy, they would present us with valuable commodities, and receive in return pieces of paper their own actions render worthless. This form of financial reparation would, of course, make our sweater industry superfluous, but all Canadians saving on their clothing bills would now be able to afford additional goods—and jobs would be created in the industries catering to these new desires.

The main sufferers from a policy of free trade are not the lower paid workers with generalized training, which is as applicable to sweater production as to anything else. They will find alternative employment at comparable wages. The real losers are the protected factory owners and the highly paid, heavily unionized workers with a great investment in skills specific to sweater manufacture. It is only they who will suffer losses unless retrained. As a result, the unions support the manufacturers in their bid for more protection and more assistance.

One of the biggest limitations on further exports to China and other less-developed countries in Asia, Africa and on the Pacific Rim is the fact that they don't have enough dollars with which to buy our exports, and they can't get our currency unless we allow ourselves to trade with them. Foreign aid, the solution to Third World poverty now popular in Canada is *not* the answer. Experience suggests aid money will probably be used to purchase limousines for the rulers and to further centralize, socialize, and distress the economy.

The motto for those really concerned with the plight of the downtrodden Third World peoples might be: "millions in foreign trade, not a penny in foreign aid." If another country can make sweaters more cheaply than we can, it makes sense to concentrate on what we do best, allow them to do the same, and then to trade. This best utilizes the special skills and factor endowments of each region of the globe. We're not going to be a very rich nation if we make people work at jobs others can do more cheaply.

Why is it, if the case for free trade makes so much sense, that we nonetheless find ourselves barricaded from affluence by high tariff walls? Although this can only be speculative, the answer seems to be in our social and economic organization. As producers, our interests are highly concentrated. It is the rare person who has more than one source of employment. Most investors focus on one or just a few industries. But as consumers, we typically purchase literally tens of thousands of items. Our interests, here are staggeringly diffuse. It is little wonder then, that when it comes to considering a tariff on shoes or toothbrushes or paper clips or bubblegum, the producers—both owners and employees—can easily mobilize on their own behalf.

Trade "protection" may cost the general public millions and be worth only thousands to the manufacturers. Yet, because of their diffuseness as consumers and the fact that the tariff will cost each of us only a few pennies, Canadians have little individual incentive to organize a resistance. The populace is so befuddled by the media blitz of the real beneficiaries of trade barriers—the protected manufacturers and unionized workers—that it has come to feel, vaguely, that trade barriers are really in their own and in the public interest. *W.B.*

FREE TRADE AND CULTURAL SOVEREIGNTY

There is a lot of talk, nowadays, about free trade. The very concept of free trade drives some Canadian political leaders into such a tizzy of fear that they substitute "freer trade" or "enhanced trade" or some other such circumlocution so that the dread name never has to pass their lips in its pure form. We the people, however, need not labour under this misapprehension. Instead, we would do well to understand the theory of free trade—in all its pristine glory—and realize that it is in the best interests of the great masses of Canadians.

One concern of those who fear an elimination of all government-imposed barriers to trade is that such a policy will lead to unemployment. They cite prospective job loss in such callings as shoe manufacture, textiles, autos, and electronics where foreigners can produce the goods at a fraction of Canadian costs. This is indeed realistic. An end to laws which protect such industries from foreign competition will mean a wholesale cutback or perhaps even the elimination of all jobs in these sectors.

But this is all to the good. Why should precious Canadian labour be expended on jobs which produce less than they might? The farmer who works at tasks that could be done as well by animal or mechanical means (plowing, hauling, lifting) will have less to show for his efforts than if he concentrated on doing things that he could do far better (running a mechanical plow, hauling by tractor, using a fork-lift). In just the same manner, and for the same reasons, Canada would be far better off if people now employed in producing shoes on an inefficient basis shifted themselves into job slots where they could be more productive.

"Any old employment" cannot and should not be our goal. Millions of jobs in Canada, billions of them for that matter, could be created if people used teaspoons, or their fingernails, to dig up our rich earth. What we want, what we *need* as a country, if we are to successfully negotiate our economic way into the 21st century, are jobs where people are freed up to do more productive things.

This was the free trade message of Adam Smith, who inveighed against the mercantilists, the economic "nationalists" of his day. He saw clearly that the "wealth of nations" was dependent on productive labour—labour directed to its most efficient employments. And as a necessary corollary, he demonstrated that this could only take place under a regime of full free trade, where government placed no obstacles whatever in the way of international co-operation, specialization, and a world-wide division of labour.

We all see this clearly in the case of maple syrup and bananas. Sure, we could produce bananas in this country. All we would need are gigantic and stupendously costly hothouses. And just as certainly, the tropical countries could produce maple syrup by erecting large scale refrigerators in which to place the maple trees. (We're talking *big* refrigerators, here.)

The very idea is ludicrous. We all see the fallacy. Far better for us to produce maple syrup, for them to grow bananas, and then each to trade for the item the other specializes in—to mutual advantage. Very few people, however, see that the same principle applies to textiles, shoes, autos, and electronic goods like television sets. But it does, it does.

There is one further bogeyman offered up by those who favour "protectionism," and this is the spectre of loss of cultural identity, or even worse, political sovereignty. These claims are without foundation. Consider the case for assuming that free trade will mean an end to Canada as a national entity. The European Economic Community (EEC) was actually proposed by some of its adherents to this end. That is, they actually welcomed a single country consisting of the European nations and saw the creation of the EEC as a means toward this end. But after decades of experience with free trade, an end to individual national sovereignty is no closer than it was at the inception of the EEC. The same is true of the Scandinavian countries; after generations of free trade between them, Norway, Denmark, Sweden, Finland, and Iceland are still individual going concerns.

If political amalgamation has not followed economic rationalization in these cases, where the one was welcomed as a means to the other, how can this occur in Canada, where most citizens vociferously *reject* any loss of political sovereignty?

What about loss of cultural identity? This too is a bogus fear. Is Canadian culture really so precarious and fragile a plant that it needs protection from the inroads of "Dallas" and other U.S. television programmes? Or *Newsweek* and *Time* magazines, or from the unregulated competition from U.S. book publishers? If it really is so weak, then it would be far better to let it go and enjoy the cultural products of America and, indeed, the rest of the world. Mozart, after all, was not a Canadian.

But this is incorrect. Canadians have their own cultural traditions. They serve us, and they serve us well. Let us consider in this regard an example very close to home, the Fraser Institute. It is extremely unlikely that this organization would cease to exist without government regulations impeding the importation of competing economic research from the U.S. Certainly, the Institute articulates the concerns of Canadians better than any emanating from thousands of miles away. But if it one day failed in this mission, and if a research institute devoted to the economic analysis of public policy located in the U.S. satisfied the needs of Canadians to a greater degree, then the Fraser Institute would deserve to go bankrupt.

The Fraser Institute creates and disseminates a wealth of public policy research and analysis dealing with economic problems which impact Canadians. Yet it does not call upon government to protect it from the competition which might develop under free trade with the U.S. Were it to do so, it would not deserve to be considered a legitimate part of Canadian intellectual and cultural life.

But what of all those artistic, musical, and literary organizations positively frothing at the mouth at the prospect of competition from abroad? To the degree that they fear a loss of business attendant upon the lowering of cultural trade barriers—and to the degree that these fears are realistic—they are not really part of

Canadian artistic life, but rather welfare recipients posing as artists.

For the most part, those who benefit from a policy of cultural nationalism are those whose incomes are in the very highest registers. On the other hand, everybody will benefit from free trade, and those in the lower income ranges will benefit proportionately more. Therefore, arguments against free trade based on cultural nationalism must be seen as self-serving to a group disproportionately benefiting from the status quo.

Another, and to some extent, more crucial point which must be made about cultural nationalism is the fact that it is self-defeating. As is well known, culture is a luxury good. The richer a nation, the more it tends to indulge its tastes for culture. The protectionist stance suggested by cultural nationalists will reduce Canada's long-term economic potential, reduce current living standards, and cannot help but reduce the overall demand for distinctively Canadian culture. The very best protection of Canadian cultural sovereignty is the economic strength which free trade will bring. *W.B.*

G

GOUGERS

Some months before the advent of Vancouver's Expo 86, in order to take advantage of the increased number of tourists expected to be swept into town on the heels of that event, numerous lower mainland hotels began increasing their room rates. Many had the audacity to jack up their rents by 50 percent to 100 percent, and even more in some rare cases. These increases were far in excess of the 9 to 14 percent deemed acceptable by the Vancouver Convention and Visitors' Bureau in its infinite wisdom.

The main beef against the "gougers" appeared to be the fear that they would give the fair City of Vancouver a reputation as a rip-off operation. "Once stung, twice shy," seemed to be the motivating cry of the city administration. If tourists are ill-treated during Expo year, they will be reluctant to come back later. The then Mayor Mike Harcourt was particularly perturbed by this concatenation of events. So much so that he used "gentle persuasion" to try to convince the hotels to roll back their rates. As well, there was always the threat of rent controls for the inns of the city lurking in the background.

To be sure, the actions and threats of the local politicians were well-motivated (no one, after all, wants to see the city come away with a black eye), but good intentions are not sufficient for wise public policy. A rudimentary knowledge of economics is also important. The best way to understand what was going on from an economic perspective is to realize that economics has a language all its own. Just as bees have a unique way of communicating to each other, so do economic actors, that is, business people.

In the present context it is crucial to understand the actual function of a price rise. It is meant to convey the information that a shortage is expected. Not only does an increased price indicate an incipient shortage, it also brings with it incentives to ameliorate the condition. With prices on the up-surge, profits are enhanced. And with greater returns to investment, more people are induced to provide the service.

In the case under consideration, higher hotel room rates can be expected to encourage the provision of a bed and breakfast industry and the creation of all sorts of temporary shelters such as trailer parks. Paradoxically, as these new supplies come rushing onto the market, the same hoteliers who are happily boosting their rates will be forced to lower them, lest they go with unlet rooms.

Greater profits in the hotel sector are thus akin to a cry in the wilderness for help. Only on this occasion the needy are not lost hikers but rather stranded tourists. The higher room rates, which are thought to harm tourists, are actually their salvation. However, just as a "decibel control" for cries for help on the part of lost hikers will do them little good, so the gentle persuasion and the not-so-gentle controls waiting in the wings redound to the detriment of the tourists.

What if hotel management had not acted in accordance with the "language" of economics? That is, suppose it had acted "responsibly" in the eyes of the politicians and had not increased room rates. No signal of future shortages would have been blasted forth onto the economic airwaves. Millions of tourists might have tried to come to Vancouver, but found there was little or no accommodation here.

If the above analysis is correct, and initially higher hotel rates call forth additional supplies, which in turn moderate or even cancel the increases, why have the hotel owners not been forced by the marketplace to rescind their announced plans? Once again government, not the free enterprise system, is the villain of the piece. Numerous legal barriers were set up against the creation of a viable bed and breakfast industry, and many local city councils in the towns surrounding Vancouver had seen fit to reject requests for zoning changes which would allow the creation of new recreational vehicle parking lots. Paradoxically, Mayor Harcourt even threatened that if hotel owners persisted in their plans to raise prices, he would let down the legal barriers which limit homeowners (and even tenants) from taking in boarders. That he could make such a threat, and that it could be found credible, is an indication of how important government interference was in the creation of an Expo housing shortage.

The "price-gouging" hotel owners were merely the messengers bring news of the incipient accommodation deficiency. However, the responsibility for this unfortunate event must rest squarely with those whose restrictions exacerbated the shortage in the first place—the politicians who sought to blame the hotel industry. *W.B.*

GOVERNMENT DEBT

Well, you finally managed to do it. After scrimping and saving—cheating on the egg money, giving up that mid-winter vacation, doing-it-yourself a little more than you really wanted to and, to some degree, letting your children do without some of the things that you would dearly love to have given them—you've paid off the mortgage. You probably had a little celebration with some neighbours who are approaching a similar happy moment in their lives. You feel a sense of accomplishment, and so you should. For most Canadians the most significant financial liability in their lives is the mortgage they acquire to purchase the family home. It is quite a natural part of the family life cycle to both acquire it and retire it.

Unfortunately, if you think you're now debt free, you'd better put the cork back in the champagne bottle. If you are an average family of four in Canada, your current financial liabilities amount to some $50,000, and they are being added to at the rate of about $4,000 per year. This does not mean loans to buy stereo equipment; it refers to the money being borrowed on your behalf by the federal government to finance ongoing expenditures.

In its budget issued in February 1986, for the first time the government provided a complete accounting in one place of the various debts it is acquiring on our behalf. The picture that emerged was not a pretty one. Ordinary accumulations of debt by the Government of Canada in 1987 amounted to $9,525 per head. Crown corporations owed a further $678 per head and, in addition, the government has provided loan guarantees to Crown corporations to a further $2,516. The latter, incidentally, are something like co-signing a loan for your nephew so he could take a trip to Tahiti. That's a total of $12,719 per Canadian—$50,876 for every family of four.

Frankly, these revelations are infuriating. While the government is busily accumulating this debt on our behalf, we are being told every evening on newscasts and in newspaper articles that we cannot cut back on social spending programmes because to do so is to disadvantage certain members of the community. We are told, for example, that payments must continue to be made under the universal social programmes—even to those who don't need the money—because universality is part of being Canadian. Meanwhile, the government borrows money on our behalf in $4,000 chunks that we wouldn't think about spending on our own families! The crowning irony of all this is that the government is borrowing this money from our children! Deficits financed by borrowing are nothing more than taxes deferred. Our children will pay, into their dotage, for the family allowance cheques given out today. If that doesn't convince you to have second thoughts about the current level of government spending and your continuing support for the so-called universal programmes and other instances of excessive government spending, then the following should.

One of the arguments for not cutting back on the size of the public deficit—the amount we add each year to the accumulated mortgage on our children's future—is that to do so would be to cause higher unemployment and economic distress. Whether you happen to agree with this or not, it is now quite clear from the evidence that has accumulated since the last federal budget that the failure to deal with the deficit has caused us to take deliberate economic actions in the form of raising interest rates which directly reduces jobs. In particular, this makes it much more difficult for Canadians to afford to purchase housing, one of the first areas to be touched by higher interest rates.

Deficits are the dry rot of our country. We shouldn't tolerate them any longer. *M.W.*

GOVERNMENT PROGRAMMES (see Market Failure)
Why aren't we more positive? Instead of simply bellyaching about government programmes and their application, why don't we provide some concrete, positive proposals for government programmes which would work? Quite candidly, that is a tough question. We do spend a great deal of time pointing out the errors in government actions and not much making proposals with which to replace those criticized. Unfortunately, that is the nature of the position to which economic analysis pushes us.

At one point in its development, economic analysis more or less accepted the commonplace observation that the market economy, being comprised of imperfect mortals, displayed many imperfections. Theoretical analysis suggested that there were many ways to correct these anomalies. If government programmes were put in place, the economy could be made to function better and the welfare of individuals would be improved. Economists have been applying that approach to issues now for the better part of four decades, and we are beginning to discover that the government programmes put in place to remove the so-called imperfections of the marketplace are imbued with their own imperfections. This is, in part, because they, too, are constructed, operated, and supervised by imperfect mortals.

More importantly, the whole apparatus by which new programmes and new controls are imposed is governed by the machinations of self-interested individuals in the political marketplace. So, even with the best of intentions, government programmes have great difficulty fulfilling the ambitions of their proponents. Further, it is very often questionable whether the programmes are adopted in the first place for the very best of intentions.

So, no, we don't propose a lot of new government programmes to solve problems. We find little evidence on the record to suggest that government programmes will solve problems. That leaves us with the unenviable task of attempting to put a positive face on what essentially must be a negative and to some extent destructive role. One can't hope to always be successful in that regard. *W.B.*

GOVERNMENT RESTRAINT

Government restraint gets bad press. The highly publicized B.C. restraint programme of Bill Bennett and his Social Credit government was heavily criticized. In the land to the south of us, Ronald Reagan's move to down-size government was stymied by farmers, welfare-rights groups, businessmen (of the "corporate-welfare-bum" variety), and other organized pressure groups. In Ottawa, our federal government seems unwilling to engage in any serious government cutbacks at all, despite a swollen and pendulous budget deficit. This is no doubt due, at least in part, to a healthy respect for the special interest groups who depend on government largess.

Given these occurrences, it is incumbent upon us to review the case for a smaller, tighter, and leaner public sector. Why should we prefer that as much economic activity as possible be assigned to the market, and as little as possible to government?

Some of the reasons for this preference can be subsumed under the following topics: resource allocation, incentives, efficiency, risk, and consumers sovereignty.

Resource allocation. When consumers want more of a product, they buy it. This raises profits and encourages entrepreneurs to shift resources away from items in lesser demand and toward those more urgently needed. Similarly, losses induce businesses to contract the manufacture of goods no longer sought by customers. This is why the transition from the horse and buggy to the automobile was achieved so easily. Had large scale government been ready to bail out the losers (in order to save jobs or promote equity) resources could never have been allocated so smoothly.

Incentives. When you own it, you take care of it; when you don't, you "let George do it." There have been crop failures, in the Soviet Union, Tanzania, Cuba, and Ethiopia due largely to forced collectivized agriculture which has played havoc with the ordinary human incentives toward hard work and reward.

Efficiency. The usual rule of thumb is two or three to one. When governments contract out to the private sector—whether for fire protection or sanitation services or health care—the typical statistical finding is that the job can be completed at a fraction of the cost.

Risk. When a private firm blunders, it does so with its own money and on a relatively small scale. When government errs, it does so with our money, and in huge proportions. Moreover, these mistakes (e.g., Mirabel, De Havilland, National Energy Program) can be repeated again and again, since the bureaucrats and politicians responsible cannot be forced into bankruptcy. Why put our money into one basket? The fewer the government enterprises, the less risk for the economy.

Consumer Sovereignty. When government runs the economy, we the people control them through the ballot box, but this occurs only every four or five years and is very costly. As well, we must vote for a package deal which includes foreign policy, unemployment, defence, mail delivery, inflation, welfare programmes, and tariffs, to mention only a few. In contrast, when most economic activity is organized on market principles, we can vote with our dollars every day. The price system gives vital information and is cheap to run. Moreover, we can focus our vote, registering our satisfaction not with the entire society nor even with whole industries. We can focus on individual enterprises. This makes them very responsive to our desires indeed.

To be sure, there is major scope for government even in the classical liberal philosophy. Courts, police, armies, prisons, roads and highways, and setting a floor under income are some of the dozens of tasks advocated by those with a limited government viewpoint. But when government exceeds its proper and vitally important mandate, two tragedies occur. One, as we have seen, is that it does a poor job, wasting precious resources. And two, it leaves undone those tasks to which it is uniquely suited. We have crime in the streets, while government spends its energies regulating the minutia of agriculture through dozens of marketing boards.

How far in excess of its limited mandate has the Canadian government strayed? In a landmark Fraser Institute publication, *Probing Leviathan: An Investigation of Government in the Economy*, the sad story is told. Some 45 percent of GNP is absorbed by government, and at least partially as a result, the black market economy may comprise as much as 15 percent of GNP. There are over 600 Crown corporations, and their numbers are still growing.

The B.C. government, upon its re-election in 1983 almost immediately launched into a programme of policy restraint which was epoch-marking in its breadth and philosophical direction. This included the abolition of rent control, freezing public sector pay, cutting jobs in the public sector by 25 percent, reduction of the level of most public services and the privatization of others, tough controls on medical and education spending, as well as changes in the province's Labour Code, and the restructuring of employment in the public sector and universities.

This Draconian programme of restraint was said to be the evil brainchild of the Fraser Institute, and the full brunt of partisan political effort was brought to bear on the government and the Institute. Meanwhile, the then premier Bill Bennett and his radical programme were being lionized by none other than the high priest of conservative economics, Milton Friedman, in his celebrated book *The Tyranny of the Status Quo*, which mentions only three courageous policymakers, Margaret Thatcher, Ronald Reagan, and Bill Bennett.

Such was the sweeping nature of the restraint programme that virtually every special interest group in the province was mobilized against the government. Even the business community rankled at the scope of the programme, and it was widely inferred by everyone that the Social Credit Party had committed a form of mass suicide. The concrete expression of this view was the so-called solidarity movement, a well-financed coalition of public and private sector unions, interest groups, disaffected academics and, of course, NDP partisans seething over their election loss to Bennett, who had vaulted over the barrage of media hostility to an increased majority on the strength of a promise of restraint as opposed to the vision of New Deal spending to create jobs.

The latter aspect of the 1983 programme and reaction to it are very important to consider since the 1986 election campaign had an echo of this past event. Ever since the restraint programme of 1983 was launched, the solidarity movement and the NDP have sought to convince the people of B.C. that the reason they were experiencing economic difficulties was the evil restraint programme. Evidently, the NDP came to believe this themselves. In the 1986 campaign they returned to the "spending for jobs and end of restraint" refrain which had been their hallmark in the 1983 election. Elect the NDP, they said, and we will end restraint and spend over a billion dollars on programmes to get the province up and running again.

The flaw in the NDP policy strategy was that the people apparently didn't buy the premise that it was restraint which brought recession. Perhaps they correctly perceived that restraint was a necessary accommodation to the recession and that claims to the contrary were motivated by the self-serving urges of teachers, hospital workers, university professors, and others directly affected by the restraint programme. It is difficult otherwise to explain the 1986 outcome, which featured an overwhelming rejection of the NDP and an even larger majority for the Social Credit incumbents.

Even those who substantially agree with the thrust of the government restraint philosophy have been heard to say that the B.C. programme was too much or too abrasive or accomplished too quickly. Since there can be no absolute measure of any of these aspects, such opinion must be based on observation of the reaction from the left. It was so strong and apparently so widespread, in their view, that the package must have been too precipitous.

But what would have been the reaction had the aspects of the package been implemented piecemeal? Take, for example, the cuts in the size of the civil service. Suppose this, together with its enabling legislation, had been the only measure implemented. What would the reaction have been?

Since the British Columbia Government Employees Union would still regard this action as an attempt to destroy it, their reaction would have been the same. Moreover, those with allied interests—unionized public servants in other levels of government and governmental agencies not affected by the first wave of reductions—would have found common cause and presumably joined the coalition against the move. And, since government employees account for half the total union membership in B.C., it is also reasonable to suppose that the support forthcoming from private sector unions and joint union councils would have been similar.

In assessing the reaction, therefore, it is necessary to remember that the core of the legislative package, namely the public service reductions, challenged the most powerful special interest group in British Columbia. That challenge might have been expected to induce a reaction in proportion to the strength of the interest threatened. Public sector unions cannot afford for this programme to become a precedent for other governments and could under any circumstances be expected to fight it as though their own jobs were threatened—as indeed they were.

While one might have arrived at this conclusion on the basis of some good old garden variety common sense, it also has a quite respectable scientific pedigree. The public choice school has analysed societal interactions in terms of the benefit-seeking behaviour of special interest groups. The essential feature of this behaviour is that groups attempt to get ahead and stay ahead, economically, by directly influencing outcomes in the political marketplace as opposed to engaging in productive economic activity. Based on the work of leading theorists James Buchanan and Gordon Tullock, we can predict that the various groups affected by the budget would react in precisely the way they have.

Rather than being an indication that the B.C. government's programme was too harsh or too comprehensive or too precipitous, the reaction should be seen as an index of the magnitude of the special interest problem. The financial and other resources brought to bear in the rallies and demonstrations against the budget were evidence of why the reductions should have been undertaken. And, they are the single most persuasive argument that the government ought not to capitulate in its pursuit of the policy. The B.C. government with its mandate for restraint and non-interventionist policy cannot be forced to back down in its attempt to cut the size of the public sector. It is hard to imagine circumstances under which that would ever be possible. *W.B.*

GOVERNMENT'S ROLE IN BUSINESS

When we consider the issue of government involvement in the economy, we have to recognize that it is, after all, only an idea. Moreover, in the relatively brief history of human economic progress, it is a recent idea. From 1750 to the present, an interval which encompasses virtually the whole of mankind's experience with sustained economic growth, only for a very limited period of time has the idea of government involvement, as we currently understand it, been an important part of the functional ideology. Functional ideology, incidentally, means the basket of ideas people take for granted and generally regard as being beyond challenge. The divine right of kings, for example, was part of Western functional ideology for centuries. And, for a relatively brief period of time, the notion of private property rights has been an integral part of our civilization.

Just because these institutions are only ideas doesn't mean they are ephemeral. We must, rather, differentiate between the idea of private property rights and the institutional, legal, and other details necessary to support it. The complexity of reality which inhibits clear thinking and very often action on the part of individuals relates to the implementation of ideas and not their understanding.

History clearly shows that there is an inevitability about the evolution of ideas. Once an idea has been discovered, it will in one way or another come to influence the course of events. That is not to say, of course, that all ideas discovered are good, self-sustaining, or what biologists call evolutionarily stable. On the contrary. The idea that governments can create wealth and can solve economic problems will be seen in the perspective of history to have been an evolutionary mistake.

The idea that government has an essential role to play in the process of economic co-ordination and development is a relatively new one. From at least the time of the publication of Adam Smith's *Wealth of Nations* in 1776, the prevailing view was that society's interests would be best served if private rights prevailed. The acceptance of this orthodoxy had many underpinnings, but important amongst them was Smith's brilliant insight into the source of economic affluence and the importance of individual action in achieving it. Moreover, Smith showed that the circumstances of those in the lowest stations of life could only be improved by raising the general standard of affluence.

This idea, though very simple, is basic to understanding why a competitive market economy produces wealth. We may have confidence in a free market economy because it is only in this context that we know with any certitude that wealth is being created. Wealth is created when two individuals voluntarily agree to trade the things they have. They make this trade because they believe that what they are receiving is of higher value or more usefulness than the thing which they are giving up. This voluntary exchange process with value added at each step is the key to economic affluence.

Properly understood, the American Constitution and the evolution of common law in the United Kingdom during the period from the mid-18th century until the beginning of the 20th century were designed to provide a legislative and constitutional framework within which this powerful exchange process could operate to the maximum advantage of all those involved. The explicit intention was to protect individual freedom of action from the caprices of collective or majoritarian law-making.

The practical significance of this idea of individuality and its enshrinement in legislative and constitutional provisions was, of course, enormous. It permeated the ethos, provided a context for popular expectations, and perhaps most importantly, set limits on the political process. It both encouraged and was encouraged by a particular sort of thinking about what was appropriate for governments to do and not do.

One of the things that governments clearly were not to do under this general conception of their role was to run deficits. Another was that they should not involve themselves directly in the commercial life of the community. An indication of the strength of the latter popular injunction can be found in a response by an American president in the latter part of the 19th century, Grover Cleveland, to the demands of some citizens for support during a commercial recession. In replying to the demands for help, President Cleveland responded that "it is the business of the people to support the government, it is not the business of the government to support the people." That Grover Cleveland could say this and that we cannot conceive of a modern president or prime minister saying it, is perhaps the best illustration one could offer of the difference between the popular perception of the role of government in the 19th century as compared to what has evolved in the 20th century.

Sometime during the latter part of the 19th century in the United Kingdom and during the second trimester of the 20th century in North America, the attitude toward the appropriate role of government began to change. Perhaps because of the natural proclivity of widely held opinions to generate conflict and finally a swing away from these ideas, the notion of the primacy of the individual began to decline. With it went the notion of the limited state.

There can be no doubt that at least in part this was due to the disruptions of and widespread misunderstanding about the nature of the Great Depression and the forces leading to the subsequent recovery. We are all aware of the crucial role which the thinking and teaching of John Maynard Keynes played in both the interpretation of and the inferences from these developments. There can be no question but that Keynes' work has had a profound impact on the subsequent evaluation of the role of government and thinking about its appropriate role. It would, however, be wrong to assume that this was the only assault upon the old idea of the role of government. There were earlier erosions in the evolution of common law relating particularly to a challenge to the primacy of private property which was posed by a new idea—the idea of the public good or the public interest.

Another aspect of the change in the functional ideology was the rise of the concept of social justice. This concept arose from the observation that not everybody shared equally in the bounty produced by the market economy. There was not equality of results in the operation of the market economy. It was urged by some, notably the Webbs and their circle in the United Kingdom (the so-called Fabians), that society had an obligation to see to the needs of those who benefited least from the operation of the market system. The concept of social justice proved to be quite infectious. In combination with the notion that there might be a public interest above and beyond that of individual interests, the concept led to a very rapid decline in the once sacrosanct position of the individual in society and a changed perception of the appropriate role of government.

While the notions of social justice and the public interest provided the moral basis for a changed view of the relationship between governments and the citizens, Keynes' work on the economic role of government provided the practical vehicle by which the collective morality could be expressed. Keynes purported to demonstrate that not only did the market economy not satisfy the moral prerogative, it also was incapable unaided of generating continued economic expansion. Keynes was able to demonstrate, at least in the public mind, that it was possible for government action to raise the level of economic activity above that which would be determined by the market and that, moreover, there was a continuing need for government involvement in the economy in order to stabilize the unreliable market process. This perceived capability, in conjunction with the emerging public morality that a nation has some collective responsibility for individuals, led naturally to a governmental imperative to do something about economic circumstances.

One of the first foundations of the old system of ideas to fall was the concept of the balanced budget. As a prominent fiscal analyst of the 1950s noted, "once Keynes had added his ideas to the conceptual stew, people began to think that it was appropriate that rather than balancing its budget government should turn its attention to balancing the whole economy." Of course, this was a task to which governments turned with some enthusiasm and appetite.

Politicians had long sought to use taxing and expenditure powers to assist them in their ongoing quest for votes. They were incapable of doing this in a thorough-going way as long as the general public regarded deficits as an evil. It was not until the idea that government could stabilize the economy arose along with the notion that there was some collective responsibility for individuals hurt by economic upheaval that governments could in fact pursue their natural inclinations.

One final aspect of the evolution of the old ideas into the present is the crucial role played by intellectuals and by rationalism. One of the most difficult things for such scholars to accept about the market process is that it happens without any rational conception of its happening. That is to say, there is no collective mind within which the market process is visualized and, hence, rationalized.

The market process is an organic phenomenon which is self-sustaining and self-coordinating. That there should be such a process was anathema to many of the emerging disciplines in universities, especially in the post World War II period. Surely a co-ordinated approach to the problem of economic development would be better than an unco-ordinated approach. Certainly the centralized planning associated with the enormous increase in production in the Second World War period provided evidence that co-ordinated activity could indeed be enormously productive.

In the rationalists' view, the free market was made up of millions of individuals operating on the basis of their own forecasts, expectations, and perceptions of their abilities. Most of these expectations and assessments would be proved wrong by the passage of events. Surely this chaos could not be superior to a system within which expectations and forecasts and appraisals were brought into some sort of planned harmony. To the intellectual rationalist, the challenge to social science was to bring order and co-ordination to the chaos.

As the 1970s drew to a close, a new ideological creature appeared on the North American landscape. These new conservatives or 19th century liberals are those who have realized that the great intentions of public benefit, of social justice, and of economic stabilization have not been achieved and are not achievable by the governmental means which have been selected. They are the liberals who have lived through the great society experiment and have seen the imperfections of humanity reflected in the governmental institutions designed to replace the imperfections of the marketplace.

As with the idea of government involvement, this counter-revolution in thinking did not occur overnight. During the dog days of the 1940s, 1950s, and 1960s, when the general intellectual establishment was rushing to embrace the new statist ideology, there were a few idea-mongers who remained true to the traditions of the 19th century. This was done not out of any reactionary sentiment but in many instances out of a well-documented cynicism with the new theology.

There was also a well-spring of research into the expansive government concept. The work of political scientists pointed to fundamental problems with public choice making. Their analyses suggested that collective choice making and the political process might not benefit most people. There was, moreover, an increasing amount of evidence showing that, often as not, the political process became the tool of special interest groups and that much of the policy enacted to pursue "the public interest" in fact reflected the age-old tradition of private interest.

Thus, for example, regulations to protect the public from the activities of unscrupulous trucking operators turn out to be an ill-disguised conduit for limiting competition and raising prices. Occupational licensure becomes a licence to print money. Marketing boards, allegedly protecting the quality and supply of agricultural products, produce just the opposite effect. Resource policies, allegedly designed to preserve resources for future generations, are adopted by governments whose single biggest legacy to future generations is an enormous public debt. Rent controls raise rents and lower vacancy rates. Minimum wage laws create unemployment for those they were designed to protect. The litany goes on and on.

The central and most important issue for thinking about how we organize our choice making institutions for the future is this. If there is such a thing as the public interest, we shall not necessarily achieve it via the suppression of private interest. The fundamental ideological mistake made earlier in this century was the assumption that because we could identify something called the public interest we could achieve it via collective action. It is in considering the failure of collective action to achieve the public interest that we are drawn back to reconsider the inherent genius of Adam Smith's insight: if constrained to operate within a system of law, private self-seeking actions will maximize the public interest. The system of choice making within the market economy does precisely that. In effect, the market system is a device for transforming some of the least attractive but most reliable aspects of human nature into a public good. The system of collective choice, on the other hand, has become a device whereby private interest has been able to subvert the public good under the guise of public benefit.

The best known disillusionment of the neo-conservative is with the capability of government to stabilize the economy. On this count, there was a relatively strong and constant opposition to Keynesianism maintained by, amongst others, Frank Knight, Henry Simons, Milton Friedman, Ludwig von Mises and

Fredrich Hayek. These and others in the classical tradition were quick to reject the Keynesian cure for economic ills on the grounds that it wouldn't work and that it would destroy one of the central underpinnings of responsible government—namely, fiscal responsibility. Their protestations fell largely upon deaf ears until the evidence against Keynesianism was too overwhelming to reject.

Currently running at over $30 billion, we are told there is no way that this monumental budget deficit can be trimmed back. The unstated assumption, of course, is that there is no way it can be cut back within the confines of the existing idea of what constitutes an appropriate level of government expenditure. As long as we permit ourselves to be contained in the straight-jacket of the old ideology, it is clear that there is no way out of our current circumstances.

The obvious way out is to abandon the currently held ideas about the role of government and to adopt in their stead the ideas which we mistakenly rejected earlier in this century. In the United States, unlike Canada and Great Britain, there is some evidence that this process has already begun. Government is no longer perceived as a source of economic stability, as a collective expression of the public interest, and as an institution seeking to achieve social justice. There is less and less discussion in the United States of making government more effective and more efficient and more and more support for outright limitations on the scope and power of government. This is a task to which we in Canada must also turn our attention. *M.W.*

HANDICAPPED (see Human Rights)

There is a group in society that normally resides under a perpetual rain cloud. The group is the mentally handicapped. The good news is that with the help of a number of voluntary and professional organizations in the U.S., they are finally beginning to find acceptance as employees in a wide variety of enterprises. Similar programmes are also in place in Canada, where success rates from the placement of the mentally handicapped have also been quite encouraging.

The most surprising feature of many of the employment situations is that the employers find that the mentally handicapped actually outperform other workers. The key seems to be matching the skills of the retarded individual to the job. Once this is done, the handicapped frequently can engage in truly competitive employment. They seem capable of unrelentingly pursuing technically unskilled work like janitorial or other repetitive tasks with almost no absenteeism. In effect, the special skill of some handicapped people is an appetite for work that others regard as monotonous. The consequence, employers say, is that if the person is matched to the job and at the correct skill expectation level, handicapped workers are superior to the teenaged employees who are often the closest substitute. Unlike many teenagers who apply for such work, the mentally handicapped are dependable, hardworking, and never suffer the boredom which leads to unproductive work performance. Associations for the mentally handicapped usually have employment placement agencies. If you are an employer, you should check them out. *M.W.*

HIDDEN TAXES

In one sense, the tax return is a completely misleading indicator of our true tax burden. For ten years or so, economists at the Fraser Institute have been engaged in a project which had the original title, *How Much Tax Do We Really Pay*. The purpose of the work is to catalogue and calculate the total tax bill of Canadians. It has been quite an exercise.

The average Canadian encounters some 51 different categories of taxation. These include the obvious ones like income, sales, and property taxes but also include some sleepers. For example, the average worker is a member of a pension plan, and most pension plans hold the shares of Canadian corporations. The taxes paid by the corporation are a direct charge, to some extent, on the accumulating income in the worker's pension plan. In the case of residents of the province of Quebec, the fact that the *Caisse de Dépôt et Placement* holds shares in corporations like Genstar means that their Quebec Pension assets are also, in effect, taxed. When the Finance Minister announces on budget night that there will be a surtax on corporate profits, the fact that this could mean less burden on personal income taxes probably causes most Canadians to heave a sigh of relief. Besides, to paraphrase a refrain from certain quarters, isn't it fair that corporations pay their share of the tax burden?

The complete accounting for taxation shows that such a reaction is based on incomplete information and is—not to put too fine a point on it—mistaken. All taxes are paid by people, and many so-called corporate profit taxes are paid by the employees of corporations in the form of taxes on their direct or indirect (pension fund) share holdings. Even those who regard themselves as quite exempt from these indirect forms of corporate tax ought to take a second look. Who, for example, do you think pays the business licence tax collected from restaurateurs? And who pays the import tariff collected from Canadian businesses when they import your favourite packaged food? It isn't the tooth fairy.

The personal income tax payments you made over the past year probably represent less than a third of your total tax bill. The rest is made up of the other 50 varieties of direct and hidden taxes which have evolved over the years as part of the revenue apparatus of government. As the forms of tax payable have increased in variety and subtlety, so has the size of the average Canadian's tax bill. From a relatively modest 22 percent of income in 1961, the average taxpayer's liability ballooned to 45 percent by 1985.

It is interesting to put this development into the perspective provided by looking at other expenditures incurred by the average family. In 1961, the largest slice, 35 percent, of a family's income was required to cover the basic necessities of life. By 1985, food, shelter, and clothing expenses were dwarfed by the tax bill. The payment of taxes had become the single largest expense for Canadian families.

Moreover, those Canadians who "made it" to an income level twice the average had to overcome an enormous hurdle posed by the tax system. The modern day Horatio Alger, starting out at an income half the average in 1961 and able to earn double the national average income during 1985, experienced a 140 percent increase in his tax bill. All young Canadians just now setting out on their earning careers will have roughly the same experience. The biggest single hurdle they will have to face as they attempt to improve their circumstances is their tax bill. *M.W.*

HOUSEWIFE PENSION/PAY

The Vatican has joined that long list of distinguished and not-so-distinguished institutions, organizations, and individuals advocating pay for housewives. A 12-article charter, which passed muster with the Pope, claims that families have a right "to social and economic order." Therefore, wives should be paid a wage for working at home.

Now this would appear all well and good. Certainly, the salary will come in handy for millions of families the world over and, in any case, who could oppose a measure that would put more bread on the table? A moment's reflection, however, will convince us that this particular apple comes fully equipped with worms at its core.

To begin with, where is all the new-found money to come from? One possibility is that those bonuses should be paid compliments of the government. But this only places a veil on the financial proceedings, as government has no money apart from what it first seizes from the private sector. So the real income transfer is from those who work for wages in the marketplace to those who can afford the luxury of maintaining an individual at home, to provide all sorts of non-taxed services to the other family members.

Apart from the possible perverse income transfers involved, this scheme also has serious allocational deficiencies. For the decision to work directly for oneself in the household sector or indirectly in paid employment is fraught with implications for the economic well-being of society. Imagine the situation that would ensue were everyone to labour at home in the direct production of consumer goods and services. We would have to do without the vast benefits of specialization, the division of labour, and the ability to pool large amounts of capital, equipment, and manpower. (On the other hand, a policy which artificially subsidizes co-operation through commercial enterprise would also reduce human welfare. Instead of brushing our own teeth, preparing our own meals at home, dressing ourselves, we would find ourselves hiring other people to do these tasks for us, with a consequent loss in privacy.)

Absent government interferences on either side, presumably, we are all at equilibrium with regard to market and non-market work. That is, the allocation of time spent in and out of the home at least roughly conforms to our desires. However, let this latest Vatican plan be enacted, and it will artificially encourage people to remain home more than they would otherwise choose to do, with a consequent loss in economic welfare. This is so because pay for work at home would encourage those on the margin between market and non-market activity to devote more time to the latter. With more than the optimal effort devoted to home work, society would suffer the loss of commercial transactions, which have been judged by the participants themselves to have been more valuable than their other options. *W.B.*

HUMAN RIGHTS (see Handicapped)

One of the most grievous difficulties associated with the establishment of tribunals and the making of laws to achieve objectives is that very often the law or the commission will produce exactly the opposite of the result intended. In fact, this is more often the case than not. Consider the submission by the staff of the Human Rights Commission in Saskatchewan that argues that a business concern that hired only the handicapped should not be exempted from the open-hiring provisions of the Saskatchewan Human Rights Code. What was at issue was the ability of the employer, a telephone sales solicitation firm, to advertise for handicapped workers. The brilliant conclusion of the staff workers of the Saskatchewan Human Rights Commission was that the firm not be allowed to advertise for handicapped workers because "a segregated work-force which relies on disabled employees to market a product contravenes the philosophy of full participation and equality as advanced by the Saskatchewan Human Rights Code."

But the real reason for the suggestion that the advertising not be permitted is to be found at the very end of the report, where they note that "endorsing a segregated work-force can only be viewed as a step backward and in conflict with the spirit of the Saskatchewan Human Rights Code." In other words, what is important is the Saskatchewan Human Rights Code and the concepts which the Saskatchewan Human Rights Commission might endorse rather than the position of the handicapped workers, who, in a time of very high unemployment have considerable difficulty finding employment in any occupation.

It is amazing, is it not, the utter stupidity of this situation? Yet it is a direct and predictable consequence of having established the Human Rights Commission in the first place. Invariably, the formulators of the laws under which such a commission operate assume that the law will be administered with intelligence, compassion, and a rational appreciation for the realities of the world. In practice, they are often vehicles for making otherwise good and intelligent people do some wrong, mischievous and stupid things. *M.W.*

I

INDUSTRIAL STRATEGY (see Planning)

Industrial strategies have three characteristics which must be examined. These are rigidity, external goal selection, and redistribution.

Rigidity refers to the fact that a plan is usually slow to change. The details must be set and widely distributed. In the case of an industrial strategy, political and administrative decisions must be made and defended and constituencies rewarded and appeased. Both of these requirements introduce lags in adjustment to changing circumstances and tend to perpetuate a given plan. As a consequence, once a plan or industrial strategy has been set it becomes part of the system and is slow to change regardless of the changing economic circumstances. Thus, for example, the National Policy established by Sir John A. Macdonald, with its system of tariffs and freight rate subsidies, continues to affect economic policy in Canada some 100 years after its inauguration.

External goal selection refers to the fact that under a system of central planning, a limited number of objectives or goals must be selected. Thus, an industrial policy inspired by the central planning view involves the selection of certain sectors or products to include in the plan. For example, a public planning strategy may be to develop secondary manufacturing in a particular area. Increasing secondary manufacturing output would be the goal of the policy. Or, the goal might be the expansion of metal mining capacity or energy production. How will these goals of the strategy be selected? Moreover, how will conflicts between objectives be resolved if they arise?

In a democratic system of government, individual wishes are supposed to be reflected via the political system. In theory, Members of Parliament represent the people and, hence, policy reflects the wishes of the people. If policy doesn't reflect the wishes of the electorate, the electorate can periodically change the government to more closely represent its interests.

A consideration of the specific issues that people are typically asked to decide in elections suggests that politics is not an effective adjunct to the detailed planning process. In fact, elections represent *prima facie* evidence that in practice the democratic process is not well-suited to the selection of central planning objectives. If deliberations about free trade are any indication, one would have to say that reliance on the open political process to establish the goals of industrial strategy would result in a ponderous and, consequently, useless planning process.

In the real world, of course, central planning objectives are not selected directly. Democracy in practice is a process in which politicians do what they think the populace will accept rather than a process of initiatives rising naturally out of the political ethos. As a consequence, the objectives that central planners pursue are likely to reflect arbitrary judgments or political expediency of a very narrow sort.

A further implication of the fact that the democratic process is not suited to narrow goal selection is that governmental industrial strategies will almost always be redistributional in form. That is to say, they will involve assisting one group in society at the expense of another. This is one of the most important and yet misleading characteristics of industrial strategies and should bear fairly careful examination.

In the real world, the selection of industrial strategy goals is not a complicated philosophical question. Basically, the goals are determined in a sectional way by pressure groups which have a concentrated economic interest to advance and who see an opportunity to gain at the expense of others. As is evident, while the political lobbying process solves the practical problems associated with goal selection, it appears that the industrial strategy evolving from political pressure is redistributional in nature and is more likely to thwart the public's will than to serve it.

Let us turn now to consider the sort of industrial strategy that would be inspired by a private planning view of the world. In doing so, we will have to re-examine some of the characteristics of the private planning process and contrast them with the attributes of public planning. The first feature we must examine is the goal determination process. The problem for central planners in a democratic, free society is the fact that goals can only be arrived at implicitly. Goals can be identified after the fact as part of a description of how people behave but, in general, cannot be known or specified in advance. People reveal what their goals are by how they act, and action is the only reliable indicator of those goals.

Thus, many people say, "I really should exercise every weekend." They might even tell this to a public opinion pollster. A planner might assume from this that exercise on the weekend is a goal of Canadians. However, observation reveals that, given the exigencies of life and the scheduling of professional hockey, football, golf, and baseball telecasts, only a small fraction of people actually exercise regularly. The fact is that life is composed of a succession of choices made in the context of conflicting goals. How the conflicts are resolved and which goals will emerge as dominant varies considerably from person to person. In the course of this very individual process of conflict resolution, people reveal what their important goals are and what actions they are prepared to take to achieve them.

Private planning is a reflection of this flexible goal-evolving process. The plan develops and changes as individuals determine their goals and shape their efforts to achieve them. This stands in sharp contrast to a rigid, centralized industrial strategy. The private planning process itself is a kind of on-going election process. When individuals decide to buy a good or service they cast a vote in favour of the good or service. This process applies equally to grocery stores and religious establishments. If people's goals change or if somebody finds a new way to achieve old goals, the voting pattern will change and the private planning process will have evolved a new scheme.

In this way, Canadians daily decide a whole range of issues. By purchasing or voting for a product, they vote for a certain income for the people involved in producing the product. Buying bread at a bakery constitutes a vote for the bread, for the salesperson, and for the baker. Indirectly, it is a vote for the flour company, the dairy, and others involved in making the raw materials.

The voting process has a wide range of unexpected implications. For example, the people who purchased a "pet rock" as a gift a few years back decided implicitly that the "inventor" should be a millionaire. In doing so, they ensured a steady supply of future amusements as other inventors labour for little or no remuneration with the expectation that they will invent other novelties to capture the public's imagination and thus be similarly rewarded.

People who choose to patronize American and not Canadian films are voting that the producers of these films go out of business or move to Hollywood. People who choose to buy an inexpensive, made-in-Taiwan shirt rather than the more expensive (higher quality?) Canadian-made shirt, vote for the Taiwanese manufacturer and against the Canadian manufacturer. (In making such a choice, people are implicitly saying that they don't want a Canadian shirt manufacturer to exist if the cost is as it appears—i.e., the difference between the prices of the two shirts.) The same sort of judgements are being made on a continuous basis by millions of Canadian consumers. Thousands of products are scrutinized for their value to the consumer, some rejected, some accepted. As a consequence, at any given point in time, the products stocked on the shelves of Canadian stores are, more or less, a reflection of these value judgements of the consumer.

Thus, private planning flexibly responds to the constantly changing goals of Canadians and in the process, it creates wealth. In voting for a product or a service, people are imbuing it with value—saying it is worth something. This stands in sharp contrast to the public planning process which, at most, involves the redistribution of wealth and often involves its destruction.

Consider the baker. Suppose he bakes one dozen fruit pies and one dozen cream pies. That week his customers decide they don't want cream pies and buy only the fruit pies. At the end of the week the baker has to sell the cream pies at a lower price, give them away, or destroy them. By choosing fruit pies, the baker's customers conferred a certain value on them by willingly exchanging some of their income for the pies. The pies which could only be sold at a discount were judged to be less valuable, while those which were given away or destroyed obviously were of less value still.

The fact that the pies could not be sold does not mean they had no potential for satisfying hunger. Indeed, it may be that unsold pies adorn the tables of the bakery staff or some charitable organization. However, it would be wrong to conclude that net value has been created simply because the pies are enjoyed. The fact is that the baker lost money. His decision to make cream pies was simply a mistake since nobody valued the pies enough to pay the baker for the time and other resources that went into making those pies. Since those resources could have been used to make other bakery goods, fruit pies for example, that people would willingly have bought, there is a net loss for the baker and for the community as a whole in the form of forgone opportunities.

To highlight the crucial role of choice making in the process of wealth creation, we can imagine a situation wherein government distributed pies at no charge to the recipient. If the government should mistakenly operate on the premise that society wanted cream pies, the result would be an enormous destruction of wealth because the resources could have been deployed in more highly valued ways. Since the government offers no choice, no one will ever know that the production of cream pies is not creating wealth.

In the case of industrial strategies, some economic activity will always result from subsidies or trade protection. However, if the products which ensue don't match the choices Canadians would have made if they had been given the opportunity, then the economic activity probably involves the net destruction of economic well-being or wealth. In every case, what is actually produced must be compared with what could have been produced using the same resources. *M.W.*

INTERPROVINCIAL TRADE BARRIERS

In some ways, Canada is really not a country at all. This does not refer to the inundation from U.S. television programming, books, magazines, movies, and other cultural phenomena. This no more hurts our nationhood than our exports of lumber, maple syrup, and energy hurt the U.S. Other small nations, such as Switzerland, Belgium, Norway, Denmark, and Iceland, are subjected to cultural influences from larger neighbours without being threatened in this way in the least.

No, Canada lacks one crucial aspect of nationhood completely apart from this usual complaint. Our problem is the widespread set of interferences with intra-national trade. Various of our provinces have erected trade barriers between themselves. As a result, in this regard, we are in some sense even less of a unified country than are the 17 separate and sovereign nations of the European Economic Community.

Consider the following facts. Canadian citizens who are non-residents of Prince Edward Island are severely restricted as to the amount of land they can legally own in that island province. Quebec has prohibited the importation of tomatoes—not from some foreign country intent upon the economic subjugation of Canada but from a neighbouring *province*, Ontario. Numerous provinces have enacted official "buy local" government policies. These effectively limit interprovincial trade. Saskatchewan requires that all bidders for major building projects in that province locate their head offices there. Even the so-called free enterprise government of the Social Credit Party of Bill Bennett has entered the fray. When a group of Ontario businessmen was interested in purchasing logging giant Macmillan Bloedel, the Premier announced that B.C. was "not for sale."

Needless to say, all these interferences with interprovincial trade fracture our country in a way movies or books from the U.S. never could. As well, they foster inefficient local enterprises to the detriment of our standard of living and our struggle against poverty. Although much of our so-called intelligentsia froth at the mouth at any mention of imports from our neighbour to the south, we would do well to borrow a leaf from the U.S. in this situation at least. In that country, all such trade barriers between states are strictly prohibited as a violation of the interstate commerce clause of their Constitution. We could do worse than to emulate this policy in Canada. *W.B.*

J

JOB CREATION BY GOVERNMENT

A scheme beloved of many politicians to lower our unemployment rate is to call for more public sector initiatives. Typically, they urge that we throw more money at the problem in order to create thousands of new jobs in public works.

But there are flaws in all such solutions. First of all, for every dollar the government spends trying to create employment, it must tax a dollar away from the private sector if it doesn't want to further fuel inflation. This destroys employment in the private sector. When we take into account the costly transfer process itself, the net result of this transfer is actually likely to be fewer job than before.

Secondly, the kinds of jobs likely to be created will be of the make-work, useless variety, while the ones destroyed are of the productive type upon which the economic health of Canada depends.

Instead of intervening further, government should rescind the laws which encourage unemployment in the first place: minimum wages, U.I.C., labour legislation, and tariffs. But some people reject this advice. They reply, "if you don't like government spending to create jobs, what are your alternatives? Don't knock our ideas unless you've got better ones to replace them."

One response is to point out that it was Hercules' task to clean out the stables of the king, not to refill them! But a more sober reaction is to point out that nobody knows where future jobs will come from, as is evident from the small businesses being created daily. It is in the very nature of such developments that they cannot be predicted. Imagine a government trying to plan for such developments! It's absurd. *M.W.*

JOB SECURITY

One of the issues in the typical labour strike is job security. Unions have made this one of their most important demands, and most people can sympathize. Who among us does not desire job security for himself, his friends, neighbours, and family? Yet, job security is in limited supply. If some of us have more of it—such as unionized public sector workers—then others of us will have less. Job security for the entire community can be increased, but only at the cost of greater economic inflexibility and retarded economic growth.

How does this work? Consider an agrarian society two or three centuries ago, before the onset of the industrial revolution. In those days things were done as they were in grandfather's time, and in his grandfather's time before him. There were no changes, no innovations, no products suddenly imported from abroad. People were born, lived their lives, and died—doing things in much the same way for their whole time on earth. Under such a system, as can readily be imagined, everyone in society had job security. With both bankruptcy and the creation of new firms practically unknown, there was much less reason to change jobs. Everything tended to be well-ordered, unchanging, and secure.

But nowadays, we live at a time of continuous change. The horse-and-buggy industry gave way to the automobile. Southeast Asians can now produce textiles more cheaply than Canadians—with the consequent loss of job security in Canadian textiles and other such horse-and-buggy industries. Waiting in the wings are robots, fifth-generation computers, genetic engineering, and a whole host of other industries that only science fiction would have taken seriously only a few years ago.

All of these new ways of doing things will immeasurably improve our lives. Indeed, the lives of billions of new human beings will come to depend upon them in just the same way that the lives of most people now living on earth would be impossible were it not for the mechanical and technical breakthroughs we now enjoy.

But these new inventions will wreak havoc on present economic methods of production. If we are to adapt to this life-giving process, job security will suffer, necessarily. If some of us are given enhanced job security through special and privileged legislative enactment—of the type sought by organized labour—the burden of adjustment to change will be unfairly shifted to the rest of us. *W.B.*

JOB SHARING

Is job sharing the solution to Canada's employment woes? While this programme has been promoted as a brave new solution to the problem of chronic unemployment, it is in reality an old solution—which has some well-known problems. There is the obvious fact that the objective of economic policy properly considered is not to create jobs. That simple objective could be achieved by outlawing mechanical devices. The real purpose of economic activity is consumption—what we call our standard of living. A shared pay cheque is one which provides less access to the good life, as most Canadians consider it. A fact which undoubtedly explains the sharp and distasteful reaction of the Canadian Labour Congress to the scheme.

Even more important, the underlying assumption of work sharing—that we are entering a new era in which the central problem is one of sharing the spoils of a technological bounty—is not met in practice. The central economic problem faced by the country is, as it has always been, to produce in the most efficient way the gross national income pie which makes the good life possible. Scarcity of all goods is not a state which we can ever, once and for all, overcome—it becomes more pressing with every extension of the human imagination and every attainment of a new level of entitlements.

The standard of living which job sharing advocates want us to take for granted would, under some conditions, begin to decline. One of these conditions is our failure to respond to the productivity challenge posed by other countries that are taking full advantage of technology to boost their efficiency levels. We should literally be shaking in our (Canadian-made, subsidized, protected) boots as we observe that productivity per head in Japan has recently been doubling every 11 years while ours has barely doubled in the past 30! Then there are the Swiss who, a few years ago in response to the economic funk occasioned by the competitive decline of their watch industry, decided by national referendum to increase the length of the work week.

But, the most devastating evidence of why all should heave a great sigh of relief at the dropping of work sharing is Italy. There, work sharing has been fervently practised, non-stop, since the end of World War II, and the effects can be plainly seen. Rather than an aid to otherwise displaced workers, the plan has been a life-support system for industrial basket cases and has left a legacy of inefficiencies which collectively deserve the label "the Italian disease." *M.W.*

JOB TRAINING

According to the provisions of the National Training Act (NTA), 82 specific skills have been designated as a national priority. Examples include electro-mechanical drafting, millwright, aircraft mechanics, electrical engineering technicians, and chemical process operators. This policy is very trendy. Instead of placing emphasis on the average out-of-work Canadian with more traditional skills, such as truck driving or secretarial training, the NTA focuses attention on the "glamour" industries: computers, electronics, hi-tech, and microchips. Says a spokesperson for the Canadian Association for Adult Education, "the Act makes official a move from trying to improve the basic skill level of the general population to investing in a smaller, more elite group."

Although this initiative leaves the lesser educated Canadians out in the cold and discriminates against women (who are proportionately under-represented in these elite areas), it was undertaken for an important reason. Previously, training programmes had been out of synch with the needs of industry. There was very little match between the skills taught by the old programmes and the ones needed to attain employment—so much so that graduates had great difficulties finding jobs.

But the worm is still in the apple. The record of the graduates of a course given in St. Lawrence College, Brockville, Ontario, is a case in point. The students were given a one-year accelerated course in electro-mechanical drafting—one of the 82 skills designated. Six months after completion of the course, 80 percent of them were still without jobs—any jobs.

The excuse given is that the new departure came just at the worst of the recession. But the real reason is quite different. The problem with retraining, of course, is that it takes time, usually a year or two, and for the more complex skills even three or four years. The needs of industry have an infuriating way of changing, and changing drastically, between the time of initial enrolment and graduation. In other words, there is a serious forecasting problem.

Our government is not without a response to this challenge. In order to mesh training with future skills' demands, the *federales* are working on a formula for long-range forecasting called the Canadian Occupational Projection System. But accurate forecasting is easier said than done, and the government's record in this regard is far from impressive—not to put too fine a point on it. As we have seen, graduates of these "new wave" courses are unable to find employment, and the government has only added to, not deleted from, its inventory of "priority" skills. The Critical Trade Skills Training programme started with six skills and now has 82. At this rate, we'll be up to our ears in retraining programmes by the next century. Things have come to such a pass that, according to the head of the Canadian Advanced Technology Association, most of the hi-tech jobs the government is currently pushing on its unfortunate clients are almost obsolete.

Clearly, the answer is to eliminate the heavy hand of government, root and branch, from this most crucial of endeavours. Instead, we must rely upon the far better record of private enterprise in this regard. In the marketplace, a school that retrained graduates for jobs no longer in existence would soon enough go bankrupt. Only those which successfully predict the future course of industrial events can grow and prosper.

This safety net, or safety valve, is unavailable to government enterprise. Whoever heard of a government ministry allowed to go bankrupt because of innumerable failures? That is why the sooner the funds being frittered away by the Ministry of Labour on retraining are returned to the private marketplace, the better the prospects for the unemployed of Canada. *W.B.*

L

LABOUR CODE (see Scab)

Provinces are continuously in the process of re-examining their labour codes with a view to revising them. In the past, such attempts have been superficial. They have placed bubble gum, band aid, and scotch tape solutions on a corpus in need of major surgery. Our legislative representatives must go to the heart of the matter in future. The health of the Canadian economy depends upon it. This analysis will entirely concern itself with the ideal labour code, with how things should be. This is crucial, for as Yogi Berra put it, "if you don't know where you're going, you'll end up someplace else."

Although many people think pickets are aimed at the struck employer, they are actually an attack on competing workers ("scabs"). Just as our laws should not and do not allow business firms to mass picket the premises of competitors, no group of workers should be able to forcibly prohibit another group of workers from bidding for jobs by picketing. A proper labour code would thus define a "legitimate union" as one which strictly limited its actions to organizing mass resignations. A "legitimate union" would eschew mass picketing, violence, and all other special advantages—legislative or otherwise—vis-à-vis its non-unionized competitors. This would end, once and for all, the legal fiction that workers who have left their jobs can yet retain any right to employment status in those positions.

Such changes would benefit the poor, who are to be found mainly in the non-unionized sector now prohibited from competing with organized labour. And it would bring about a modicum of labour peace, as union leaders would have to think twice before calling a strike. If they did not exercise caution and reserve strikes to only the most severe situations, they would have to pay the penalty—in the form of severe loss of union membership. Were this one basic change in labour relations made, society would have to re-think a whole host of unjust and unwise elements now embodied in present labour legislation.

Wage restraints should be ended. This would be an unconscionable interference with the rights of legitimate unions to engage in collective bargaining. And, as the Fraser Institute study, *The Illusion of Wage and Price Control*, makes clear, they misallocate labour, reduce productivity, create black markets, and do not cure inflation.

Boycotts. An alderman in Canada once voted to contract out the municipal garbage collection to the private sector. Because of this, a union withdrew its funds from a bank—his employer. As a result, he resigned his seat on the city council. Mean? Yes. Cheap? Yes. Petty? Again, yes. But this union, and all other depositors for that matter, have the right to withdraw funds at any time and for any reason. Boycotts of whatever type are simply a refusal to deal with certain people. Everyone has the moral right to choose his friends and business associates. Any attempt to stop such behaviour would be a severe violation of our human rights , and this goes for the secondary boycott as well.

Applying anti-combines legislation to unions. A favourite of union bashers, this too would be inapplicable to legitimate unions. Yes, unions attempt to withhold service and to jack up wages (just as corporations attempt to reduce output and raise prices). But as long as these activities are not buttressed with force or the threat of force, as long as competition, even potential competition, is allowed, these activities do no harm. And because of the invisible hand of the marketplace, they may even do some good. (See another Fraser Institute book in this regard, *Competition Versus Monopoly*, by Donald Armstrong.)

Imposing "democracy" on unions. This is another widely accepted means of reining in unwarranted union power, but it would be improper when applied to legitimate unions. Such organizations would be akin to private clubs, which should be free to set any rules they desire. It would be no more justified to subject legitimate unions to democracy than it would be to impose the secret ballot, government supervision of voting procedures, or limits on political activism on any other voluntary organization such as the corporation, the faculty club, or the Roman Catholic College of Cardinals. There have been abuses with regard to voting for decertification, but the answer would not be democracy. Rather, it lies in making sure that unions are limited to organizing voluntary walkouts and are not in any way allowed to interfere with "scabs." Then, those who do not wish to join the union strike may simply remain at work, without benefit of any voting at all.

Back-to-work orders. This would be an infringement upon the right of free men to withdraw their labour services. Under an ideal labour code, it would be no exaggeration to interpret this practice as a form of involuntary servitude or slavery. In such a situation, the only proper options open to an employer facing a labour walkout are to accede to the union demand or hire replacement workers. Fines, jail sentences for labour organizers, and imposed loss of check-off privileges would be completely unwarranted interference with the only tactic at the disposal of legitimate unionism. *W.B.*

LEVEL PLAYING FIELD

A new phrase has entered the common lexicon, "the level playing field." It sounds like sports jargon, but it is not. Instead, it refers to a rather technical aspect of international trade negotiations which took place between Canada and the United States. In this dialogue, the level playing field alludes to a situation where the citizens of neither country have an unfair competitive advantage over the other. If trade between nations can be represented by a playing field, then according to this doctrine it should tilt neither one way or the other, nor should the wind be at the back of either team, nor the sun more in the eyes of one side rather than the other. (In sports such as football, basketball, hockey and soccer, the goals are switched around half-way through the match to equalize any disadvantage which might result from an uneven playing field.)

The practice of particular concern to advocates of the level playing field is that of subsidizing exports. The Americans, for example, were worried about the price of lumber sent to their country. Low lumber prices, they contended, were due to low rates of stumpage, a form of tax levied by government. Without this advantage, our lumber industry would not be able to compete so efficiently. The U.S. wanted a level playing field where the Canadian government did not help its citizens to compete "unfairly" against Americans.

In a superficial analysis, this point of view makes sense. After all, there are specific losers—the American lumber companies who suffer directly from Canadian stumpage policy. But if we look a little deeper, we can see that insisting on a level playing field makes no economic sense at all. In order to prove this, let us ignore such situations where our bureaucrats pursue a policy which in effect, if not by intention, allows us to sell products more cheaply to the Americans than would otherwise be possible. Let us instead consider an extreme hypothetical case where the Canadian government encourages us to *give away* our goods to them for free!

For example, suppose that a law were passed tomorrow permanently subsidizing, to the rate of 110 percent all free gifts of lumber to the U.S. That is, for every $100 worth of wood products we sent across the border at a zero price, our government would give us $110. Let's pass lightly over the objection that this would bankrupt Canada in short order, even faster than at the present furious pace, and ask only what effect this would have on the economy of the U.S.A.

It is easy to see that although this policy would drive the entire American forest industry into bankruptcy, it would be a boon to their economy as a whole. They could have just as much wood as before (compliments of Canada) while freeing up large numbers of workers and whatever capital could be transferred to other occupations. In this way, their standard of living would rise with no additional inputs. Moreover, this is roughly how the war-torn economies of Europe were rebuilt after World War II, thanks to the generosity of Marshall Plan aid. If they wished to remain logically consistent, the Americans could hardly turn around now and refuse such aid were it offered to them.

This is all that an "uneven" playing field consists of—an offer from one country to subsidize the economy of another. Instead of objecting to other nations pursuing such policies, each should encourage others to tilt the playing field in the direction of subsidizing exports even more. Yet, the economic level of sophistication that commonly prevails in North America holds the very opposite: that is, that each nation should protest when its neighbours subsidize it. *W.B.*

LIABILITY INSURANCE

If you haven't been watching closely, you would have missed it, but there is a certain irony about the crisis in liability insurance. The furor started several years ago when the courts in the United States, under the influence of a so-called activist judiciary, began to stretch the interpretation of liability law. In what was an essentially ideological leap, the court system increasingly reflected the judgement of the activist left to the effect that there was one law for the rich and another for the poor. The apparatus of the court, they said, was just one more manifestation of how the system was stacked against the average person and in favour of the well-to-do and corporations.

The result of this judgment in the area of civil tort (the area of the law which includes liability for bodily injury and economic damages) was to stretch the interpretation of liability so that corporations and insurance firms became liable for events heretofore regarded as simply the vicissitudes of life. Increasingly, such legal contests were regarded as the ordinary person versus the corporation. The legal system became an instrument of those who sought to create the "just society." These were, in many instances, the same well-intentioned folk who pursued the "just society" via the route of government regulation and intervention in most aspects of our lives.

Now, however, the worm has turned. The campaign to attack the wealthy via the courts is coming home to roost. Legal principles, having been stretched to get the wealthy and corporations, begin to reach into the ordinary areas of our lives. We are beginning to discover that unlimited liability protection is very expensive.

Recent headline-making increases in the cost of liability insurance for groups ranging from day-care facilities to municipalities have caused people to focus their attention on this usually esoteric and obscure aspect of the economy. For the most part, however, attention has been devoted to determining who should be blamed for this escalation in cost. The usual bogeymen have all been dragged out and thrashed for their antisocial behaviour. Insurance corporations have been accused of gouging and ripping off the unsuspecting public, an impression which is heightened by the fact that some municipalities have decided that in the light of the increase in costs they will now insure themselves against risks. The insurance companies, for their part, deny all corporate culpability and indicate that the upward surge in the cost of insurance is due simply to the rise in the number of claims and their increased dollar value.

Central to the claims of insurers is that their customers have been very lucky in the past half decade or so in that the cost of insurance settlements was in part being met by the very high interest rates that were available on the money insurance companies have invested. While critical commentators haven't denied that fact, they have alleged that insurance companies have been making too much profit. The question is, who is right in this imbroglio?

The excess profits story doesn't make sense. The reality is, we do not find capitalists stumbling over each other and rushing to invest their money in the insurance liability business because of the lucrative profits that can be had there. On the contrary, the very escalation in the insurance rates is an indicator of the fact that there is widespread concern about the viability of existing insurance companies and, therefore, no attraction for new capital to move into the industry.

A much better indicator of the extent of profitability of an industry than some journalist's rendition of the high profits to be made there is the extent to which people and capital gravitate toward it. For example, a few years ago when real estate markets were in their heyday and the profits of development companies were the media's target, large groups of people responded to the lure of huge profits by investing significant amounts of money in real estate. Some of them were even successful, although the promise of profit was highly overrated and the skills necessary to earn it under-appreciated. The fact that there is no such rush to invest in insurance is a prime indicator that the excess profit charge is probably not warranted.

Of course you've heard the expression "buyer beware!" Many believe that this doctrine of the marketplace was a crafty invention of greedy capitalists seeking yet again to exploit the hapless consumer. Recent developments with regard to liability insurance, however, serve to remind us of the very important reason for the development of the *caveat emptor* principle. Essentially, the notion of buyer beware is that consumers ought to decide by their own actions in buying it and using it whether or not a product should be purchased. Such an attitude imposes on the consumer the responsibility to inquire about the safety and other aspects of the products they buy. The so-called consumer protection legislation enacted by governments during the last three decades has in part been a reflection of the fact that consumers cannot be trusted in their buying decisions. Consumers, in the judgement of governments, cannot be relied upon to avoid purchasing products that may be hazardous to their health and safety and that of others. Never mind that these same consumers as electors are held to be quite capable of sorting out the complex issues necessary to make appropriate choices when choosing amongst political candidates.

While consumer protection legislation calls into question the competence of the customer, it does not remove the basic presumption that the buyer should retain responsibility for his or her purchasing choices. Recently, however, in the courts in the United States and increasingly in Canada, there has emerged a new doctrine, "seller beware!" It is this doctrine, ultimately, in its various forms that lies at the base of the current insurance liability explosion.

Consider the following description of events. Joe Bloggs is driving his car down a steep incline. Suddenly a bolt snaps, the brakes fail, and Joe Bloggs crashes into a concrete wall erected by the local municipality. Poor Joe is left a paraplegic. Joe's lawyer says, "we can't fix your back, Joe, but we sure can make somebody pay for the mishap." The manufacturer of the 10-cent bolt is sued for selling a faulty product, and the municipality is sued for erecting a concrete wall at a point where someone could run into it. This is a fictitious case, but hundreds similar to it have recently and frequently been decided in favour of the injured party and against the bolt manufacturer and the municipality.

The effect of these kinds of court decisions is to transfer the risk from the consumer, or user, of a product, to the producer. It is a risky business to drive an automobile; there are thousands of parts which may malfunction—not because of any negligence on the part of the manufacturer but simply due to chance. By assessing the liability for such accidents on the manufacturer, the courts are in effect providing the purchaser with a no-limits guarantee as to the safety of the product being used. In every case, this will mean an increase in the price of the product to cover the increased cost of insurance. In some cases, manufacturers or service suppliers will simply eliminate the product. We've already seen municipalities react to the circumstance by limiting the activities which they permit in municipal parks, for example. Meanwhile, of course, liability insurance premiums have gone up. Nobody said a risk-free society would be cheap.

The liability insurance crisis is spreading into every area of our lives. Insurance companies, faced with the prospect of having to pay out hefty future claims arising from current accidents, are boosting their rates. Where rates can't cover the potential losses, they are simply refusing to provide the insurance at all. This is a perfectly predictable response to the increased generosity of awards and the increasingly wide interpretation of liability by the courts. It is, however, producing demands by some groups, such as Ralph Nader's Public Interest Research group, that government step in to keep the cost of insurance from rising and make sure that insurance continues to be available. They allege market failure and demand further government action.

Two aspects of this require further scrutiny. First, there is no market failure. The fact that insurance rates are rising is just the bad news from the market about the cost of the attempt to provide people with unlimited guarantees and to create a risk-free society. The market isn't refusing to provide the insurance out of a fit of pique but rather because the uncertainty of what the courts will do next makes it impossible to set rates that are related to the risk.

Secondly, higher insurance premiums are a signal to firms that they now are in a very hazardous business. If the courts decree day-care operators are to be held absolutely and completely responsible for any mishap which affects their young charges, of course liability insurance will be more expensive. If parents expect such responsibility, they should be willing to pay for it. Otherwise, they must press government to constrain the court's interpretation of fault and liability. Government-provided insurance would treat the symptom, not the cause. *M.W.*

LIBERATION THEOLOGY

Liberation theology may be characterized as the cutting edge of the religious Marxists interest in Third World economic development. First developed by Roman Catholic priests in Latin America, it then spread its way to the rest of the Third World, and to leftist Catholic and Protestant circles in Europe, the U.S., and Canada.

In this view, the reason the downtrodden peoples of the earth have not bettered their secular lot is because of colonialism, capitalism, and the attendant economic exploitation. The rich grow richer by trampling down the poor, as the liberation theologians see things. Liberationists, such as Gustavo Gutierez of Peru, Jon Sobino of El Salvador, and Gregory Baum of Canada, believe they can adopt the Marxian techniques and outlook—shorn of Marx's atheism, of course—and apply it to help improve the economic conditions of the poor in the Third World. And for a while, these views were sweeping through the seminaries and schools of Divinity where new religious leaders are trained.

But, of late, there has been a re-thinking of the Marxist-oriented liberation theology. Economists, such as Lord Bauer of the London School of Economics and recently elevated to the House of Lords in Great Britain, have established through a series of scholarly studies that poverty in the Third World is due to lack of initiative brought about by central economic planning of the Marxist variety. He has shown that the closer the relationship between the capitalist nations of the West and a Third World country, and the more reliance placed on the marketplace, not foreign aid, the richer the country in question.

Theologians such as Michael Novak of the American Enterprise Institute and Richard John Neuhaus of the Rockford Institute have demonstrated that reliance on democracy, on the family, and free enterprise—all bourgeoisie values—have been a mainstay in Latin American economic development. These three, and other Fraser Institute authors, have undertaken a decade's long empirical, spiritual, and theological critique of liberation theology.

Most recently, there has been a report by Joseph Cardinal Ratzinger, the Vatican's chief theologian. It was authorized by none other than Pope John Paul himself, who has already spoken out against advocating violence for social change and building theology on a Marxist foundation. But Cardinal Ratzinger's report, published in *30 Giorni*, the authoritative Italian Catholic monthly, goes even further. It aggressively attacks the liberation theologians' penchant for embracing Marxism and transforming spiritual concepts into political ones as a serious doctrinal error. Liberation theology may be good Marxism, but it is certainly bad economics and, it would appear, poor theology as well. *W.B.*

LIBERTY

It is crucially important to make clear the connection between economic liberty and political liberty. If we look around us at the nations of today or consult history, one thing will become perfectly clear. Economic freedom (free trade, private property, profits, competition) is a necessary, but not sufficient, condition for political freedom (free press, free speech, freedom of religion, freedom of association, freedom of conscience, and democracy). Without economic freedom, political freedom is well-nigh impossible. No nation, all throughout history, has ever enjoyed the various political freedoms unless much of its economic activity was organized along the principles of the free marketplace. But economic liberty is by no means a sufficient condition for political liberty. There are many nations in the world, including countries of Southeast Asia and South America, which do organize their economic systems at least roughly along marketplace lines and yet suffer from a lack of political liberty.

There is an important reason for the interconnectedness of economic and political freedom. When the government owns or controls the overwhelming majority of goods, services, capital, and resources of a society, there is little scope for individual initiative in the economic sphere. If the individual cannot earn a living independent of state authorities, his political liberties are to that extent proscribed.

Lech Walesa, for example, along with virtually every other Polish citizen, perforce must work for the state apparatus. There are precious few alternatives. It is a tribute to this man's rare courage and conviction that he is able to overcome these severe limitations to the degree he has. Imagine, if in Canada all employment was on government account. Would this stifle dissent? Would it limit the expression of religious, economic, or political opinions at variance with those maintained by government leaders? To ask these questions is to answer them.

Right now, in Canada anyone is free to purchase paper, ink, and a printing machine to set up his own newsletter. And there, within very wide parameters, he is free to express his own opinions, no matter how unique or objectionable to the powers that be. If he can attract enough subscribers, he can even earn his living in this manner and be independent of the authorities for his livelihood. Under public ownership of capital goods such as paper, ink and printing machines, such an option would be impossible. This is why, in the name of protecting political, religious, and civil liberties, we must always resist encroaching interference with our economic liberties. *W.B.*

LICENSING

On December 27, 1985, in a stroke of a pen in the form of an Order-in-Council, the Government of British Columbia ended one of the most remarkable and inappropriate pieces of legislation on the books of that province. The 61-year-old law was a licensing system covering every theatre and movie projectionist. Among other things, the legislation provided that projectionists had to be licensed under the Fire Commissioner's Office. The origin of the law was that in the 1920s motion pictures were encoded on highly flammable cellulose nitrate film. Allegedly, in order to become proficient in the handling of such film, a prospective projectionist had to apprentice without pay for a minimum of one year and pay a fee of $1,000. Having been licensed in this way, the projectionist would then have to become a member of the Projectionist's Union to work in most of the theatre chains.

While cellulose nitrate hasn't been used in theatres for decades, the advent of safety film was not followed by an abolition of the nonsensical licensing provision. One of the reasons is that such an abolition was hotly opposed by the B.C. Projectionists' Union because the existence of the restriction gave the union effective control over the movie marketplace. Of course, the abolition of the law will have no momentous effects on movie goers, because in most cases, particularly in the chain theatres, unions also have a closed shop arrangement. It will, however, affect independent theatres and the ability of new theatres to spring up in the future. Now that licensure of projectionists is gone, there are only several hundred occupational licensures remaining, and most of them are as useful as the projectionists' licensing was. *M.W.*

LITERARY PROTECTIONISM

Remember when there used to be a Canadian *Time* magazine? It was really the *Time* international edition with eight pages or so of Canadian content tacked on at the front. It was used by Canadian advertisers because it was widely read. It is still used by Canadian advertisers on a limited basis, even though they aren't allowed to count the costs for tax purposes—not since Bill C58 which legislated that advertising could not be a deductible tax expense unless it appeared in a periodical that is 75 percent Canadian-owned and has 80 percent Canadian editorial content.

Of course, the effect of this law was to greatly advantage Canadian magazines like the then-monthly *Maclean's*. The Maclean-Hunter publishing empire was quick to capitalize on the new restrictions, changing *Maclean's* to a weekly and boosting its circulation to the present level of about 650,000 per week. Meantime, *Time's* circulation has deteriorated but still stands at a healthy 360,000 per week.

But there is an attempt to revive a Canadian edition of *Time* by a deal worked out between Time Canada Limited and Canadian-owned Comac Communications Limited of Toronto. Already the fur is beginning to fly. Arch nationalists like Mel Hurtig and the 230-member Canadian Periodical Publishers Association and Maclean-Hunter are beginning to talk about the demise of the Canadian publishing industry if this new, improved Canadian edition of *Time* is allowed equal treatment with the existing Canadian magazines. David Orlikow, federal New Democratic Party's communications critic, set the tone of the debate by remarking that, "I don't think *Time* is concerned about the welfare of Canadians or the Canadian magazine industry." While the *Globe and Mail* has quoted Mel Hurtig as saying: "surely we have been through this before. There's no justification to reopen this after C58. Why turn the clock back?"

What is the principle that should guide our thinking? First of all, it must be loudly and clearly said that what *Time* Canada is seeking is not preferential treatment but merely equal treatment under the law which at the moment applies to magazines such as *Maclean's.*

Secondly, the villain in the piece is the government legislation itself, which sets limits on the kinds of magazines that may seek to finance their operations by offering advertising to their readers. While it may look like the law is protecting Canadian culture, what it is really doing is protecting the potentially mediocre and inferior Canadian magazine producers from the competition they richly deserve. This is particularly true in magazines which purport to provide a world scale or to be international in their scope. Canadian consumers and not the government should decide what kinds of news magazines they wish to read and what style of editorial content they prefer. In answer to publishers like Mel Hurtig, Canadians should clearly say, "let's wind the clock back and eradicate Bill C58, because Canadians have the right to be exposed to all views, not simply those which past muster under Bill C58." *M.W.*

M

MAKE-WORK PROJECTS

What real harm can it do to provide somebody with a job, even of a mind-numbing make-work variety? There is an old adage that it's better to have somebody working at something rather than having them unemployed. Unfortunately, this piece of old husband's tale is just that. It doesn't fit reality. The reality is that employing an individual in such a make-work task has many bad side effects.

First of all, it makes that person unavailable for active employment in a worthwhile occupation. Secondly, the fact that many of these tasks are very well-paid (sometimes not much less than skilled or other interesting work) means that much of the incentive that the individual would have to improve his own circumstance is removed. After all, what incentive does a flagperson, making $8 an hour have to upgrade his skills so that as a tradesperson he can make $9 per hour? Aside from destroying incentive, employing somebody to do nothing at high wages also encourages unrealistic expectations about other employment possibilities and his or her future in the work-force.

The next time you see a flagperson apparently doing nothing on a roadway, don't permit yourself to think that is better than doing nothing on unemployment insurance. It may be better should they receive the modest compensations from unemployment insurance or welfare which would still leave them an incentive to find productive and more enjoyable work. *M.W.*

MARKET FAILURE (see Government Programmes)

Many professional economists subscribe to what might be called the argument for market failure. In this perspective, the market is imperfect, and therefore the government is justified in intervening in commercial activities, in order to improve matters.

This view has not gone unchallenged. First of all, any attempt to justify government regulation of business on this ground violates a distinction which is axiomatic in economics, that between the normative and the positive. Justification is by its very nature a normative, value-laden procedure, but economics is a value free subject. There is nothing in the value free corpus of economic science that could possibly justify anyone doing anything. Economics as such is limited to describing, explaining, understanding, and perhaps predicting behaviour. The justification of action is entirely outside its realm.

Secondly, even if there were any such thing as market failure and economics could somehow justify acting so as to obviate such a phenomenon, it by no means follows that its mere existence would justify state activity, for there is such a thing as government failure (the inability of state bureaucrats to act efficiently, due to a lack of the proper profit and loss incentives) and in any given case the latter might outweigh the former. In ordinary parlance, the cure might be worse than the disease.

Thirdly, there has been no definitive demonstration that any real world example of market failure exists. The major candidates put forth by the proponents of this doctrine include monopoly and pollution. Let us briefly consider each.

Trusts, or combines, or monopolies are said to misallocate resources when they attain too great a degree of control over a given industry, but economists cannot even unambiguously define an industry. There may be only one widget producer in a given city, but if the whole province, the country, or the entire world is defined as the relevant market, the concentration ratio (the proportion of sales, employment, or profits accounted for by the top few firms) can be made to appear very low. Similarly, the more all-inclusive the definition of the good in question, the less "control" there can be. One is far more likely to find monopoly in the industry limited to colas than in the one which includes all beverages, and yet there is no unambiguous way to define the industry.

As well, the misallocative or dead weight losses described by some economists are solely a product of their narrowly constructed blackboard economics. Firms depicted in these models are timeless and static, while those which earn a living in the real world are forced to act in a dynamic setting. Nor is there an independent criterion (the perfectly competitive result, beloved of the blackboard economist) against which to measure the actual operation of a business concern that might run afoul of combines legislation. Rather, the proponent of such legislation must claim the contrary to fact conditional that were such an industry to exist, it would have arrived at a different pricing and quantity decision than the defendant accused of restraining trade. But here the firm finds itself in a "Catch 22" no-win situation. If it charges more than its competitors, it can be found guilty of monopolizing or profiteering. If its prices are lower, it can be fined for cutthroat or predatory competition. It cannot escape even if it proves it did neither, for then it stands condemned of engaging in collusive behaviour.

Pollution is claimed as another instance of market failure. The charge, here, is that the business firm need only calculate the costs of its inputs—land, labour, and capital—and can safely ignore the costs of smoke, wastes, and pollution, since these are imposed on others. It is for this reason, claim the critics, that the capitalist system is earmarked by excessively dirty air and water and by noise inundations.

There is a failure of some sort that explains these unfortunate circumstances, but it is not market failure. On the contrary, it is government failure, in this case the neglect of the courts to carefully define and assiduously protect the property rights of those victimized by polluters. Were the state to have awarded injunctions to the plaintiffs in the early 19th century pollution or nuisance cases, our entire experience with smoke prevention devices and technology would have taken a far different turn than it has and our environment would have been far more adequately protected.

There may well be market failure in the sense that commerce is conducted by flesh and blood creatures who are imperfect and, hence, given to error. But no one has shown the existence of any market failure in the real world apart from the fallibility of human beings. *W.B.*

MARKETING BOARDS

As economists, we are often asked how people can best invest their money to avoid the effects of inflation. Often as not, they expect to hear about gold or, until the market was bunkered, silver. The more sophisticated are inclined to expect esoteric tips on land markets or insight as to the real impact of the interest rates on oil stocks. Imagine their surprise when we confidentially whisper "eggs," or "chickens," or, upon occasion, "milk" into their disbelieving ears.

Many have sauntered off shaking their heads and mumbling about how work strain ultimately takes its toll or asking when we last read a financial page. However, the few who stayed to hear the explanation would have profited quite handsomely. Take eggs, for example. An investment of $300 in eggs in 1975 grew to nearly $3,000 in 1981, and there is no sign that this appreciation will abate. Where else could one have realized a tenfold increase in one's investment in the short interval of six years? A similar, though less lucrative story could be told about milk and chickens.

Why have egg investments been so lucrative, and how can such investments be made? First of all the how. Contrary to initial impressions, an investment in eggs would not be made by purchasing futures contracts on a commodity exchange. Nor would such an investment necessarily entail knowing anything about egg production. All that an investor had to do was to purchase quota rights, that is, the right to produce eggs. These quotas are issued by provincial egg marketing boards across the country under the auspices of the Canadian Egg Marketing Agency. Unfortunately, one cannot simply go to the local egg board and purchase a quota because it is strictly limited in supply. At any given time, all of the available quota will be owned by existing egg producers.

The first clue as to why the egg marketing quota has increased so dramatically in price is to be found in the fact that its supply is strictly limited, and for good reason. By its very nature, the egg marketing quota is supposed to limit the total amount of egg production possible in a given area. In effect, the quota is a licence to produce eggs and entitles the holder to a membership in the egg producing cartel. Obviously, if everybody had the right to produce and sell eggs, the cartel wouldn't be very successful.

Purchasers of quota don't have to worry that the value of their investment will be eroded by maverick producers. Unlike cartels that arise from time to time in the private sector, the egg cartel is backed by the force of law. And, on more than one occasion in the past, producers trying to produce more eggs than they had quota for have had their chickens seized by officers of the law. Neither do quota holders have anything to fear from low cost competition from south of the border, since the egg cartel also has the power to control egg imports. All in all, the quota is a pretty safe investment in terms of holding its value.

However, control over the market and the ability to use the force of law against those who threaten the investment in quota don't in themselves explain why the value of quota has risen so dramatically. For that, we need the added clue provided by the fact that the cartel also has the power to set the price of eggs. Needless to say, that power is also enforced by the full clout of the sanctioning government.

How does the cartel persuade governments to permit it to set prices in such a way as to ensure the yearly appreciation of the value of quota? And, how does the ability to set price lead to increasing value for quota in the first place? The price of eggs established by the egg marketing board is based on the cost of production. In their representations to government, the marketing board can claim that the price of eggs is rising because the costs of production are rising. Since the price is based on a formula involving the various costs of production, the egg board can completely document its claims. Moreover, if the government in question becomes nervous at the high price of quota—as indeed they should be—the marketing board can triumphantly point to the fact that whatever may seem to be the case, the cost of quota is not included in the formula used to set prices. Ergo, rising quota values don't cause rising egg prices. Neat!

For the prospective investor in egg quota, this leaves somewhat of a puzzle. Why are egg farmers willing to pay heavily for quota rights if the cost of quota cannot be retrieved by them in the price they receive for eggs? Remember that the formula allegedly sets prices on the basis of the cost of production, and quota costs are not included in the formula. For a farmer to be willing to pay for quota, he must feel that he can produce eggs at a lower cost than the cost allowed for in the formula. Is there any reason to suppose that is the case? Fortunately for the investor, that is precisely the case.

The formula used by the Egg Marketing Agency to determine the price of eggs is based on a theoretical "model" farm assumed to be located in Manitoba. The costs of production are calculated on the basis of the costs that such a producer would face if he or she existed and operated according to the model established by the egg board. If an actual egg farmer is more efficient, and thus has lower costs than those predicted by the model farm, profit can be earned. The fact that many egg producers in B.C. are willing to pay dearly per case for the right to sell eggs at the egg board price is *primafacie* evidence that at least in their judgement there is considerable excess profit to be made on each dozen eggs sold.

The egg marketing board presents not only an economic issue but a moral one as well. Imagine, if you will, a courtroom: the accused stands quivering in the dock; the judge, manifesting every vestige of the power of law which resides within him points the accusatory finger and intones, "Mr. John Bloggs, it is alleged that on the morning of March 1, 1983, you did willfully and with premeditation sell eggs to the Tara Natural Food Stores. You are, therefore, accused of the heinous crime of selling uninspected eggs. How do you plead?" Poor John Bloggs, having been caught in the act, as it were, and being a normally law-abiding, God-fearing citizen, pleads guilty. The judge then passes sentence according to the provisions of the Act.

Sound like a wholly improbable circumstance? Not at all. In fact, precisely this sort of thing occurred in Kingston, Ontario. Farmers sold their eggs directly to health food stores. Apparently, the consumers who frequent these establishments prefer eggs bought directly from the farmer to those purchased after a ponderous bureaucratic process from the Egg Marketing Board and their supermarket. Not only that, but they are paying about 50 cents a dozen more than the price at supermarkets. The heinous crime of which John Bloggs stands accused is that he allegedly sold uninspected eggs and, under the law of Ontario, eggs must be inspected for health reasons.

It is very strange that farmers may sell their unprocessed eggs directly to the consumer, but if they should dare to sell them to consumers via the intermediary of the health food store or any other commercial outlet without first having the imprimatur of the Ontario Egg Marketing Board, they are in trouble. Evidently, it is not the protection of public health that really is at issue; rather, it is a question of selling eggs via a commercial outlet which does not participate in the marketing process established by the marketing board.

What we have here, masquerading under the guise of consumer protection legislation, is really one of the bricks in the complex wall agricultural producers have built up around their markets to inhibit potential competitors. We can only look forward in our wildest dreams to the day when the Ontario Egg Marketing Board and the British Columbia Egg Marketing Board and all the others will stand in the dock accused by the judge for conspiring against the interests of consumers. *M.W.*

MEANS TESTS

Most of the beneficiaries of the co-op and non-profit housing programmes are, in fact, middle or upper income Canadians, not those with incomes below the poverty line. Many people will regard with disdain, shock, and even horror the revelation that at a time when the federal government is running a large deficit it is spending hundreds of millions providing housing subsidies to those with incomes above the average. Little do they realize that this, quite apart from being an exception, is the rule for government programmes. Such hallmark social welfare programmes as Unemployment Insurance convey more than half of their benefits to Canadian families whose incomes are above the average.

This is not an accidental occurrence but a direct result of the fact that Canada, like many other so-called welfare states, has completely eschewed the use of means tests in the disposition of public funds. There used to be long and hard debates about whether or not taxpayers' money should be ladled out to whoever sidled up to the trough—whether there shouldn't be some sort of income-testing stile over which prospective recipients had to pass before being able to sample the state's largess. Somewhere along the line it was decided that such tests were demeaning and, in consequence, the whole apparatus of social welfare spending became devoid of a compass to keep it on the course which had originally been set. The system which sets out to play Robin Hood has been transformed into one which taxes Maid Marion and pays the result to the Sheriff of Nottingham. *M.W.*

MEDICAL LICENSING

According to U.S. Representative Claude Pepper (Democrat, Florida), over 10,000 "doctors" are practicing in that country without benefit of proper medical licensing. These are not people with questionable credentials or graduates from diploma mills or physician's assistants or nurses practising beyond their qualifications. We're talking about outright impostors here, individuals who have no official qualifications at all. Apart from this, fully 10 percent of the 450,000 duly licensed physicians practising south of our border are incompetent. This, at least, is the opinion of Dr. Robert Derbyshire, past president of the Federation of State Medical Boards, and is seconded by Dr. David Axelrod, New York's Health Commissioner.

What is the situation in Canada? There are no official estimates of fake doctors in this country, but according to the College of Physicians and Surgeons of Ontario, a random sample of doctors from that province showed that 13 percent either practised medicine in a way that caused "serious concern" or kept poor records. This crisis applied mainly to family doctors, not specialists, and to elderly doctors. Thus, the situation here might even be worse than in the U.S. However, even if the usual ten-to-one rule of thumb applies, this would mean that about 1,000 practising doctors in this country are outright frauds, and another 4,500 are unskilled—despite their legitimate credentials.

How could this possibly be true? Are not this nation's doctors subjected to a complete and up-to-date medical school education, an exhaustive system of initial pre-diploma testing, and airtight procedures which ensure competence throughout their careers? This, at least, is the theory. But the practice is far different. The function of medical licensing in this country is not so much to ensure physician quality as it is to limit entry into the field, so as to increase the income, power, and prestige of those doctors already in practice.

According to Fraser Institute research, the Canadian medical establishment at one point or another in its history has: (1) banned price and other advertising for licensed doctors; (2) set minimum price schedules; (3) acted to prevent "overcrowding" or an over-supply of physicians by setting up a whole host of irrelevant criteria for licensing—examples include a knowledge of grammar, mathematics, Latin, history, philosophy, and other academic studies, language requirements, and citizenship; (4) outlawed the uncontrolled study of medicine, even for those who do not intend to practise; (5) placed roadblocks against foreign doctors practising in Canada where they would compete with domestic physicians; (6) been content with imposing entry examinations only (for if the certification of quality were the true goal of these exams, they would more likely be required of practising physicians at least every decade or so; there is little guarantee—certainly not on the basis of testing—that a doctor of 70 years of age is still qualified, merely for having successfully sat an examination 40 years earlier); (7) fought against pre-payment contract practice, opposed doctors testifying for plaintiffs in malpractice suits, and discouraged charity work as undermining minimum fee schedules and professional prestige; (8) raised medical student fees in order to increase the costs of entry into the profession; and (9) succeeded, from time to time, in raising physicians' income levels beyond that of other, equally skilled, professions in Canada.

These changes are a part of the Canadian historical record with which most people, even doctors, may not be familiar. The evidence will thus come as a distinct and uncomfortable surprise to most Canadians, and for good reason. This is because the typical doctor in this country is not at all involved in limiting entry into the field as a means of feathering his own nest. On the contrary, the average physician works long, hard hours (Winston Churchill's oft-quoted remark about "blood, sweat, and tears" is a particularly apt description of medical practice) and has as his main concern the practise of his profession, not the financial exploitation of his patients.

Thus the truth or falsity of these claims cannot be based on the experience of individual physicians who do not perceive themselves to be engaged in restricting their competitors. On the other hand, the leadership of the medical profession in conjunction with well-meaning, though paternalistic, bureaucrats has been doing just that for a century.

If the present licensing system has failed, what can be done about the epidemic of doctors who are either incompetent and/or sheer frauds? The public policy recommendation which follows from this analysis would be to install a system of competitive certification in place of the present system of monopoly licensing. Under licensing, if the applicant fails the test, he cannot practise (as in the motor vehicle licence). Under certification, a rejected applicant can still practise (a non-chartered accountant may legally help people fill out tax forms), but he cannot pass himself off as certified.

The problem with monopoly licensing (as with all other coercive monopolies) is that if the responsible institution does a poor job, consumers have no alternative. Under competition, there is an incentive system for all competitors to try to outdistance each other in terms of quality control, innovations, and cost-cutting. The weakest producers are forced to the sidelines, the strongest can expand the scope of their operations to the ultimate and ongoing improvement of the industry.

Although provision of knowledge to health care consumers about the skill, qualifications, experience, and general trustworthiness of doctors may not appear at first blush to be an "industry," the effects of competition operate here as well. How might competition work in the medical profession? Were government so minded, it could announce that at some time hence (say, ten years) it would call a halt to the present monopoly system of licensing doctors. This would usher in a competitive certification system to begin at present, to co-exist with licensing for the next decade, and to be launched on its own at that point.

What kind of firms might undertake such an endeavour? One likely scenario would have various certification agencies—the Canadian Medical Association, the Royal College of Physicians and Surgeons of the provinces, the McGill University Medical Faculty, and major insurance companies—all competing with each other as to which might best be able to ensure the quality of physicians to the general public. Under such a system, the cost of physicians' services would fall and the quality of medicine and the extent of monitoring medical practise would improve—to the great benefit of the health care of the Canadian populace. *W.B.*

MEGA PROJECT

The Montreal Olympic stadium cover is the largest retractable fabric roof in the world and is a tourist attraction. It is a monument to Mayor Drapeau, and generations will marvel at its engineering and those who built it. Of course, the really incredible aspect of the building is the fact that by the time it is paid for in 1993, it will have cost $1.4 billion. To put that in context, the stadium will cost an amount equal to three and a half times the deficit experienced running Expo 86. Undoubtedly, the Olympic stadium will be the most expensive such building ever constructed. The puzzle is why the author of such a financial disaster is revered as a kind of hero?

Mayor Drapeau, unfortunately, is not alone in attaining this paradoxical status. Joey Smallwood, the father of Newfoundland confederation, was revered as the country's longest sitting premier, in spite of the fact that his government was the sponsor of an unbroken string of the most absurd economic development ploys which often involved considerable human dislocation and disappointment. And then there is the still fondly remembered Pierre Trudeau, who dashingly charmed and mesmerized Canadians into cheering as he built the social and economic edifice for which he will be remembered and for which our children and grandchildren will pay.

Why we make heros of such people is hard to say. Perhaps it is because of the argument that convention centres, stadiums, and other mega projects, even if they lose millions of dollars, still benefit the cities in which they are located, because even more millions of tourist dollars will enter the cash registers of the local businessmen and find their way into the city's coffers through taxation.

But this is fallacious. First of all, it ignores the experiences of such places as Montreal with its Olympics and New Orleans with its World's Fair. Both places lost money hand over fist; yes, tourist dollars came flocking in, but to a lesser degree than expected, and at far below the rate of loss on construction.

Secondly, this argument commits the fallacy of "the seen versus the unseen." To be sure, there is a job multiplier effect engendered by the construction of the convention centre and by the jobs created in order to run it. Tenants buy things in the local economy (food, shelter, and entertainment). It is also true that these people go out and spend this money, again creating a further ripple of jobs. All of this is "seen."

But what about the "unseen?" What would have happened to all these millions of dollars had they not been forcibly seized from the taxpayers and funnelled into the mega project in question? It is hard to say. Probably, people would have spent this money as they always do: on paper clips and bobby pins, toasters and frisbees, on ballet lessons and tennis racquets, and on apples and toothpaste. These expenditures, too, would have created a "multiplier effect," but one not so easy to discern. In evaluating the mega project, it is not a "seen" multiplier effect against—nothing. Rather, it is a "seen" multiplier effect against an "unseen" one. That is what always makes them look so good.

In addition to consumption, there is the money consumers would not have spent but would have saved. This, too, creates jobs, production, and wealth. More savings mean lower interest rates, and this leads to investment projects unfeasible at the old, lower rate of saving.

Does this mean that mega projects are never justified? Not a bit of it. Entrepreneurs are always casting about for ways to earn a profit. When in their eyes a convention centre can be a going concern, they will invest their own funds and invite the public to help out by floating a stock issue. There are great advantages to such projects—when engaged in by private interests. Business makes the investment with its own money or with money which must be repaid. Hence, graft, corruption, and inefficiency tend to be reduced. The market, moreover, has a way of rewarding those who make wise (mega) investments and punishing those who engage in foolish ones. It rewards the one with profits and penalizes the other with losses. This means that on any given occasion, the millions of dollars which must be spent will tend to be controlled by people who have made wise entrepreneurial decisions in the past—not by photogenic politicians who talk a good line nor by bureaucrats who may have no socially redeeming qualities at all. *W.B.*

MIDWIVES

The power governments have given to the medical profession to control who may engage in the practise of medicine is nowhere more evident than in the case of midwifery. From an economic point of view, the medical monopoly exercised by physicians is comparable to a marketing board—the kind that regulates the supply of chickens, eggs, milk, and dairy products. To market eggs, one must receive an egg quota from the marketing board. To sell medical services, a certificate from the Medical Council of Canada must be granted. The difference between the farm boards and the medical board, however, is that members of the latter have the power to eliminate all potential competitors. Midwives, for example, can't practise in most Canadian cities. They may, however, practice in northern and isolated areas where there are no physicians.

Once more using the farm marketing boards analogy, not only can physicians limit the supply of chicken, they can also make sure that nobody is allowed to eat pork, beef, or other forms of protein. Medical marketing boards, no less than the barnyard variety, are against the public interest and should be dismantled.

Now let us consider an objection to the foregoing. According to some people, to allow midwifery is to be guilty of promoting a dangerous practice. The delivery of children in the home via the natural method is a dangerous, life-threatening, and often fatal situation for about 4 percent of the population. It is therefore irresponsible to encourage such behaviour. However, support for midwives to gain official recognition in no way implies encouragement for home delivery. On the contrary, it is based solely on the view that certified midwives ought not be prevented from practising by a licensure requirement which shields physicians from competition. In the current situation, midwives are legally allowed to practise. This almost invariably means that women who choose to have a midwife rather than a physician attend the birth of their child must have the child at home since midwives are not allowed to practise in a hospital setting. The full legalization of this occupation would provide the possibility for the attendance of midwives at birth in hospitals. There, modern technology and the more technically skilled obstetricians and surgeons would be available for those 4 percent of cases where difficulties develop in the course of delivery.

The thought that midwives may be allowed to practise in Canada and, therefore, have access to hospital facilities is not some outlandish, off-the-wall proposal. It is, for example, the current situation in Sweden, so often held up as a standard to which the rest of the world ought to compare itself in social welfare matters. Canadian women should be able to choose whether to have a midwife attend the delivery of their children. If they make this choice, they should not be regarded as engaging in a quasi-legal act, as at present. Nor should they be denied access to a hospital under those circumstances. *M.W.*

MINIMUM WAGE LAW

Even some of the most ardent free enterprisers in our midst will often be found supporting the minimum wage law. In fact, public discussion of the subject generally has been limited to assertions that the minimum wage level is not rising fast enough. This is particularly unfortunate since the long-run effect of minimum wage legislation, paradoxically, is not to raise the take-home pay of workers with lesser skills but often to make it well nigh impossible for them to find any jobs at all.

The major impetus behind the minimum wage enactment is the fear that, in its absence, employers would be completely free to dictate the level of wages paid. In this view, it would be a calamity for governments to leave remuneration decisions for the lowest paid workers to the tender mercies of capitalists, an entirely understandable stance. Enlightened opponents of minimum wage laws do not deny that employers will try to pay as little as possible. On the contrary, opponents of this law fully accept the self-serving attitude of employers. After all, you can always rely on others—whether capitalists or not—to put their interests before yours.

But we must also accept the harsh reality that there is an inexorable tendency for wage levels to reflect the productivity of workers. Wage levels below worker productivity are pushed up, and those above are pushed down, by self-serving employers. Take, for example, an employee who creates value of $3.00 per hour and who is now being paid only $2.00 per hour. This person's employer makes a pure profit of $1.00 for each hour the worker toils. This sounds bad for the worker but it is a situation unlikely to exist in the real world, and even if it did, it would be completely impossible to sustain. It could not last because the $1.00 profit per hour would act like a vacuum, sucking in competing uses of such profitable labour.

Other employers, in the ceaseless quest for profit, would like nothing better than to woo this worker away from his present boss and seize these extraordinary profits for themselves. In order to do so, they must offer a slightly higher wage. And so the upward march of wages toward $3.00 per hour would cease only when the profits to be gained by attracting such a worker begin to fall below the costs of seeking him out and employing him. Therefore, we must conclude that in the absence of minimum wage laws, a worker worth $3.00 per hour will earn, at the very least, a wage not significantly below this $3.00 productivity level.

But what happens with the passage of a law that says that if a firm hires this sort of worker it must pay him $4.00 per hour? Will these people now find a job? The answer is that some may, but the vast majority won't. For the prospective employer, taking on these labourers would be a financial disaster: $4.00 per hour would have to be paid out while only $3.00 per hour would be taken in. A firm might decide to act so unwisely in a few cases, perhaps out of charity, but if the firm persisted on a large scale, it would succeed only in driving itself toward bankruptcy.

The tragedy and the shame is that if given a chance of employment the low productivity worker can usually raise his skill levels and, hence, his productivity level by on-the-job training. With minimum wage legislation, he is effectively barred from employment in the first place. Since many of our young people are effectively barred from on-the-job training in this way, is it any wonder that the problem of youth unemployment is so prominent? *W.B.*

MORTGAGE RATE RENEGOTIATION

In 1982, people signed mortgage contracts calling for interest payments of between 18 and 20 percent. Subsequently, market rates fell, and these people were understandably upset. Many pundits may think it entirely reasonable for government to be concerned about, and consider intervening in, such a situation. Obviously, those who negotiated their loans at 18 percent or so are paying much, much higher amounts than they could pay under later circumstances to borrow the same amount of money. And, since the banks have lots of money, why don't they renegotiate and give people a break?

But the fact of the matter is that the banks have no money of their own. The money we're talking about that was lent to those people at 18 percent or more was deposited in the banks by other Canadians who received comparably high rates of interest. To the extent that the banks had exactly matched their portfolios for every individual who has an 18 percent mortgage, there is some other person who has a guaranteed investment certificate or other term deposit bearing interest at close to that rate. In other words, the bank was not making 18 percent on the money but only the difference between the 18 percent that it was charging on the mortgages and the amount it has to pay for the money it lends.

Accordingly, any government interference would have to coerce the banks to continue to pay interest at 16 percent on term deposits while, at the same time, charging only 12, 13, or 14 percent on mortgages which they insist the banks renegotiate. The implications of this are so absurd and so unjust it is ridiculous to contemplate the government seriously pursuing it. The only way government can force the banks to reduce mortgage interest rates on those past contracts, while at the same time not expropriating part of the bank's income, is to permit the bank to declare null and void the interest contracts which they have with the Canadians who provided the money which has been lent out. Of course, if they attempted to do that, there would be a deafening political outcry. *M.W.*

N

NATIONALISM

It is agreed on all sides that a policy of free trade with the U.S. will be to the economic advantage of Canadians. The ability to sell to a market of 250 million people instead of a mere 25 million, the opportunities to enhance the continental division of labour and specialize in the things we do best while trading with the Americans for products which embody their particular excellences, guarantee an economic improvement for this country. All this is so blatantly obvious that even opponents of reduced trade barriers concede that Canada has to pay a price, a real price, for the status quo.

But the Canadian nationalists have an arrow in their quiver which is even more powerful than a finely honed calculation of dollars and cents advantages and disadvantages. They claim that closer commercial ties would put at risk our cherished political sovereignty. It is as if, along with the cheap goods and services which will come flooding into Canada, there would be hidden platoons of U.S. soldiers ready to pounce on the RCMP and take over the country. But when the argument is stated in this nuts-and-blots manner, it is easy to see the flaw it embodies. Ronald Reagan does not need free trade to take over Canada militarily. If he wanted to do so (a ludicrous proposition), he surely has the means at his disposal under the present regime of trade barriers.

With this argument in tatters, the nationalists have a second one to fall back on. Free trade may not mean an actual loss of political sovereignty but a loss of the Canadian soul. And what, you may well ask, is the Canadian soul? It is to be found—you had better be sitting down when you read this!—in the unique Canadian spirit or character as expressed by no less than the arts community of this country.

This proposition, too, is hard to defend. For apart from a few hundred Canadian writers, painters, and musicians in this country who make it on their own without subsidies from government, there are no artists in this country. The several thousands of people who line up at the Canada Council, Canadian Film Board, CBC and numerous other public troughs for grants are only welfare recipients whose "salaries" are a means of disguising the true reality. No doubt, some of these people could prosper in a free artistic marketplace, but we'll never know for sure until the welter of government arts grants is ended.

Who says that only homegrown art can express the culture of a nation? Mozart and Bach were not Canadians. The Bible, the works of Shakespeare and the paintings of Rembrandt were not created in the "true north, strong and free." The U.S. is self-assured enough not to "protect" itself against foreign films, books, magazines, orchestras, ballet companies, and so forth. Canada will never attain any comparable level of artistic maturity and self-confidence if it continues to hide behind a system of subsidies for domestic artists and restricts the import of the products of those living abroad. The way to save the national soul is to allow our artists to compete with foreigners for the allegiance of the Canadian public. Full free trade can only hasten the coming of this glorious day. It is to be applauded on both pocketbook and artistic grounds.

There is no real danger that a demolition of trade barriers between us and the Americans will lead to a dissolution of Canadian culture. There is strong evidence from the European Economic Community, which has a much closer economic relationship between its members than is being anticipated between Canada and the United States, that cultural independence is not threatened.

There is no indication whatsoever that free trade or closer trading ties have weakened the ability of member countries to maintain a separate cultural stance or a separate ideological stance on policy matters, as is evident in the government of France. The strongest public case of cultural independence is the United Kingdom and Ireland. Free trading arrangements between these two countries have in no way jeopardized the ability of Ireland, Southern Ireland at least, to conduct its own cultural activities. Even within Canada, where we have some semblance of free trade between the provinces—although not as much as exists between the members of the EEC—it is important to remember that there are still great cultural differences. There are very distinct communities in Newfoundland, we have the distinct cultural heritage of the Acadians, and the Quebecois—all of whom have maintained strong cultural identities, notwithstanding very close economic ties in all directions. *M.W.*

NO-FAULT AUTOMOBILE INSURANCE

One of the ideas currently making the rounds is that of no-fault automobile insurance. No-fault insurance would radically change the way in which the problem of compensation for damages works. At the moment, if you have an automobile accident and there are serious injuries involved, the injured parties both in your automobile and in the other automobile may sue you for damages. The extent to which they can extract damages from you depends on the extent to which you are found to be liable for the accident, that is to say, the extent to which you are found to be at fault. If the total amount of damages involved in an accident is $1,000,000, and you are found to be 50 percent liable for the accident, you would be liable for 50 percent of $1,000,000 or $500,000.

The legal proceedings involved serve two purposes. They serve the purpose, first of all, of establishing fault—who is guilty, whose actions caused the accident. Secondly, they establish the amount of damage. Both aspects of the suit are complex and require careful examination of evidence and, hence, a considerable amount of time.

The proposal under no-fault is to eliminate this discovery of guilt and damages process and replace it by a finding of no-fault. Secondly, there would be an elimination of the process whereby the amount of damages is fixed. Instead of the latter provision, there would be what amounts to an injured party compensation board which would examine the facts and set the damages at some prescribed level. While many people seem to have found this an attractive notion, as they see within it an elimination of the fees charged by the lawyers involved, is no-fault insurance a good thing or not?

We answer in the negative. In the first place there is the fundamental question of retaining a system of accountability in which individuals who cause damage are, in fact, made liable for those damages, hence providing an incentive for people to avoid causing damage. People are sensitive to cost; their behaviour reflects what they believe will be the consequence of their actions.

But a more important reason for objecting to a no-fault insurance programme is the way in which it will deal with the losses people suffer. When you are injured in an automobile accident at present, you can go to court and seek compensation from your injurer for the income loss you suffered as a result of the accident. Suppose, for example, you have been rendered a paraplegic or lost a leg or the use of a hand; in each of these cases the income loss which you will experience will differ. Moreover, the income loss suffered by you will vary according to your capabilities, both demonstrated and potential. Under the system proposed, however, you would be treated the same as everybody else—a great averaging homogenizer of the insurance board would award you a standard amount based on a formula.

If you are unfortunate enough to be a student and have not yet demonstrated your capabilities, you would be subject to a universal rule of 90 percent of the net income derived from the average wage. If you are a minor, that is age 16 or less, you would be condemned to a lifetime income of even less. No-fault insurance, an idea whose time has come only within the narrow confines of the world typified by George Orwell's *1984*, is certainly not a system which our society of individuals should welcome with open arms or, indeed, even accept. *M.W.*

NUCLEAR POWER

The death of 84 men with the sinking of the oil drilling rig *Ocean Ranger* off the coast of Newfoundland was a great tragedy. It's one of many accidents in energy industries which claim human lives. All the more reason, then, to re-examine the widely publicized misgivings about the health hazards of nuclear energy foisted upon us by the "ecology" movement.

The *Ocean Ranger* tragedy was not, unfortunately, the first energy-related accident to claim numerous lives. Rather, the non-nuclear energy field has been plagued with a series of similar mishaps.

Other recent offshore oil drilling rig mass fatalities include the capsizing of the 10,000-ton *Alexander Kielland* accommodation rig off Norway in the North Sea in March 1980, with the catastrophic loss of 123 lives; a November 1979 oil rig collapse during a storm in the Bohai Gulf of northeast China which killed 72 workmen; and a blow-out in October 1980 of the U.S.-owned rig *Tappmeyer* off Saudi Arabia in which 18 people perished.

Coal mining, too, has been marred by numerous large-scale accidents the world over. In Canada, the Nova Scotia coal mine Springhill was the site of a disaster which claimed 39 lives in 1956, and another 74 in 1958. In the U.S., roughly 200 coal miners die in the line of duty every year; and in addition to cave-ins, coal miners have long been subject to the dread "black-lung" disease, which has crippled many and directly or indirectly killed many others.

If this past record looks bleak, the future bodes ill as well. Despite ever-improving technologies, as the quest for offshore oil continues apace into evermore inhospitable environments, the only rational expectation is for more of the same, only more so. The same holds true for coal mining. If energy prices rise, one source of additional coal supplies may be to dig deeper—into increasingly more dangerous terrain. Strip-mining of coal nearer the surface brings in its wake the risk of water run-offs and slides and other hazards—all vociferously pointed out to us by the self-styled ecologists. Other alternative energy supplies come with dangers of their own. India, for example, suffered a hydroelectric dam disaster which drowned thousands of people.

What of nuclear power? Despite the widespread media led wailing and gnashing of teeth which accompanied the meltdown at Three Mile Island in Pennsylvania, the plain fact is that not a single solitary radiation-related death has occurred in the West in the quarter century of commercial nuclear power generation. (The contrast with the Chernobyl event is stark. There, the lack of double containment and a lower level of safety precaution produced a much larger public sector type disaster.) And yet the litany goes on. Protestors at nuclear power stations continually attempt to halt operations—and are accorded a respectful-to-fawning hearing by the nation's press. Although trespassers on private property, the protestors are given credit for "morality" and "concern."

Based on the well-attended movie *China Syndrome*, starring political activists Jane Fonda and Jack Lemmon, the impartial observer would be led to think that oil, gas, coal, and hydroelectric power were cheap and safe energy sources, while nuclear energy was a mass killer. Can anyone imagine how the media would have reacted had the victims of the *Ocean Ranger* instead perished in a nuclear accident? There is little doubt that the nuclear industry would have been brought to its knees. A sea of front page news coverage would have made the publicity accompanying the repatriation of the Canadian Constitution seem pale by comparison.

It is long past time to redress this imbalanced analysis which has been perpetrated upon society. This does not mean, of course, that we must bring the same unreasoning passion to bear on the traditional energy industries that the left-wing "ecologists" have long aimed at nuclear power. This would mean a serious curtailment of all energy supplies—and the death of millions of consumers who are dependent upon energy for their very lives. On the contrary, a more sober and measured evaluation would appear to be in order, one which looks carefully at the evidence before launching into public policy recommendations. When this is done, the conclusion is inescapable that nuclear power must be allowed to compete fairly with all other energy industries, without fear of favour on either side. *W.B.*

O

ORGAN TRANSPLANTS

According to recent reports, the black market value of a kidney which can be transplanted is $13,000, which translates to roughly seven times its weight in gold. Such a fact may occasion all sorts of references to King Midas, who was supposed to have been turned into a statue of solid gold. But behind this rather dramatic way of characterizing the value of human organs lies a story of untold and tragic human suffering.

There are hundreds and even thousands of Canadians whose lives could be vastly improved could they but have the use of a healthy kidney. Paradoxically, there are other thousands of people who die each year, taking perfectly healthy kidneys to the grave with them, who have no financial incentive at all to bequeath these organs to those in need. Why, it may well be asked, cannot potential donors presently be given a pecuniary reward for doing the right thing? What precludes a businessman from purchasing the future rights to a kidney from a potential donor and then selling these rights to those suffering from kidney disease?

The problem is, it is illegal to harness marketplace incentives in order to encourage kidney donors. Anyone who set up a business of this sort would be summarily imprisoned. Instead, our society must resort to all sorts of inefficient stratagems toward this end. Famous personages have exhorted us, in the event that we suffer untimely death, to make a posthumous gift of these organs, and medical schools coach their students on the best techniques for approaching next-of-kin. The difficulty is that they must ask permission at the precise time when they are least likely to be given it—upon the sudden demise of a loved one.

All of this has been to little avail. While potential recipients languish on painful kidney dialysis machines waiting ghoulishly for a traffic fatality which may spell life for them, the public has refused to sign cards in sufficient numbers giving permission for automatic posthumous donor status. Things have even come to such a pass that there are grotesque fascistic plans now being bruited about which would allow the government to seize the kidneys of accident victims unless they have signed cards denying such permission.

The free enterprise system, were it allowed to operate in this instance, might well be a godsend to the unfortunates who suffer from diseased kidneys. A legalized marketplace could encourage thousands of donors. Would you sign a card donating your kidney after death for 13,000 big ones, right now, in cold, hard cash? There are very few people who would turn up their noses at such an offer. If sufficient supplies were not forthcoming at this level, prices would rise even further until all demand was satisfied. Given free enterprise incentives, we would be up to our armpits in kidneys. This is the tried and true process we rely on to bring us all the other necessities of life: food, clothing, and shelter. We do not depend for the provision of these goods and services on voluntary donations. We know this to be a relatively unreliable system, notwithstanding the fact that it is flogged by numerous opinion leaders in the case of organ transplants.

There is no doubt whatsoever that those presently responsible for preventing a free market in kidneys take these actions with the noblest of motives. To them, legalizing the purchase and sale of human organs would be the ultimate in degradation. Far better, from their viewpoint, that people donate their bodily parts for free so that thousands of kidney disease sufferers may live normal lives. However, no matter how benevolent the intentions of the prohibitionists, it cannot be denied that the effect of their ill-conceived actions is to render it less likely that those in need shall be served.

It is long past time for our society to put aside its archaic and prejudicial opposition to the marketplace, so that we can relieve the suffering, and in many cases, lift the death sentence we have inadvertently placed on as hopeless and hapless a group of citizens as ever existed. *W.B.*

P

PARITY PAY

There is a catch phrase going the rounds in labour-management relations called "parity pay." According to this doctrine, at least from the point of view of the union sector, it is incumbent on the firm to offer the same pay scale to all its employees, no matter where they may be located. In the words of one spokesman for organized labour: "our members deserve wage parity; it simply isn't fair to base wages on plant location."

One difficulty with this precept is that it is really a disguised demand—not for parity but for a wage boost. Parity could as easily be achieved by decreasing the highest salaries offered by a corporation until they were equated with the lowest as by raising those at the bottom of the scale to match that paid at the upper end. Since organized labour never asks for the former, only for the latter, it is easy to see that parity is really a call for business as usual.

But let us take this latest demand seriously, even if its proponents do not, and analyse the case for wage parity on its own merits. Consider the situation of a nation-wide firm with plants located in several different provinces. Assume that it hires a labour force with average skills, so that its workers can shift, without insuperable difficulty, in and out of its employ in response to changing wage differentials. Under these conditions, if it implements a system of wage parity, it will endanger its very existence.

With a pay scale that is invariant all over the country, it must of necessity pay less than the prevailing wage in some places and more in others. If the business concern in question offers a salary package that is not as attractive as obtainable elsewhere, it will have a great deal of trouble attracting a work-force at all. This will depend upon just how big the differential called for by the parity scheme is in any specific case. If the company does succeed in hiring employees, it certainly will not be able to pick and choose; rather, it will have to be satisfied with whoever deigns to work for it at the below-market wages it is offering. Certainly parity will put it at a competitive disadvantage compared to other business concerns which are not similarly constrained.

Now consider the opposite case. Here, parity forces the business establishment to pay wages higher than the prevailing rate. Under such conditions, it will have no trouble at all attracting a labour force. On the contrary, it will have far more applicants than it can handle. Certainly, it will be able to pick and choose to suit itself. The only problem is that it will again be uncompetitive, for its wage bill will be greater than it need be. Local concerns and national companies not hemmed in by a parity scheme will be able to obtain just as competent a labour force—at a lower price.

If the idea of parity is uneconomic in the labour market, it is equally so in any other field as well. One acre of land, even of identical fertility, has a far different value in Ontario and Saskatchewan, in British Columbia and Prince Edward Island, to say nothing of the Yukon and Quebec, and it is not too difficult to see why. An acre is an acre is an acre, but some physically identical acres are worth far more than others, if for no other reason than that they are closer to population centres and thus require lower shipping charges to bring their produce to market.

For similar reasons, a quart of milk or a dozen eggs or a pair of socks or a chess set costs far more in the Northwest Territories than in the Golden Triangle. Transportation expenditures are far higher.

The same can be said for the costs of labour. Wages vary greatly over this vast country of ours, even for labour which would be equally productive were it but located in the same place. The productivity of a worker in remote regions must be discounted by these additional transportation costs if his salary is to bear any resemblance to economic reality. Nor is the difficulty of hauling the final product to the consumer the only determinant of geographically diverse wage rates.

This may come as a surprise to parity advocates, but some areas of Canada are far more hospitable than others. There are those which are mild and relatively comfortable all year round while others suffer from extremes of heat and cold. Some are already settled, replete with friends and family schools and churches and other accouterments of modern society; others are as yet only barely scratched-out places in the wilderness. Naturally, others things equal, most people prefer the former settings to the latter. Indeed, they can only be induced to live in the less desirable parts of our nation if they are compensated, through higher wage rates, for doing so. How else can we understand the great remuneration offered to Canadians for working in the Territories or, for that matter, in Saudi Arabia? The differences in this regard between Vancouver, Calgary, Winnipeg, Toronto, Montreal, and Halifax may not be as great as in the foregoing examples, but the same principle operates there as well.

Other causes of non-parity pay for equally productive workers are even more subtle. For example, Alberta has a multibillion dollar heritage fund. Some of it was used to pay off the debts of municipalities. This enables the municipalities to keep taxes below the levels which might otherwise obtain. To the extent that this is true, employers in Edmonton can offer lower wage rates and still attract a sufficient labour force. In this case, the explicit portion of the compensation is received by the employee in his pay packet, but the other, hidden part is received in the form of lower municipal taxes.

Finally, the adherents of the parity position ignore one further aspect of how an economy works, that is, the function of wages in allocating labour. It is through the continually shifting pattern of wages that employees are led, as if by an "invisible hand," to leave off working in those industries whose products consumers no longer value so highly and to move toward those which are now seen as more important.

Take the example of how the automobile supplanted the entire horse-and-buggy industry. When Henry Ford first introduced his "horseless carriage," in addition to all the other challenges he faced, he had to somehow entice people to leave their previous employments and come work for him. This he accomplished by the time- and tradition-honoured expedient of making a better offer than that which was previously available.

The point is that, at bottom, entrepreneurs are no more than agents for consumers. The business which persists in manufacturing item "A" rather than "B"—despite the fact that the consumer has registered a clear preference for the latter—courts economic disaster. But if the structure of production is to be geared up to satisfy this new preference for "B," workers must somehow be induced to leave "A" where they may have been comfortable, and enter into "B," which is new and unknown. What better way to encourage such behaviour than by offering higher wages?

Innovations are seldom introduced at the same time throughout an entire country. Henry Ford's operation was clustered around Detroit, for example. Often, then, this process of introducing new products will give rise to what appears to be irrational wage differentials based on geographical considerations. If wage parity becomes embedded in public policy through legislation or labour-management practise, then economic progress will be stultified. *W.B.*

PICKING WINNERS

Every industrial strategy ever penned has indicated that its intention is to help identify winners and throw the full weight of government behind them. But this is a puzzle because, of course, it is precisely the winners who do not need assistance. It is they who would, in the competitive struggle, ultimately survive and produce economically meaningful production whether in high-tech areas or elsewhere. Quite apart from the lack of any demonstrated ability of governments to produce winners, even if they could today pick the winners, there seems to be little justification for subsidizing them. *M.W.*

PLANNING

Strategy implies planning, intelligence, and rationality. In common parlance, strategy is a kind of foregone conclusion in the sense that most people like to think of themselves as acting in a deliberate, rational way. The familiar meaning of industrial strategy is of a similar form; it implies a plan—an articulated scheme for economic development. Moreover, the general public takes for granted that this plan exists in some form and that the actions of government are guided by it. This common sense attitude is motivated by the judgement that since private behaviour without planning is chaotic, concerted national economic development must surely be unattainable unless there is a national plan.

That this perception of planning and economic development is widespread cannot be denied. It constantly lurks beneath the surface. It motivates newspaper editors, businessmen, and scholars to deplore the lack of leadership evidenced by government, and it tragically misinforms the pundits who call for more planning and more schemes as a response to each emerging problem.

It is fair to say then, that what most people mean by industrial strategy is public or central planning of some sort. There is, however, an entirely different view of industrial strategy. This is based on the notion that while we certainly need planning, that planning must be done on a private basis. According to this conception, not only is public planning not required, it is to be regarded as counter-productive. An industrial strategy based on private planning would be completely concerned with the process of economic change and would have no explicit master plan in view. As a matter of fact, it would not even have a specific goal in the sense that public planning must have a goal.

Public and private planning can appropriately be viewed as ends of a spectrum. A world in which there was no public planning at all would be a libertarian utopia. A world in which there was no private planning would be a totalitarian, absolutist utopia (even if its utopian aspects were obvious to only a few). To determine an industrial strategy for Canada, we must make a selection from the public/private spectrum. To do that, we must first look more closely at what the two polar cases imply.

Public planning is one of the oldest institutions known to man. It has assumed a variety of forms through the ages. In primitive times, the ritualistic sharing of the proceeds of the hunt and the various traditional allocations of responsibility amongst tribal members were a form of central planning. The monarchial forms of government in Europe, with their associated mercantilist economic systems, were centrally focused and reflected the wishes of the relatively few members of the ruling elite.

While it may seem strange to classify all pre-market activity and command economies as central planning, this becomes more obvious when one considers that the polar opposite is individual planning. The essential difference between the two poles on the planning spectrum is the extent to which they involve the desires, judgements, and freedoms of the individual participant. Ritualistic or traditional systems of organization offered almost no latitude to any of the participants while command economies restrict freedom of action to varying degrees.

Ideology has been a powerful motivator for those who propose the adoption of central planning or its more limited variants, but there are proponents who would claim ideological neutrality. These are the rationalists—people who believe that the undirected interaction of individuals is unlikely to yield the best outcome for society. According to this view, because there is no rational conception of the whole economic process in, as it were, one mind, the economic process can only be effective by chance.

Since individuals make judgements and initiate economic activities according to their expectations and forecasts of the future, the lack of a central forecast or public expectation implies that people will largely make wrong decisions and poor judgements. By the very nature of things, only one forecast can be correct. The others will be wrong and lead to inappropriate behaviour. Hence, the existence of the plan and its self-fulfilling forecast would actually facilitate private planning, make it more accurate and, hence, more effective.

On a cursory level, this is a very appealing notion. It attains the best of both worlds. On the one hand, a central plan provides everybody with a correct forecast of all industrial, commercial, and consumer needs. On the other hand, all participants in the market will have this information at their disposal and, hence, will have expectations compatible with everybody else's actual behaviour since the forecast will be self-fulfilling. There are, unfortunately, some rather serious weaknesses in this grand design—most of them stemming from the fact that *homo sapiens* are willful, unpredictable, imperfect creatures.

The most significant weakness is the assumption that the goals of the process are known or knowable in advance. It is a straightforward matter to show that a plan of sufficient complexity to be useful would have to have a fairly detailed articulation of the objectives toward which individuals are striving—not just how many cars or boats or houses are wanted, but what sort of work people will want to do, where they decide to live, and much more. Moreover, these objectives and the extent of their attainment would have to be provided in minute detail. Most important, some objectives would have to be ruled inadmissable. In other words, a fixed number of objectives would have to be selected, since only a limited number would be obtainable.

This raises the very knotty issue of how the limited set of objectives will be selected and how, once they have been selected, people will be persuaded to conform to them. If the plan says only 10 'garben-spangles' should be produced and there is a demand for 20, how will the 10 extras be produced or the demand for the additional 10 be channelled elsewhere?

Without pretending to solve the problem of objectives, we can raise another question and that is the possibility of forecast error. If, perhaps because of the foregoing issues, the public forecast is wrong, what then? All the crystal balls are in one basket since,

P P P P P P P P P P P P P P P P P P P P P

for the sake of consistency, private expectations have been reined in to conformity with the public forecast, the central plan. What mechanisms will operate to correct the error that will then be institutionalized?

So much for the public planning end of the spectrum. Let us now briefly consider the private planning process—how and why it works and what its weaknesses are. Private planning is as old as economic activity. As long as there have been individuals interested in repetitive trading arrangements, a series of expectations, forecasts, and plans have influenced people's behaviour. However, it was not until the 18th century that people became aware of how this private planning process worked.

While economists may dispute who made the discovery, most would agree that Adam Smith, a Scottish political philosopher, produced the first complete articulation of how the private planning process works. In an inquiry into what caused nations to be wealthy, Smith discovered that by following their own interests people were led, as if by an invisible hand, to produce results that fitted into a constantly evolving, coherent scheme. And, Smith observed, the freer people were to pursue their interests and the more directly they bore the costs or reaped the benefit of their activities, the more effectively the system worked.

The most incredible thing Smith noted is that the system of private planning requires no external co-ordination. The co-ordination function is performed by prices and wages changing in response to changing supplies and demands. Thus, there is no need for a central plan to determine a certain target output of iron or coal or pins. Rather, people voluntarily choose to produce more or less of these items as time passes according to how much profit can be realized. At the same time, users of the products adjust their use on the basis of changes in price. In this way, the economic process gropes ahead into the future, coping with changing circumstances with no outside direction.

With the benefit of the history that has elapsed since Smith published his *Enquiry into the Wealth of Nations*—we can clearly see that the private planning process works. In fact, the most fantastic economic progress that the world has ever seen was achieved with no central plan—no public direction of consequence.

This is not to imply that the process is perfect, indeed it is very imperfect—as imperfect as are the human beings who participate in it. As a consequence, the process frequently produces errors. Expectations and forecasts are frequently not realized and, hence, economic decisions prove to be wrong. Over-production and under-production occur as producers incorrectly perceive the demand for their products. Occasionally, conditions of over-population and under-population persist for some time as information is slow to spread and people are reluctant to change their behaviour.

The imperfection of man will haunt whatever sort of planning scheme is erected—whether public or private. The saving feature of the private planning system is its self-limiting or error-correcting nature. Individuals or firms who err bear the direct consequences of their mistakes. Therefore, they have great incentive to plan carefully and react immediately if forecasts prove erroneous. If the error is large, the firm may cease to exist or the individual may be forced to change occupations. The loss associated with the error is, thus, as localized as it can be in that it is limited to those directly involved in the activity.

This contrasts sharply with the public planning process where government initiatives may be sustained for decades after an error is discovered. In many instances, strategy errors become enshrined in new policies to protect them. This has been true of many Canadian industries encouraged by public design. Once a public initiative has been launched, whether in the form of protection for a private firm or a direct public enterprise, it is very difficult for government to scuttle it. Political factors and not economic rationality are the dominant consideration in most public decisions. As a consequence, obviously unviable projects are propped up with public funds and what would have been a narrow, localized loss under the private system becomes amplified, broadened, and sustained.

The essential point is that the system of private planning has evolved as a process for dealing with errors—a system based on the imperfectness of mankind. The system of public planning, on the other hand, involves an assumption of knowledge about the future. For that reason alone, it is inherently unworkable. *M.W.*

POLITICS

An American humourist, journalist, and political pundit by the name of Henry Louis Mencken once noted that politics and, more precisely, elections are a kind of futures market in stolen property. What he meant by this comment is that the art of politics consists of drawing lines through the polity so as to create groups of beneficiaries, or winners, and groups of losers that were to the benefit of the politician's electoral standing. During the course of an election campaign, a politician curries support from the electorate by creating groups who perceive themselves to be winners.

Given that the politician is not capable of creating any new wealth, in order to create this group of winners he has to create a corresponding group of losers. The trick is to ensure that this group of losers is sufficiently diffuse or unaware of the fact they are losers that their adverse reaction politically does not offset the positive reaction from those who are the targeted beneficiaries. This model of politics applies very well, and we can all find thousands of instances of it from everyday experience. This warrants us referring to this comment of Mencken as being Mencken's law of politics.

Protectionism falls nicely within the confines of Mencken's law and, in fact, is almost a made-to-order political product in this sense. In order to see this, consider the case of a manufacturer of socks in Welland, Ontario. The manufacturer finds that over a period of time he has been losing sales. He is told by his sales staff that the problem is the arrival on the scene of cheaper but equivalently good socks coming from foreign suppliers. The reaction of the manufacturer is fairly predictable. First of all, he calculates that the difference between his product and the product of his competitor is a few cents a pair. If he can somehow boost the price of socks, he won't have any further difficulties. Having received his MBA from the University of Western Ontario, he knows precisely what to do about that—he has to go to Ottawa.

Since he is a significant manufacturer and employer in his constituency, the M.P. and cabinet member is only too happy to entertain the sock manufacturer and listen to his woes. Now, the manufacturer doesn't talk about his declining profit levels. He talks in terms of declining job possibilities in his plant and declining possibilities for campaign contributions during the course of the next election because of his failing economic circumstance. The politician is impressed by these cogent arguments, and he does some quick calculations of his own.

He reckons that while the sock manufacturer has every incentive and every interest in petitioning for some governmental relief for his problem, the consumers of socks have no particular interest, from a financial point of view, in providing any political reaction. The politician quickly calculates that if the government were to erect a tariff barrier or other device for foreign sock manufacturers, so that the price of socks in Canada were to go up by three or four cents, this would not cause any immediate reaction from consumers. Consumers are widely dispersed across the country, and the increase in the cost of socks at three or four cents doesn't make it worthwhile for them to object. The difference in price doesn't even cover the cost of a postage stamp for them to write a letter to their M.P. to object.

From the point of view of Mencken's law, the chemistry of this situation is just perfect. A concentrated benefit is provided to the sock manufacturer who in turn will distribute that judiciously to his employees who will also be happy. The cost is distributed widely across consumers in the whole of Canada, and it is a cost most consumers will simply not be able to distinguish from ongoing increases in prices caused by inflation.

The important thing to note about this protectionism and the calculus used by each of the participants is that it is effectively a device whereby the politician and the manufacturer contrive to create a benefit for the producer or manufacturer at the expense of consumers. It is the consumer who loses and the manufacturer and employees who benefit from the tariff. It is important to have this clearly in mind, because it casts protectionism within the political mould and shows that it has very little to do with the third country which may be exporting socks to Canada. Whether protectionism will be imposed or not depends on the political chemistry in Canada and on whether the producers and manufacturers can contrive, via the political process, to in effect get a benefit from consumers which they are not able to get via the marketplace. It is a form of "theft" in the Mencken paradigm, to put it in the least contentious terms possible.

It is also important to note that in most instances the political chemistry is very unfortunate from the point of view of the consumer interest and from the point of view of third parties attempting to export to Canada. There is an imbalance in the political interest in the sense that the manufacturer or producer normally has a very highly concentrated gain to be made from exercising political pressure for the acquisition of protectionism, whereas consumers bear a disaggregated and dispersed cost, the individual amount of which does not provide any incentive for them to engage in countervailing political action.

There will be some countervailing political action in the form of activities by consumer unions and consumer federation groups. However, their actions can at most be effective against tariffs on one or two products—not against the tens of thousands of possible protection targets. *M.W.*

POVERTY

Many people draw a sharp contrast between the haves and the have-nots and imply—as has been done so effectively in comparisons of the rich and poor nations of the earth—that those who enjoy the good life are in some sense responsible for the plight of those who do not. Nothing, however, could be further from the truth. The reasons for the existence of poverty are as numerous as the poor themselves.

In some cases, what sociologists refer to as core poverty is simply a reflection of the fact that the sufferers were dealt an unlucky intellectual or physical allocation from the roulette wheel of genetic inheritance. Others suffer physical handicaps due to no fault of their own. These unfortunates are the normal objects of private charity. Obviously, their position in life is not due to the success or failure of others who have been more fortunate. However, they are dependent on the success of the more fortunate for their maintenance. It is only the successful who generate the income that supports those who are unable to support themselves. That is true whether the vehicle by which the help is provided is private charity or public welfare. Far from being the cause of their depredation, the success of the wealthy and the maintenance of a generally affluent environment are important for the maintenance of the unfortunate.

There is a probing social commentary suggested by the current plight of the poor. That is the puzzle as to why we still have considerable difficulty delivering aid to those unfortunates who are poor through no fault of their own. One of the reasons is that there are many people who are classed as poor in Canada who are in that position through choice rather than chance. The total welfare bill is trying to service their requirements as well as those who are more deserving.

At the moment, the welfare apparatus makes no distinction between people demanding welfare because they have been irresponsible and those who have simply been unfortunate. The failure to make these distinctions means that there is less available to support the deserving poor, but it also means that we are creating a monstrous problem for the future.

While we may commiserate with people because of the consequences of their actions, we must also recognize that the unthinking insuring of people against the consequence of behaviours that only they can control is likely to have very damaging side effects. While such unwise behaviours obviously include the abuse of drugs, they also include social decisions of an increasingly common nature such as divorce. If two people who have had an average family income decide to divorce and as a consequence of that act have an income below the average, does the state really have an obligation to replace this loss? *M.W.*

P P P P P P P P P P P P P P P P P P P P P P

PRICE CONTROL

It is alleged that there are some conditions under which wage and price controls would make sense, but this depends on what causes inflation. Wage and price controls seem to be motivated by a feeling that inflationary pressure arises from cost-push or price-push. Both are very popular explanations of inflation because they seem to conform to everyday experience.

On the cost-push side, every businessman has been faced with increased wages, increased costs of raw materials, and increased costs of transportation. When you ask the businessman why he is pushing his prices up, he will simply explain that he is increasing his prices to cover his increased costs. On the other hand, if you talk to a union leader about why he is pushing for higher wages, he will tell you that he is doing so to cover the higher cost of the commodities that his members must buy. And so it goes, with prices pushing costs, costs pushing prices, and prices pushing costs. Since it does not finger governments as the cause of inflation, this theory is very popular in Ottawa.

The most popular of the cost-push arguments seems to be the greed or monopoly power theory of inflation. According to this theory, some large power group, either unions or corporations, arbitrarily increase the price of their service or commodity and effectively extort that price from a seemingly witless market. Based on this view, it would appear that during the period from 1960 to 1964 Canadians were, on average, a fairly happy-go-lucky crowd and certainly were not grabby or greedy. As a consequence, the inflation rate was stabilized in the 1 to 2 percent range. However, in 1965, owing to a still unidentified cause, the extent of Canadian greed began to grow at a very high rate. This growth in greed proceeded unabated until 1970—1970 will go down in Canadian history as the year of brotherly love, since greed was totally absent and, as a consequence of that fact, inflation fell back to the 1 to 2 percent range again. Canada did not long enjoy this lull in greed however, and in 1971 the old greed urges came on stronger than ever and pushed the inflation rate to unheard of double-digit figures.

This is the kind of description one would have to give if one subscribed to the greed theory of inflation. On a more serious level, we realize that the greed theory of inflation suffers from the old fallacy of composition: what is true for one element of a population need not be true for the population as a whole. If Mr. X stands on his tippy-toes to see a parade, he may well see better. But if Messrs. A, B, and C, standing in front of him, also rise up on their tippy-toes, nobody will see any better than they did before Mr. Xs unilateral action.

In the case of a greedy union or corporation, the net effect of a unilateral increase in the price of a good or service is a smaller output of the good or a smaller use of the service than would otherwise have occurred. This leads to a greater relative supply of other goods whose prices, correspondingly, will be lower than they would otherwise have been. Economic theory tells us that the net effect of the original "greed grab" is no change in the average level of prices but rather an increase in the relative price of the affected commodity or service.

Another of the cost-push theories has to do with specific prices, such as those for oil or food. It is popular, for example, to suppose that the unilateral increase in the price of oil or the reduction in the supply of oil by the OPEC countries has increased the inflation rate in North America and in the world. What is involved here, however, is not inflation but a straightforward reduction in the Western real standard of living. Of course, an attempt by government to temporarily avoid the inevitable consequences of such a radical change in the supply of a basic commodity may well produce inflationary consequences.

The actions of the OPEC countries in 1973 and 1974 were not a unique event in recent economic history. One has only to go back to the reparation payments following the First World War to find a similar sort of money transfer between nations. Effectively, Lloyd George and his colleagues were bent on extracting the full cost for the First World War from Germany. The reparation payments involved essentially a transfer of real resources from Germany to the Allied countries—a transfer that amounted to about 85 times Germany's total exports. In the first year, the payments were supposed to have amounted to $1 billion, or 2.6 times Germany's total exports. Germany was unable to accept those reparation payments. As a consequence, Germany inflated its money supply to cover the loss in real income that those reparation payments represented. The cause of the German inflation was the money printed to cover up the effects of the reparation payments. The same is true of inflation resulting from OPEC.

By far, the most widely accepted theory of why we get inflation is the monetary or monetarist theory. It says that inflation is caused by growth in the money supply at rates faster than the real sector of the economy can grow. The result is "too many dollars chasing too few goods." The four periods of inflation identified earlier are coincident with four different episodes of monetary growth. Furthermore, if one superimposes monetary growth rates for the previous year over the price performance of any given year, the correlation is quite remarkable.

Another popular theory which went the rounds in the debate about wage and price controls sees government expenditure as a cause of inflation. Again, as economists, we have to take a serious look at that theory since it seems to have a fair amount of support. There are some theoretical and even commonsensical reasons for believing that government expenditure and government deficits might produce inflation in the long run because of the distorting effects they have on the capital structure in the country. But in the short run, government deficits only produce inflation if those deficits are financed by increases in the money supply. It is quite clear that if the expenditures are financed by taxation or borrowing, the government expenditure simply displaces private sector expenditure and the total level of aggregate demand in the system is about the same. Of course, if the government borrowing is done abroad, the expenditures themselves may be inflationary if the influx of foreign currency associated with the borrowing leads to domestic money creation (and it frequently does via the interaction of the Exchange Fund Account with the Consolidated Revenue Account of the government). But the usual argument about government expenditures is simply that the deficits themselves represent some sort of irresponsible behaviour and, hence, lead to inflation. This is incorrect.

The only real danger involved in giving undue attention to such a theory is that it may distract attention from the true source of the inflationary pressure arising from government expenditures, that is, the fact that the money supply is increased as the government attempts to finance its expenditure programmes. An illustration of this is to be found in statements by numerous politicians. Many have defended the high level of government expenditure as being essential. Because government expenditure was for "essential services" they said, there was no possibility of reducing very substantially the net inflationary pressure provided by the government. The fact of the matter is that the government could very well reduce its inflationary impact without reducing the level of essential services. All it need do is finance those expenditures through direct taxation and not through the "hidden" taxation of money supply creation.

Unless the "greed theory" of inflation is correct, wage and price controls cannot be a very useful policy. According to several authors of Fraser Institute publications, wage and price controls never have worked under circumstances similar to the ones that we experienced in Canada. In fact, they have never worked under any circumstances. Economists are skeptical about the beneficial effects of wage and price controls, largely because they do not get at the roots of inflation.

Wage and price controls seemed to have been successfully applied during the Second World War. "If wage and price controls don't work, how come they worked during the war?" is a typical objection to the view put forth here. In this regard it is interesting to compare the inflation rates during the First World War, when there were no controls, and during the Second World War when there were. These periods of war are not strictly comparable. We are told by economic historians that the extent of the commitment during the Second World War was substantially greater than the commitment during the First World War and that the percentage of the total output of the economy that was directed towards the war effort was increased in the second conflagration.

These facts notwithstanding, the overall end result of price inflation after each of the wars was roughly comparable. During World War I, the cost of living rose from 1.00 in 1913 to 1.89 by 1920 and then back to 1.53 by 1923. In World War II, the cost of living rose steadily from 1.00 in 1939 to 1.59 in 1949. The ascertainable difference is that the controls during the Second World War succeeded in damping the rise in prices associated with the attempt by government to reallocate resources by bidding them away from private sector uses. It is largely on the basis of a comparison of these two sets of numbers that people conclude that wage and price controls were successful during the Second World War.

From other research we learn that the main effect of the 1970s series of wage and price controls in the U.S. was to reduce the quality of the output that firms produced. Was there a similar deterioration in the quality of the commodities produced under wage and price controls during the Second World War? The answer is yes. Not only was there quality reduction to avoid the controls, but this was enforced as part of the overall mobilization effort. It is hard to know exactly what the effect of that enforced quality reduction was. A fairly modest effect would wipe out the total gain achieved with controls during the Second World War. One commentator on the subject, then (1946) President of the Canadian Economics and Political Science Association, K.W. Taylor, regarded the quality reduction, or at least the cost saving as a result of the quality reduction, as being substantial and absolutely critical to the war effort. He also explicitly stated that the reduction in the resource content of goods was, "very considerable and undoubtedly of major importance in enabling the Board to 'hold the line' effectively." Now, if this is true one has to assume that the extent to which the reported price series over-reported quality and hence under-reported the true price could have been very substantial indeed. Our conclusion is that even during the war, wage and price controls didn't work—except to cover up the true rate of inflation. *M.W.*

PRIVATE HOSPITAL MANAGEMENT

A profit-making hospital is almost as rare these days as a sympathetic bureaucrat from Revenue Canada. That is why great interest is now developing in the Hawkesbury District General Hospital in Hawkesbury, Ontario, near the Quebec border. American Medical International Canada Inc. of Beverly Hills, California, has managed to pull Hawkesbury Hospital, formerly haemorrhaging red ink, into the black. In the eight short months of its management, AMI has taken an operation with perennial yearly deficits of $500,000 and made it into a money earner to the tune of $400,000 annually. This is a turn-around of almost $1,000,000 on an annual basis.

How has AMI performed this minor financial miracle? Part of its success was due to streamlining a previously inept and wasteful management system. Then, too, it was able to avail itself of numerous volume discounts. As well, budget planning, better money management, and an improved accounting system saved thousands of dollars more. For its expert services, AMI receives a $300,000 management fee plus a 50 percent share of any profits above $750,000. While AMI brings business-like techniques to the management of hospitals in the form of a system which has been perfected over a period of 27 years in some 115 hospitals around the world, the control of the hospital remains in the hands of the locally elected hospital board.

Extendicare, a Toronto-based provider of long-term hospital care, has been appointed by Alberta's health minister to be the administrator of Athabasca's General and Auxiliary Hospital which had been wallowing in financial mismanagement. Under the terms of a three-year contract, Extendicare will function as the hospital's administrator and answer to the publicly elected board of trustees.

These sound like developments that would be applauded by every responsible commentator. But if you thought so, you reckoned without some ideological opponents of private efforts in health care. The NDP opposes making profits in health care—no matter what the results. Says one spokesperson, "Hawkesbury is the way into the market for private companies. If they get a larger share of market over time, there will be a deterioration in health care." Another has denounced the move because it involves making profit off sick people. A third "progressive" warned that this was the beginning of the end for publicly funded health care. He conceded that private management teams have shown themselves to be more cost effective than public administrators in managing small hospitals and that using such teams to manage our hospitals would save money which could then be used to provide more and better hospital care or smaller deficits. But he doesn't like the increasing privatization of hospitals because the employees could ultimately be unorganized rather than committed to the ranks of the hospital union by virtue of their employment. Some progressive!

This phenomenon should be distressing to all taxpayers since, by their very nature, these contract management organizations (of which AMI is only one of several attempting to establish in Canada) usually set their sights on the least well-managed hospitals. It is at these institutions that the potential for turn-around and, hence, profit are greatest. Correspondingly, here also is the greatest unnecessary drain on the health care budget.

At the moment, the single biggest component of total health care costs in Canada is the cost of running hospitals. In many areas, the response to an unavailability of sufficient funding has been cutbacks in the level of service provided. Contract management clearly provides an alternative adaptation to these financial pressures. It may be time for provincial health ministries to take a more careful look at the options provided by the business management approach. At the very least, every province ought to have at least one hospital under a private management contract, if only to provide a benchmark against which to measure the efficiency of the conventional hospital management approach. *M.W.*

PRIVATE PROPERTY

Consider the buffalo, an animal equipped by evolution with a magnificent apparatus for survival against the worst that nature could provide. However, it proved incapable of surviving shortsighted government policy. Anyone who has ever observed thousands of head of beef cattle roaming the range lands must wonder why cattle have survived but the buffalo didn't.

The reason the buffalo didn't survive is because they belonged to everybody. Since they belonged to everybody as a natural heritage, it wasn't in anybody's particular interest to ensure that they survived. Cattle, on the other hand, have always been private property. The buffalo, like many other of our natural resources, simply succumbed to the "tragedy of the commons"—an economic reality summarized by the old adage that everybody's business is nobody's business. And, of course, it wasn't politically attractive then to designate buffalo rights any more than it is today to designate forest rights. *W.B.*

PRIVATIZATION

In 1976, the Fraser Institute published a small book by Nobel Laureate Milton Friedman which dealt with aspects of Britain's economic problems. One of the topics he canvassed was how to get rid of the nationalized industries. His immediate and insightful reply was, "give them away!" This book, meanwhile, was read by some people in British Columbia, and they were inspired to suggest the option to the provincial government, which responded with the privatization of the British Columbia Resources Investment Corporation in 1979. This privatization was the second largest share offering in North American history. As such, it attracted great attention. One group of people who paid close attention were the experts from the British Energy Department who visited Vancouver to observe firsthand and to get a copy of the Fraser Institute book about how firms could be "BCRICed." Soon after, Brit Oil was privatized and others, including the British Telephone System, have followed as the idea of privatization spread. Soon somebody in Ottawa will wonder whether we should import this idea from Britain!

And it looks as if the French have already done so. With the defeat of France's Socialist government the privatization epidemic which is sweeping the globe will be given another great push. Unlike most other countries, France has had the experience of wholesale nationalizations. For example, in 1981 newly elected Socialist President Francois Mitterrand confirmed the worst fears of the international business community by nationalizing what was left of the private banking system. His objective was to sever France's links with capitalism. The resultant economic upheaval formed the base of Mitterrand's electoral defeat and provided the words for the election slogans of the opposition. As Alain Juppe, economic spokesman for the then opposition alliance, put it before the election, "our aim is to change the course of French economic history."

How do they intend to do that? In the words of Michel Noire, the industry spokesman, "in principle, no activity in the competitive sector should be in the hands of the state." Their objective was to rid the public sector of about $26 billion in assets over the five-year life of their government. In pursuing it they will have the sterling example (no pun intended!) of Margaret Thatcher's government which has privatized billions of dollars worth of British nationalized industry. They will also face the reality that after years of public ownership there is not much of a private shareholding tradition. As a result, like Mrs. Thatcher, the French may have to rely on the sale of their enterprises to foreign stockholders. Not impossible, but tricky.

Privatization has by no means been limited to Crown corporations. Services traditionally supplied by government at municipal, provincial, and even federal levels have been moved into the private sector, for example, firefighting services, garbage collection, road maintenance, and the like. There is even an experiment in Hong Kong with the use of in-vehicle monitoring devices which would ultimately make possible the privatization of the road system.

Consider the privatization of firefighting. It turns out that the private provision of these services not only is cheaper but is more effective than the public variety. Proof of that particular pudding, incidentally, is to be found in the reaction of casualty insurance companies and the rates they set for residential home insurance. The insurance companies have now seen fit to reduce the insurance rates they charge customers upon the emergence in their municipality of a private firefighting organization.

The most exciting privatization news is the current effort to move in the direction of privatizing the road system. While developments are at a very early stage, an increasing number of people in Connecticut are convinced that the route to solving the state's transportation problems, recently exacerbated by the collapse of a major bridge, is to create a state highways corporation which would manage the road system in much the same way that Crown corporations in Canada produce goods and services. While the initial response to the road problems in Connecticut was the well-known knee-jerk response of governments—namely, abolish all tolls and take more direct government action to solve the problem—the bill which would have abolished the tolls has been vetoed by the governor who, at the outset, was a strong proponent of it. Consideration is now under way to establishing a more sophisticated tolling system based on the in-vehicle monitoring device being tested in Hong Kong.

A key consideration for Connecticut is the fact that the firm which manufactures the monitoring device is located in that state and, of course, the project there would be a marvelous demonstration project for other states and other jurisdictions. It may be too soon to say that private roadways are the way of the future, but only just. *M.W.*

PRODUCTIVITY

Everywhere one looks, journalists, politicians, and pundits are preoccupied with productivity in its various guises—what causes it, how technology affects it, what it does to workers, what it does to a nation's competitiveness, and, of course, what it does for profits. Nowhere is the discussion more prevalent than in the public sector. Here, productivity bargaining has become a panacea for excessive wage growth and a solvent for management/employee relations.

Generally speaking, productivity bargaining is regarded as a conservative adventure. After all, if we're going to have a public service it should be productive, shouldn't it? And, if it is productive, how can we complain about it? Productivity bargaining is ensconced squarely in government and labour rhetoric and even in the language of agreements. In the United States the notion is rearing its pointy head in the school system where the merit principle of compensation is increasingly being adopted.

However, as a moment's reflection clearly shows, the concept of productivity bargaining in the public sector or productivity or merit pay is hard to defend. This is because the notion of payment for value received does not characterize the public service in any of its aspects. To see the truth of this, one has only to observe how merit pay operates in the marketplace. In the private sector, employees really must be paid what they are worth or their employers will lose money and ultimately cease to exist. In that situation, it is the consumer who ultimately holds the power of determination. It is consumers, by evaluating the products of private firms, who determine the merit of the product itself and, hence, the merit of those who manufacture it. If employees in a private manufacturing enterprise decide unilaterally that they are being more productive and, hence, deserve higher wages (and which of us does not!), they will ultimately answer to the consumer of the product for the higher prices those higher wages would imply if no increase in productivity was forthcoming. Was their extra work worthwhile or not? Only the final consumer of the product can tell.

What about the public sector? It is possible to devise all manner of measurements of productivity: number of pages typed, number of application forms completed, number of park benches painted, and so on. But these, it should be clear, are not measures of value or productivity in any real sense, but only measures of work. A public employee who spends all day making mudpies is judged to be working (and Statistics Canada dutifully records his piemaking as increasing the gross national product). If he produces 12 more mudpies a day, has his productivity gone up, down, or remained the same? The answer, of course, is that since no value is being produced there is no productivity at all, and the only thing measured by the productivity measure is the extent to which the individual is working.

It is unfortunately the case that the consumers of products of the public sector usually have no ability whatsoever to indicate their approval or disapproval or their appreciation or lack of appreciation for the value claimed to be produced by government. The attempt to take into the public sector what in the private sector makes eminent good sense (namely, productivity bargaining) leads to an undue level of confidence in the process of determining compensation and a notion that public sector managers are doing all right by the taxpayer by forcing such productivity bargaining. Don't be misled by this particular nonsense. *M.W.*

PROFITS

"Profit" is a dirty word in the view of many people. "Obscene profits" is considered a redundancy in some quarters. For, in this view, profit is always and ever an example of exploiting other people and, hence, a moral disgrace. Even some businessmen who earn profits are infected by this notion. Instead of being proud of the profits they earn, these businessmen are apologetic. Many are embarrassed by their profits. Their public policy announcements feature pie charts showing how small a sliver of the consumer's dollar goes toward profits. Their defence against the charge of profiteering is to claim that profit levels are moderate and reasonable.

This is all so tragically wrong! Profits are an integral part of free enterprise. The marketplace is centred on the profit-and-loss system. So let us subject the concept of profits to some serious analysis to see if the critics have any case.

We begin by asking, "what are profits?" On the most commonsensical level, profit is the difference between the value of what we give up in order to obtain that which we want and the value of the item we want. In the typical business example, if the price of an orange is 50 cents and the total costs, including charges for land, labour, and capital, come to 40 cents, then a 10 cent profit is earned. The entrepreneur must give up a value of

40 cents. Since he obtains, in return, a value of 50 cents, he earns a profit of 10 cents.

But profits are much more widespread than this archetypical example would imply. According to our definition, consumers earn profits every time they shop in the local supermarket. Let's carefully consider what they do. As they select items for purchase, they choose only those for which they have a value in excess of the price. If the consumer buys an item for 50 cents, it is because he or she values it more than the 50 cents forgone.

At what rate do consumers value the item? They might be truly desperate to have it. They might be willing, if pressed, to pay as much as $2.00 for it. They might do so if this particular item were the only one to be had. If so, then the profit they earn on this purchase is $1.50. This is the difference between the 50 cents they must part with for the product and the price of $2.00 that in their heart of hearts they would have been willing to pay.

So, the businessman and the consumer each earn a profit: one by producing and selling, the other by purchasing. But who exploited whom? The answer is neither. In the marketplace, *both* parties to a trade earn profits. Instead of a dirty word, profits are a marvelous testimonial to the working of voluntary association.

Profits also have an information function. A dramatic increase in profit rates is a signal to entrepreneurs everywhere that investments made in that field of endeavour will yield good returns. The presence of high profits probably means a shortage of supply or reflects a sudden upward pressure on demand in the market. The excess profit initially earned is the mechanism which signals to entrepreneurs to invest capital there, create more of a supply there and, hence, ultimately stabilizes prices in that area. Mr. Gorbechev's policy of *perestroika* is a recognition of the signalling function played by profits. The next time you read one of those stories about excess profits, remember that even if profits are escalating dramatically, the reason is that the economy needs a signal to allocate more resources to that sector.

These beneficent marketplace profits must be sharply distinguished from those which are the result of state activity—tariff protections, bailouts, licences, subsidies, and favours. These are exploitative profits because they are coerced by legislation and not the voluntary expression of consumer valuations. *W.B.*

PROPERTY TAX

One seemingly beneficial aspect of the property tax rate system is that it provides municipalities with the ability to levy different rates of taxation, different mill rates, on different kinds of property. On the surface, this legislation seems to be highly desirable in that it imparts to municipalities greater flexibility in dealing with the complex problem of taxing a wide variety of different kinds of property. Flexibility, it has been said, will lead to greater fairness. But is that the real reason?

An alternative explanation is to be found in Colbert's advice that if you're going to grill the taxpayer you ought to do so in a way that will elicit the least amount of opposition—in this case, political opposition. The variable mill rate is a device for accomplishing precisely that. In the absence of such a provision, when a municipality wished to raise taxes from property it would do so by raising the rates on all taxpayers. The consequence is that everybody is made aware of the government's appetite for revenue and is led to question the desirability of that development. However, with the marvelous invention of the variable mill rate, it is possible to pick off taxpayers on an isolated one-by-one basis. The tax base will be split up and, given the desire of everybody in political life to avoid political backlash, there will be an obvious tendency to tax most those who can least effectively voice their opposition. At a time when everybody is concerned about the burdens of government and the taxation which it implies, it is a master stroke to divide political opposition and thereby effectively conquer it.

In addition to real property taxation, businesses in many provinces are also subject to a machinery and equipment tax. The more machinery and equipment contained in a particular building, the higher the property in total is taxed. Suppose you are a manufacturer and have two buildings both valued at $100,000—one of which was used to manufacture furniture and the other to store the manufactured products. Without this additional assessment, the property tax on each of the buildings would be the same. But the building used to manufacture the furniture contains $400,000 worth of machinery and equipment. If there is another tax on these factors of production, i.e., the Machinery and Equipment Tax, it could amount to almost doubling the tax levied on the property alone.

What is the effect on the bottom line? A building which is used as an idle storage facility could be taxed at only about one-third of the rate which is levied on a productive installation of comparable size. This is simply an incredible situation. At a time when practically every jurisdiction in the world is attempting to attract industry within its borders, the existence of a tax which specifically punishes those who make productive use of the land on which they locate is an obviously counter-productive and ill-conceived measure. *M.W.*

PROTECTIONISM

The United States, the land of the free and the home of the brave, is supposed to be the bastion of free enterprise, especially under President Ronald Reagan who crooned about the "magic of the marketplace" in solving economic problems and bringing prosperity to all. In theory, the U.S. is a living embodiment of the principles of Adam Smith. The People's Republic of China, in contrast, is presumably anything but a country which supports economic freedom. Its official ideological position is some variant of Marxism, and it is thus not expected to be open to the arguments for free markets and free trade. So much for the theory. In the real world things can be far different.

A case in point is a trade dispute over textiles that has erupted between the "communist" Chinese and the "capitalist" Americans. Peking threatened to retaliate against Washington over U.S. protectionist interferences with textile trade. According to the official Chinese news agency Xinhua, Chinese Ambassador Zhang Wenjin is unhappy with the U.S. "country of origin" rules. This measure means that U.S. customs agents will reject clothing manufactured in Hong Kong based on materials and semi-completed garments originating in mainland China. Mr. Zhang protested against this rule, which he said will threaten $2.2 billion worth of textile exports to the U.S. He stated that "hundreds of factories and about 60,000 jobs would be harmed in his country's southern provinces alone, and that this would be a grievous blow to China's industry, employment, trade and economic development."

What goes on here? In point of fact—as opposed to theory—the U.S. is a rather protectionist country. In order to make this claim, one need do no more than mention the infamous Smoot-Hawley tariff of 1931, which exacerbated the Great Depression. But even in the 1980s it has clamped down increased tariffs or set quotas on goods and products such as motorcycles, steel, autos, and, as we have seen, Chinese textiles. As well, it had continually threatening to deal more harshly with Canadian potash and forestry products. Lip service to the ideals of free markets is not enough. Actions speak louder than words. If the Reagan administration wishes to benefit its own citizens and those in the rest of the world, it should begin dismantling the tariff walls it has been erecting around itself—and with all due deliberate speed.

Trade barriers needlessly diminish economic welfare. If the peoples of the earth cannot join with one another in friendly trade, they will all miss out on the benefits of specialization and the division of labour. Why not produce those things we are good at and trade for the products other nations can produce more efficiently than we do? Adam Smith must be spinning in his grave. Imagine, a country devoted to the principles of capitalism and free markets erecting barriers to trade—and the Communists protesting.

But our hands in Canada are far from clean with regard to protectionism. Politicians and pundits have protested vociferously about Japanese automobile imports, hiring Korean engineers, purchasing beef from the EEC, being overrun by U.S. products, and the sale of hundreds of other foreign goods and services in this country. This may serve the special pleaders and narrow interests of some Canadian producers, but it certainly lowers our standard of living. Worse, it is a violation of the right of the Canadian consumer to purchase in the cheapest markets. *W.B.*

PUBLIC INSURANCE

The Insurance Corporation of British Columbia is a monopoly created by government to pursue the benign intention of giving B.C. the best insurance at the lowest cost—a motivation shared by the management and staff. When people join the employ of ICBC they abandon the normal human concern for themselves, their salaries, and careers and are transformed from self-seeking, self-interested individuals into altruistic drones, concerned only about the well-being of the province's motorists.

Unfortunately, the monopoly is not easily operated in the motorists' interests. Lacking competitors to keep them cost conscious, managers find themselves with large staffs and even larger costs. Critics have been able to point to the fact that while the number of autos insured dropped by 52,000, the staff of ICBC grew by 20 percent between 1980 and 1982. ICBCs social concern notwithstanding, hirees were not added at make-work type salaries. The average head office employee costs the corporation about $43,000 per year—even altruists have to live. As if this were not bad enough, people are beginning to make invidious comparisons between the rock-bottom rates offered by ICBC and the somewhat lower ones available to motorists in other provinces.

Responding to this and other concerns, and noting that "there is some legitimate concern" over the future of the corporation, ICBCs president began pointing to hidden benefits the megacorp confers on B.C. Before his selfless enthusiasm was restrained by the minister responsible, he had begun a public information programme to convince British Columbians of the apparently not so manifest advantages of a B.C. based, B.C. nurtured, and B.C. controlled organization.

But perhaps the critics see the advantages from the cost rather than from the benefits perspective: the fact that $181 million of taxpayers' revenue has been written off and the reality that ICBC does not keep reserves of the kind that are compulsory for private insurers. This means that ICBC could not pass a standard solvency test. Perhaps economy-conscious observers count the taxes—on both premiums and profit—which ICBC does not pay. Finally, perhaps motorists are beginning to wonder whose interests are served when management and the monopoly union representing the staff join forces to convince the public not to support the dissolution of *their* insurance corporation. *M.W.*

PUBLIC PENSION FUNDING

Which institution is the single biggest investor in Canadian stock markets? Unbeknownst to many, it is the *Caisse de Dépôt et Placement.* That is the quasi-independent holding pool for assets of the Province of Quebec, including the assets of Quebec's equivalent of the Canada Pension Plan. The crucial but relatively silent and obscure role played by this financial giant is immediately evident in its large size. Tipping the calculator at $23 billion, the *Caisse,* as it is fondly referred to, is larger than Alberta's heritage fund. Consideration of the *Caisse*'s performance in the management of the Quebec Pension Plan suggests some lessons for the Federal government in its conduct of the pension affairs of the Canada Pension Fund.

The *Caisse* has been able, on the average, to realize a yield on pension assets 2 percent above the level chalked up by the Canada Pension Plan on its portfolio of government bonds—mostly IOUs of the provinces, other than Quebec. And, when the investment is in the billions, that 2 percent is sizeable. But the most important lesson for the Canada Pension Plan isn't just the straight management issue, it is, rather, the question of how the funds are invested. The *Caisse* invests in real productive assets, like the factories of Genstar and Domtar, whereas the Canada Pension Plan is invested in government bonds—the proceeds from which may or may not have been productively employed.

The important difference between these two approaches is the fact that the money taken from Quebec citizens to support the Quebec Pension Plan is being channelled back into the private sector through the investment decisions of the *Caisse.* In this regard, the Quebec Pension Plan very much resembles private plans. The Canada Pension Plan, on the other hand, has no such reverse flow. Money contributed to the CPP stays in the public sector and is used to finance current spending of government. A potential problem is that as more and more pension savings are channelled through the public sector, less and less will be invested in the productive assets that will be needed to produce the income requirements of future pensioners. That is not to say that none of the money contributed to the Canada Pension Plan will be used to create useful capital. Roads, for example, are obviously important for the future. However, none of the public uses of capital are forced to pass the test of earning a competitive rate of return, and it is that selection process which ensures that our scarce savings are best employed. *M.W.*

PUBLIC POLICY (see Quotas)

Those of us who advocate a radical restructuring of government involving sweeping changes in the way we organize our public and private affairs are often told that what we propose is not realistic, that it is too Utopian in nature. However, we are always ready to admit our Utopianism in that we like to propose solutions to problems which will only be half adopted or vaguely pursued. The reason is that unless we keep a firm focus on where we're trying to go, we'll never get there. Notwithstanding that view of the world, we are always struck by the extent to which people who regard this approach to the world as unrealistic are blind to many of the idiocies and incomprehensibilities of the existing system. Let us consider three instances.

Vancouver artist Tony Onley found himself in the position of having to threaten to burn his unsold prints because the government wanted to assess and tax them in the same way that it taxes lawyers, accountants, and other professionals on the basis of work in progress. One would have thought, of course, that the difference between the work of lawyers or accountants and artists was rather obvious and that the bean counters in Revenue Canada would have little interest in pursuing an artist for his work in progress. The problem is, of course, that Mr. Onley is a *successful* artist. While the government has no compunction whatsoever in doling out large dollops of money in the futile attempt to develop indigenous Canadian art, whenever the marketplace happens to discover a successful artist he must be singled out and penalized in order to satisfy some bureaucrat's sense of homogeneity in the tax system.

Secondly, there is the fact that we have a gigantic bureaucracy of individuals in our departments of agriculture across the land whose specific role it is to encourage agricultural output. At the same time we have marketing boards penalizing farmers for producing milk, eggs, and chickens and, of course, sending the RCMP out to confiscate hens which have been raised "outside the law." Of even greater hypocrisy is the spectre of some bureaucrats subsidizing tobacco growers—while others spend millions in an effort to convince us not to smoke.

Thirdly, there is the billion dollar boondoggle of foreign aid—the policy which is designed, allegedly, to help the denizens of the Third World. It would not be surprising to discover that the aid in kind—skim milk and the like—often shipped to these countries would be occupying the same ship upon which clothing, shoes, or textiles produced in that less-developed country are being returned to it because they were imported into Canada without a quota. Various aspects of our trade policy in Canada effectively block the economic escape routes the Third World has open to it via trade. Meanwhile, we substitute a paltry amount of foreign aid which, while allegedly in the interests of these people, is very often used for political and other purposes and has little if any effect on the living conditions of the average Third World resident.

Yes, we Utopians are pretty silly, all right, especially by comparison with those real world pragmatists who are currently designing our policy edifice. Couldn't you just pull your hair out?
M.W.

PUBLIC SECTOR UNION

The importance of public sector unions cannot be over-estimated. One out of five people in the active work-force is employed in the governmental sector and some nine-tenths of them are unionized. As a direct consequence, nearly half of the total union membership in Canada is employed by governments. Public administration is the most heavily unionized of all the major sectors in our economy. It follows, then, that the laws pertaining to the rights and obligations of public sector employees are some of the most important enacted by our parliaments.

Although there are still some significant differences between labour policy for the public and private sectors, Canada's public employees have virtually all the unionization rights given to the private sector. In sweeping changes to federal and provincial legislation during the mid-1960s, wages were made subject to collective bargaining everywhere, and the strike weapon was made legally available to many public sector workers.

By comparison with the United States and, surprisingly, the United Kingdom, these developments represented quite a radical departure. In the United States, federal and most state government employees are prohibited from striking and are not permitted to bargain over wages. In Britain, wages in the public sector are not normally determined by bargaining but rather by strict adherence to private sector comparability guidelines.

The principle motivating this extension of private sector labour legislation to the public sector was that employees in the public sector should be treated in the same way as employees in the private sector. On first glance, equal treatment seems to be a just principle. Upon reflection, however, and now upon the basis of bitter experience, it is obvious that there are fundamental differences between the public and the private sectors. The failure of much existing legislation to take these differences into account lies at the root of many of the current problems.

The first and most important difference between the public and private sectors is the nature of the services supplied. In almost every case, services provided in the public sector are there in the first place because of their avowedly essential nature or because of the supposed, but seldom demonstrated, unreliability of the private sector in providing them. Governments are monopoly suppliers of these services and, as a consequence, the personnel involved in their delivery are in a unique position to "hold the public up to ransom" in support of wage and other bargaining claims. A service which is supplied by government as a reflection of the public's will can be withdrawn on the decision of a very small number of self-interested public employees. The public is then faced with the necessity to bargain for its return. In principle, and even on the basis of common sense, this is a ridiculous system. One is driven to ponder how ever our elected representatives could have led us to such circumstances.

Even if this essential flaw did not exist, there are differences between public and private employment that should suggest the inappropriateness of private wage determining procedures in public settings. For example, wages in the public sector are not subjected to any sort of market test. Higher wages are not reflected in higher prices and, hence, lower demand for government services—at least not directly—and unions can, therefore, make their demands knowing there will be no direct economic consequence. In fact, in many instances the economic effects of a wage increase are lateralized and forced on some other aspect of public service. Thus, higher wages for teachers may well lead to less expenditure on sports equipment or grounds maintenance rather than fewer jobs for teachers. It is precisely these prospective economic consequences of wage demands that provide the stabilizing feedbacks in the private sector wage bargaining process. Their absence in the public sector means that the bargaining process is not firmly anchored in economic reality.

A second major difference between public and private wage bargaining is the nature of the bargainer the union encounters at the bargaining table. The private sector employer is forced to bargain on the strength of profit and loss calculations that take into account a wide range of realities both domestic and foreign. At the end of the day, a private employer must have created more value than the value of the labour, capital, and materials he used to produce his products—otherwise he will have to go out of business. In short, he or she is a value or profit maximizer and brings this perspective to the bargaining table.

By contrast, public sector employers, to the extent they can be identified at all, are politicians attempting to maximize their voter appeal. As a consequence, a not too well-hidden, indeed perhaps the only, agenda item in public sector bargaining is the political appeal of the stance adopted by the public employer. Economic considerations pale by comparison with the necessity to get re-elected. The political orientation of the public sector bargainer has, in recent history, meant that public sector wage settlements have been very generous. They have been generous because the tax cost of the wage increases, being spread over time and many taxpayers, have been judged less important politically than the interruption of services to a relatively large number of well-identified, noisy, customer voters. However, the process has also worked in reverse.

Once it has perceived that the public is more sensitive to tax increases than the interruption of public services, the public employer is inclined to do a complete flip-flop. Generous wage settlements are replaced by impervious fiscal rectitude; passive acceptance of the most outrageous pension and working arrangements is replaced by public outrage and excoriation of the bargaining tactics employed by the union. The end result is that the wage bargaining process is no more rational and economic in its orientation when the cost to the taxpayer is uppermost in the minds of the public sector bargainer than when the tax cost is ignored. These inherent contradictions of existing legislation suggest that a radical restructuring of public sector labour legislation is required.

The right to strike over compensation must be withdrawn from public sector employees. Compensation in the public sector must be determined by a wage board selected on a broad basis and enjoying complete independence by virtue of long-term appointment. In setting wages, the board should be guided by the desire to achieve comparability between private and public wages—bearing in mind all of the distinguishing characteristics of employment in the two sectors.

Withdrawal of the right to strike over compensation, though difficult to accomplish, would remove the basic inconsistency in current legislation relating to the provision of government services. Wage determination by a wage board would not only serve to protect the taxpayer from excessive gains by public employees, it would also protect public employees from inappropriate measures taken against them by government during periods of public sector belt-tightening. Thus, curtailment of their bargaining rights may be in the long-term interest of public employees.

Secondly, since the right to strike over non-compensation issues must be retained, existing legislation must be altered to strengthen the ability of public sector employers to protect public services provision and to retaliate against striking employees. The package of necessary changes includes contingency planning to provide backup services, the right to lock out rotating strikers, limiting security clauses to the Rand formula, the right to lay off employees idled by strikes, and the right to hire replacements for striking employees.

A common response to the sort of root and branch restructuring suggested here is that it is too naive and fails to account for the realities. One must agree that it is prudent to be aware of practical difficulties. It is, moreover, important to acknowledge that justice demands a delicate, complicated balance between the power of public employees to influence their working conditions and the protection of the public interest. However, current legislation has within it the potential for a massive breakdown of public services—a potential which picketing government employees regularly bring to public attention. *M.W.*

PUBLIC SERVICE

Let us be clear at the outset. We do not believe public servants are lazy, malicious, or incompetent, or at least, no more so than the rest of us. We do, however, believe that the institutional organization in which they find themselves may well predispose public servants to act in ways which are not contributory to the public interest.

At the bottom line (to use one of the most abused and little understood clichés of our time), whether public servants are productive or not depends on whether they are producing something which the public wants and would willingly pay for if it had a choice in the matter rather than simply paying en masse for public services via taxes. Given the extent to which government attempts to hide the cost of public services, we can probably assume that people would not readily pay for at least some of these services if they had the knowledge or option.

In the ordinary conduct of our daily affairs we all make value judgements about things. We express these value judgements in terms of our decisions to purchase or not to purchase goods and services, to view or not to view particular television programmes, and to patronize one form of entertainment rather than another. When it comes to determining the creation of value in the private sector, we have no great philosophical difficulty. All we have to do is add up the amount of money people have been willing to spend on the various items they buy. That is an expression of the value people place on them.

Of course, not every provider of these products in the private sector will be contributing to value. Some firms, thinking they are providing just what their customers want, will lose money because they are failing at this task. So, when we add up the total amount of value produced in the private sector, we subtract losses incurred by unsuccessful businesses. As a result, private sector workers are productive in the sense that they are involved in the creation of value which is tangible, measurable, and beyond question.

Some of the services produced in the public sector are also of this sort. If government was not involved in the business of producing health care, education, transportation, and utilities, these goods and services would be provided by the private sector and people would willingly pay the price for them. But there are two points about the way we account for the production of value in the public service which require further attention.

There is, first of all, the matter of the cost of producing these goods and services. If the cost of producing a service in the public sector is higher than that which would be incurred if the service were provided by private contractors, the amount of value creation in the public sector is the total amount spent minus the excess cost incurred. For example, current research in Canada and the United States shows that municipal garbage collection by public employees costs about twice as much as that service performed by private contractors. Although garbage removal is a necessary service for which we would all willingly pay if it were not provided by government, that does not mean that the value of the total productivity of the municipal garbage collectors is equal to the total amount of money spent on this task. The total productivity is equal to the total amount which would have to be expended if the service were provided by the private sector. The difference between these two costs is, in effect, a loss which is being imposed on society but which, unfortunately, very few recognize. To the extent that public servants are involved in this loss-making garbage operation, they are not productive but are rather contributing to a societal loss. This does not mean that public servants are lazy or incompetent; it is only that the system of production in the public service itself is unproductive.

The other aspect of civil service productivity relates to the value of those goods and services which would not be produced in the private sector even if government stopped producing them. In this case, there is a very curious difference in the way we account for value. Rather than adding up the total amount which people have spent for the goods and services, we account for the value of government services on the basis of the amount the government spends to produce them.

In the private sector, if a person gets a great idea to produce left-wheeled 'garben-spangles,' invests money in the 'garben-spangles,' and ultimately discovers that nobody is willing to buy them, the person will make a loss equal to all the resources used in their production. The total contribution of this effort to the nation's productivity will be measured as zero, since the payment of wages and other costs will be offset by a loss of the money invested.

Suppose, however, that a senior government employee gets the same idea and, after voluminous reports indicating that 'garben-spangle' production is in the public interest, is successful in having government spend money on such a project. While the 'garben-spangles' produced in the public sector have no more value than the ones produced in the private sector in accounting for the total value production in society (the so-called gross national product), statisticians in Ottawa will dutifully record that the gross national product is higher because government spent money on 'garben-spangle' production.

There is a fundamental anomaly in the way in which we account for government services which makes it difficult if not impossible to determine when the public sector is incurring losses. It is, therefore, very difficult to know for certain whether value is being produced in the government sector or not, and if so, to what extent. *M.W.*

Q

QUOTAS

While Canadians are going about their business of living, earning, spending, and bringing up their children, our elected representatives in Ottawa are conspiring against the public interest. It's no big deal as far as these things go. The end result will probably be only a slight rise in the price Canadians shall be forced to pay for clothing made of denim in the years to come. But, in microcosm, their actions are an indication of a policy which afflicts the Canadian economy today.

What is bothering the Ottawa mandarins? Hong Kong, it would appear, has been stepping up its exports of denim to Canada in recent years. This has our politicians all agog, since denim is produced in central Canada and the government is much beholden to the votes and contributions of producers and organized textile labour in Quebec and Ontario.

If their request to Hong Kong to limit its exports was presented as a straight matter of political patronage, well and good. There would be a certain amount of charming honesty in the scam, and Canadian voters could register their reaction at the next election. Needless to say, no such honesty is emanating from Ottawa. Instead, they are cloaking their actions in the Canadian flag, representing this request as an attempt to save Canadian jobs and strengthen the Canadian dollar.

But denim from Hong Kong is not some commercial fifth column, ready to strike at the vitals of our economy. If Hong Kong can produce this cloth at a lower price than that available domestically, consumers will be able to buy clothing more cheaply. Not only that, with these savings Canadians will make additional purchases, creating more jobs, or save the extra money, making these funds available for new job-creating investments.

Consider what the people of Hong Kong will do with the Canadian dollars they receive for their additional denim exports to us. Canadian dollars are no more acceptable in Hong Kong than are dollars of this British colony in our own country. If the new owners of these Canadian dollars want to use them, there is only one place in the world, ultimately, where they are acceptable. Right here. When these funds come back to us, they will be for the purchase of goods and services. This will create still additional domestic jobs.

If the inhabitants of Hong Kong were perverse and refused to spend their Canadian dollars here, either by stuffing them into mattresses or by burning them, this would greatly benefit us. It would be as if Hong Kong had granted Canada a gift, or foreign aid, consisting of denim cloth. It can hardly hurt us to be the recipients of such largess. If the Hong Kong exporters spend their Canadian dollars in a third country, such as France, then the French will either spend the funds here, creating jobs, or keep them, in effect making a free gift to Canada.

No matter how you slice it, trade between consenting adults benefits both parties to the deal, otherwise it would not take place. The exchange of Canadian dollars for Hong Kong denim cloth is no exception. There is simply no justification for Ottawa to negotiate import limitations with Hong Kong, or with anyone for that matter. The sooner they cease such anti-social behaviour, the better off will be the Canadian economy.

But quotas do not only hurt the domestic economy. This is almost as nothing compared to the harm imposed on the economies of our trading partners, many of whom are impoverished Third World countries. Consider in this regard the decision by the federal Cabinet to impose a measure restricting shirt imports from storm-ravaged Bangladesh. That unfortunate country ships about 800,000 shirts to Canada a year, and it is one of only a few products Bangladeshians produce that is of interest to Canadian purchasers. The government has been trying for more than a year to convince Bangladesh to cut its exports by more than two-thirds, to a maximum of 200,000 shirts a year.

In an almost incomprehensible defence of this action, Canadian textile importers have indicated that the beneficiaries of this cutback will not be Canadian producers of shirts but rather exporters of shirts from other countries such as Taiwan, South Korea, and Hong Kong who can threaten to stop importing from Canada if trade barriers against them are tightened. So their story goes; their quotas will be preserved at the expense of Bangladesh.

This is a classic red herring. The real question is why there are quotas in the first place and why Canadian consumers are being forced to purchase shirts produced in Canada at a price far above the level they would have to pay if Bangladesh, in its struggle to achieve even a minimal level of economic subsistence, was able to sell its shirts to us on a freely competitive basis. The story is even more bizarre than it appears, because the shirts themselves are a measure of the success of previous Canadian foreign aid programmes. For example, the Canadian International Development Agency indicated that $41.5 million has been spent on economic assistance, including aid to an organization which trains rural women in the textile industry.

We have, on many occasions, commented on the inconsistency of Canadian policy which on the one hand proclaims a desire to help Third World countries by direct foreign aid and on the other hand imposes quotas on articles imported from those countries. In the particular case of Bangladesh, we have actually managed to bring those policies into direct conflict by creating a supply of shirts which we now refuse to buy. For shame! *W.B.*

R

REDISTRIBUTION

Government policy nowadays serves the dictates of "social justice" as that concept has come to be evolved. But surely, if we are to learn anything from the experience of the last two decades, we should acknowledge that the direct pursuit of egalitarian objectives is likely to be destructive. It is our opinion that the move toward more redistribution represents a serious miscarriage of justice and a miscalculation of the public mood to boot. By all means, government should remove subsidies to high income Canadians but should use the proceeds to reduce the deficit or cut the overall level of taxes. It ought not perpetuate the pretense that the public interest is served by the "redistribution of income." The interests of Canadians will be better served by renewed economic growth than by confiscatory income redistribution.

We have made a calculation (based on income tax data in a recent year) which indicates the real limitation imposed by income redistribution and the veritable bonanza to be realized from economic growth.

If all Canadians' income above $30,000 was to be confiscated and given to those filing a tax return whose income was less than $30,000, the payment before tax to each of those persons would be $126.25. That is not a gigantic sum and clearly illustrates that redistribution has important limitations as a means of improving the lot of the "average" Canadian.

By comparison, a minuscule 1.4 percent growth in total income, even if distributed in the same way as it is currently, would yield an equivalent or superior income increase for all Canadians. There can be no question that causing growth and creating the conditions that facilitate it are much more important for the furtherance of the public interest than a policy of income redistribution. *M.W.*

REGULATION

There is a marvelous line in Gilbert and Sullivan's *H.M.S. Pinafore* to the effect that "if you stay on shore and never go to sea, then you'll become the ruler of the Queen's Navy." Now, most listeners to this piece of lyrical advice to success in the British Navy may have thought it a trite or perhaps even silly observation. The fact of the matter is that Gilbert and Sullivan were extraordinarily prophetic. The proof of their carefully followed personnel management advice is daily to be observed in the pages of our newspapers.

The evidence has to be extracted by carefully sifting through the announcement photographs in the business section of the paper. There you will find case after case in support of W.S. Gilbert's insightful pyramid-climbing instructions. Typical is a recent announcement by Warm As Toast Energy Transmission. In their blurb, they proudly reveal that Joseph K. Bloggs had been appointed Vice President of Strategic Planning. They note that Mr. Bloggs came to his position with an illustrious pedigree. First, a Bachelor of Arts degree, next a Bachelor of Laws degree, and finally, a Master of Laws degree from the, ahem, London School of Economics. In all, nine years of education but, of course, not a second of practical experience in Warm As Toast or any other firm even vaguely engaged in a real world economic activity.

While lacking in industry experience, Joe Bloggs, of course, did have a deep steeping in the reading and writing of laws and the interpretation of their fathomless complexity. He was, therefore, an excellent candidate to work with lawmakers and had found himself a ready career in the federal government. The announcement also indicates that Joseph Bloggs has had experience in private industry. He'd been a regular user of natural gas, for example. Moreover, thanks to an industry/government exchange programme, Mr. Bloggs had spent a year rattling around inside a large oil company trying desperately to learn the etiquette of the company's executive dining room.

No, it is quite clear that Joe Bloggs' main attraction as an employee and Vice President of Warm As Toast Energy Transmission is that he is a bureaucrat and interpreter of laws *par excellence.* Having ascertained that, we can't help but be puzzled. One might have thought that a strategic planning position in an energy firm as large as Warm As Toast would have required knowledge of and experience in the problems of energy extraction and development. But, judging from Bloggs' pedigree, it appears that the most significant strategic problem the firm faces is dealing with laws and their interpretation—in effect, dealing with government.

Aside from providing interesting insights as to areas in which young, aspiring rulers of the Queen's Navy ought to engage themselves, this trend is a sad commentary on the evolution of incentives within our economy and society. It says, if you want to get ahead, learn to be a regulator, learn how regulations rule the land, rather than being an innovator, a producer, or an entrepreneur. In effect, stay on land and don't put to sea.

While many are beginning to recognize the difficulties associated with excessively large governments, the realization has not yet dawned that one of the most significant by-products has been the growth of a regulation and intervention "industry." This is an industry peopled by those in government and those in the private sector who must negotiate with them. The success of the intervention industry and those within it depends directly on an increase in the size and complexity of the regulatory apparatus. In turn, the self-interest of the Joe Bloggs inside and outside government mitigates against its being dismantled. It ensures that there will be considerable inertia whenever government entrepreneurs attempt to effect a change in policy direction—particularly when it threatens the jobs in the regulatory industry. More pointedly, we can all guess the sort of advice Joe Bloggs will give his president when asked to comment on the strategic aspects of deregulation or governmental down-sizing. What advice would you give if you were Joe Bloggs?

Consider the machinations of the CRTC and its failure to allow the new pay television networks to offer free service to potential subscribers as an advertising gimmick. This is really a dark episode in the history of Canadian regulatory affairs. The CRTC responded to charges by the Canadian Broadcasting Corporation and the Canadian Television Network by saying that pay-TVs offering of a free month of viewing to potential customers was, in fact, unfair competition.

This really is an interesting case because it exhibits the true reason for the existence of the CRTC which, we are sure, many Canadians think is to protect the consumer interest. After all, we have all been subjected to the platitudinous comments about the role of the CRTC to protect our cultural heritage and ensure that the undiscriminating Canadian mind is not subjected to too much in the way of culture shock by American TV programmes. From an economic point of view it is alleged that TV networks are given a monopoly, and in order to protect the Canadian consumer from outrageous behaviour by these licensed monopolists, the CRTC must tightly regulate them.

There is an alternative view of the role of regulatory agencies. The 1982 Economics Nobel Prize winner George Stigler, a Fraser Institute author, a wit, and an incisive social critic, framed a law which others have called "Stigler's Law." This states that regulation exists in the interests and the support of those who are regulated. A more clear indication of Stigler's Law in application could not be found than this decision of the CRTC. It is clearly the consumer who suffers, as a result of the decision not to allow the loss-leader programming month by the pay-TV networks, and the existing two networks which gain. Consumers will be denied a month of top quality entertainment. They will be denied the free information about what exactly pay-TV is all about, which they would otherwise have received from the network. They are now forced into the position of paying to discover whether pay television is their cup of tea or not.

While it is disgraceful that the public has been denied this benefit, the positive side of the experience is that it reveals the CRTCs true spots, and that's worth something! *M.W.*

RENT CONTROLS

If governments are serious about solving the housing crisis, they will make the removal of rent control one of their highest priorities. Since tenants outnumber landlords and are usually convinced rent controls are in their best interests, it may prove "politically impossible" to act in any such a manner. But do it they must, otherwise today's politicians will reside over the ruination of the Canadian rental housing market.

Like any law that freezes prices or causes them to rise at lower rates than otherwise, rent control is a market signal. What it indicates to the entrepreneur is that no new rental housing units should be constructed. While it is true that new rental units are specifically exempted from coverage by all provincial rent enactments, investors are too cautious (perhaps too smart) to put their faith in rental housing—believing that they may well eventually be hit, despite the present assumptions. A question we often ask rent control advocates is: "Suppose you inherited $1 million, or won it in a lottery; would you invest it in an apartment building at a time when tenants are clamouring for more and stricter rent controls? Would you advise your elderly parents to place their hard-earned cash in this highly risky field?"

Some analysts have attempted to account for the shortage of residential rental construction and the near zero vacancy rates in many parts of Canada not in terms of rent control but as a result of other factors. Alternative explanations include high interest rates, increased costs of construction (labour and materials), and immigration and population growth. But there are grave difficulties in each attempt.

Other things equal, an increase in the interest rate leads to a decline in all long-term capital investments. But why, then, have high interest rates not punched as serious a hole in the construction of office buildings, factories, warehouses, and commercial space? While vacancy rates for residential rentals in Vancouver hovered at zero levels in October 1979 (when rent control was in existence in B.C.), empty space in office towers amounted to about 8.9 percent. A similar analysis can be applied to rampaging building costs. They harm all building, but commercial, non-rent-controlled construction remains, curiously, almost exempt.

Immigration and population gains can be the occasion for temporary reductions in vacancy rates, but markets can usually be relied upon to adjust over the long haul. Any lengthy shortage of housing is an indication of special problems. It is no accident that the average residential vacancy rate in Vancouver was 1.03 percent in the seven years after the imposition of rent control in 1972, while it was 2.75 percent over a similar period before this legislation was enacted. This was a 62.5 percent reduction. Nor can this be explained away by population growth. The number of people in British Columbia grew by only 2.1 percent per year after rent control versus 3.1 percent before.

Existing rental units do not fare very well under controls. Even with the best will in the world, the landlord cannot afford to pay his skyrocketing fuel, labour, and materials bills, to say nothing of refinancing his mortgage out of rent rises he may legally charge. And under rent control, he no longer has the best will in the world. The incentive to supply tenant services he had under free market conditions is reduced.

His allowable rent rises are now arbitrarily set by outside political forces. They no longer depend, as they do in other fields of endeavour, on the market situation and on the standards he maintains. The result is often improper maintenance, poor repairs and painting, grudging provision of services, and a gradual slide into housing deterioration. The sitting tenant is "protected" by rent control, true, but he receives no real bargain. The enjoyment he can derive out of his dwelling space tends to be reduced to a level commensurate with his controlled rent.

Why is it so difficult to educate tenants and other members of the public about the economics of rent control? One would have thought this to be an easy task, given the unanimity of opinion on this subject on the part of professional economists. (This agreement cuts across the usual debates, and ranges from Nobel Prize winners Milton Friedman and Friedrich Hayek on the "right" to their fellow prize winner Gunnar Myrdal, an important architect of the Swedish Labour Party's welfare state, who claims that "rent control has in certain Western countries constituted, maybe, the worst example of poor planning by governments lacking courage and vision" to socialist economist Assar Lindbeck who states that, "in many cases rent control appears to be the most efficient technique presently known to destroy a city—except for bombing.")

But the popularity of rent control is such that right now it affects virtually all Canadian communities. Only Alberta and B.C. have made a clear decision in favour of dismantling controls. The average voter either has not heard the economist on rent controls or will not listen.

Although this can only be speculative, one explanation for the durability of this law may be because of the sheer durability and immovability of the large residential structure. No one in his right mind advocates a price control on carrots in order to ensure a lower priced supply. Everyone realizes that the farmer would switch production to other vegetables, leading to a shortage of carrots. Likewise, when governments have attempted to place ceilings on the incomes of doctors, they have been faced with a brain drain to other freer countries. While the farmer can easily change to a new product, and labour is mobile at moderate cost, people see it as exceedingly difficult, if not impossible, to move a big apartment dwelling into a non-controlled locale. The average man may think he can have the "benefits" of rent control without the attendant destruction.

This is a mirage. When the market signals a lower need for apartments by holding down rents, entrepreneurs will take every step at their disposal to comply. They will attempt to convert rental units to condominiums and to build single detached units, which have never been controlled, for rental purposes. They will allow the slide of the rental housing stock into deterioration if it cannot otherwise be made into a paying proposition.

These phenomena, however, are rarely seen by non-economists as the result of rent control. They occur years after enactment and are often interpreted as the results of other social forces. Voters and politicians should not confuse appearances and reality. They must come to realize that however immobile residential buildings seem to be, economic law grinds on inexorably. As the Fraser Institute study *Rent Control: Myths & Realities* concludes, based on the experience of six countries over the past 50 years, "the lesson of the essays for legislators is, if you have thc best interest of tenants in mind, don't control rents, and, if you already have control, then decontrol as quickly as possible." *W.B.*

REVERSE DISCRIMINATION

When our Constitution was repatriated in 1982 we included a Charter of Rights. These protections of individuals from the overwhelming power of the state were only half-hearted, however, and do not provide the kind of inviolable rights we might have hoped for. For example, the Charter of Rights explicitly permits discrimination in the workplace because there is a provision for affirmative action programmes to correct alleged past discrimination against women and minorities. In other words, reverse discrimination or employment preference for these groups will not be sufficient cause for a person to seek protection under the Charter, even if they are hurt by the preference. So, if you are leapfrogged by one of your fellow workers in a government job you will not be able to charge discrimination on the part of your employer if the leapfrogger is a member of a group given the right of employment preference in the Charter.

As a result, the Manitoba Human Rights Commission was able to act not on behalf of a discrimination-free society but in favour of one segregated on the basis of gender. Claudia Wright, head of the MHRC, attended a female-only conference on the media and participated in one of the workshops, despite her acknowledgment of the fact that the Manitoba Human Rights Act prohibits sex discrimination.

The event was put on by the Manitoba Action Committee on the Status of Women and Media Watch, groups which at least heretofore had been opposed to sexual segregation. According to conference organizer Lynne Gibbon, men were excluded because a number of male journalists had already been interviewed on the subject of the media. Evidently, the male reporter who tried to cover a weekend session but was told to leave was not one of those who had "already been interviewed." Ms. Gibbon went on to explain that this "was an attempt to include women rather than exclude men." Put that in your pipe and smoke it, male chauvinist pigs of the world!

Nor did this bit of illogic exhaust the explanatory powers of the women's movement. According to one Debbie Holmberg-Schwartz, managing editor of *Herizons*, a new national women's magazine located in Winnipeg, the decision to exclude men was a form of affirmative action: "It's really important that women catch up in this field, and of course the logical place to give them opportunity is at a women's conference."

Can anyone imagine the response of the Manitoba Human Rights Commission, and all others in the "human rights" biz, had a group of male white Anglo-Saxon Protestants used a similar line of argument to justify the exclusion of females, or gays, or native peoples, or handicapped persons, or Francophones, or indeed, any other group favoured by current prejudices? The double standard, so long reviled in Canada, would appear to be alive and well. *W.B.*

RIGHTS

In the last decade or so, we've been hearing a lot from the "human rights" industry. This includes human rights commissions, boards, committees, and associations spread out all over Canada. Their complaints are widespread, shrill, and even, it almost appears sometimes, omnipresent, but their underlying philosophy is deeply flawed. If we were to apply our "truth in advertising" legislation to these people, they would be exposed as the impostors they are.

In order to show this, we must first distinguish between positive and negative human rights, for this is the key to understanding the whole concept. In the classical liberal tradition, the view made famous by Adam Smith, David Hume, and John Stuart Mill, the only human rights were negative rights. People had a right not to be murdered, not to be raped, not to be enslaved, not to be kidnapped, not to be tortured, not to be stolen from, not to be victimized by fraud, pickpocketing, assault, battery, trespass, and any and all other invasions of person or private property. Other people did indeed have obligations under this theory of negative human rights. This obligation was merely to refrain from perpetuating any of these evil deeds upon innocent parties.

A strong defence of this notion is required, for nowadays the trendy lefties have sought to define a whole host of new positive rights. What are these new so-called positive human rights? They range widely, depending upon which particular philosopher is holding forth. What they all have in common is a request or a demand for wealth—always for the property or rights of other people. Examples include the right to food, the right to housing, the right to clothing, the right to challenging and interesting employment, the right to high pay, the right to meaningful relationships with other human beings, and, most relevant to the human rights industry all throughout Canada, the right to demand that people deal with you on terms they offer to others, whether or not they wish to deal with you at all.

Notice how different are these new positive rights from the negative rights of classical origin. In this view, the obligation of other people is not merely to refrain from invading person and property. Not at all. Here, the demand is that other people provide the food, clothing, and shelter that is their right. But this, it should be obvious, is merely a disguised way of demanding the products that other people have earned, produced, and created. It is an attempt to smuggle compulsory income redistribution into the language—under the guise of human rights.

There are other disparities too. Negative human rights can all be attained simply by an act of will. If we all resolve, henceforth, never again to rape, murder, and pillage, human rights can be entrenched at one fell swoop. That's it. We could attain full human rights, in their proper sense, merely by a mass refusal to ever again initiate violence.

The contrast, here, with the counterfeit idea of positive human rights is stark indeed. No resolve in the world, be people ever so well-intentioned, could suddenly feed, clothe, and shelter the five billion human beings now inhabiting the earth to the level regarded by Canadian advocates as the right of all citizens here. Certainly, this could not have been accomplished 200 years ago, when we were all much poorer. Legitimate human rights, negative rights, that is, could have been entrenched any time in human history. This is because they do not depend in any way, manner, shape, or form on levels of wealth or prosperity.

Let us consider an example. Suppose a person, shipwrecked in a sudden storm through no fault of anyone else, were to suddenly find himself washed up on a small desert island. And suppose that the food, clothing, and shelter available on this island were far below levels demanded by our so-called human rights activists. An accurate way of describing this person's plight would be to say he is poor. That he lacks wealth. But it would be a travesty to say that his human rights had been violated, for there are no other human beings in the picture who could have done any such thing. Human rights, real human rights, have nothing to do *per se* with income levels. Our shipwrecked sailor may be poor, he may even be dying of starvation, but not one shred or iota of his negative human rights could have been violated, for there is no one else there who could have assaulted him. Yes, his positive human rights are violated, but this just goes to show how nonsensical a notion that is.

One further disparity. If A has more of his negative human rights met, B does not suffer any diminution in his. That is, if no one murders, assaults, or enslaves A, this in and of itself does not constitute murder, assault, or enslavement of B. Human rights are not additive. It's not true that there is only so much of them, and that A can only get them at the expense of B. But this *is* true in the case of the bogus positive human rights we are considering. If I have more of my rights to food met, you, of necessity, have less of your rights respected, given that there is only so much food or wealth in existence at any one time. If you are forced to deal with people you would prefer to avoid all together, their positive human rights are increased while yours are decreased. *W.B.*

S

SAFETY LEGISLATION

A cynic, we are told, is a person who knows the price of everything and the value of nothing. Economists often get labeled with this tag because of their preoccupation with the analysis of costs and benefits. You'll never find an economist worthy of the name talking about the benefits which accrue from a particular activity unless they also acknowledge the costs of that activity. There has to be a concept of net benefit.

One of the areas where economists get themselves into the most trouble in popular discussions about net benefit is in the area of life and death. For most folks, the very mention of the notion of net benefit in this connection is perplexing because, after all, isn't life an infinite benefit? And, from a personal point of view, there is nothing more important under ordinary circumstances than one's life. However, choices are made all the time which involve the implicit assignment of a value to people's lives, and that value is far from infinite.

Take, for example, level railway crossings. The risk of collision between automobiles and freight trains can be completely eliminated by doing away with all level railway crossings. We don't do so because of the cost; that assigns an implicit value to the human lives which are, as a result, put at risk. For the most part, we don't acknowledge explicitly that such a net benefit in terms of human lives is being calculated. Perhaps it is just as well, since many of these decisions are made by politicians, and it's simply impossible to imagine one of them out on the hustings arguing about the costs and benefits of lives. However, in many areas of public policy, just such a net calculus is absolutely necessary.

Increasingly, there is no such calculation of net benefit concerning risk to life, and this is a potentially destructive development for society. The reason is that removal of risk is typically expensive. Moreover, the cost is often measured in terms of indirect loss of life which isn't included in the analysis. That is clear in the case of level railway crossings because the money spent on the overpass isn't available for hospital construction. It is less clear in the case of occupational health regulations and the installation of machines to purify air, for example.

The American Society for Risk Analysis cites studies which show that the construction of safety equipment valued at about $33 million will cost about 6,000 lost person-days or one death. Accordingly, unless more than this level of life preservation is anticipated, the installation of the so-called accident prevention or safety equipment would, paradoxically, actually produce an increase in the extent of death and disablement. The unfortunate fact is that in many cases equipment of this sort is forced upon industry by well-meaning regulations which simply have not taken into account the indirect safety effects.

Nor is it clear that safety legislation on behalf of workers is the sacred cow it has long been taken to be. Consider in this regard the nuclear workers who go into a nuclear plant's radioactive area and do repairs to the power generators. They are sometimes called "minutemen" because they can only stay in the radiation area for a very short period of time before their exposure limit is reached. The limit is set by the U.S. Nuclear Regulatory Commission at three REM. Most private companies, however, insist that employees leave the contaminated area once the limit of two and three-quarter REM has been reached. That's the equivalent of about 110 chest X-rays in a year.

For most people, the thought of exposure to radiation is unnerving. Regular minutemen know that the risks they face are somewhat less than those faced by coal miners, asbestos workers, and those who handle dangerous chemicals in the chemical industry. In any event, they make their choices on the information available and willingly derive the benefits therefrom. But if the Anti-Nuclear Environmental Policy Institute in Washington, D.C. had its way, the jumpers wouldn't be allowed to engage in what they regard as high tech feudalism.

The question ultimately, of course, is who should be allowed to decide? In our view, only individuals can make such decisions, because only individuals can make the delicate trading-off of costs and benefits which every human activity requires. *M.W.*

SCAB (see Labour Code)

In the field of labour relations, the crucial issue is the strike. Actually, this is a misnomer, as it refers not to one act, but to two. A strike is, first, a withdrawal of labour in union from an employer on the part of the relevant organized employees. To this, there can be no objection. If a single individual has a right to withdraw labour services, or to quit a job, he does not lose this right merely because others choose to exercise their identical rights, at the same time. There is a second aspect of the strike, however. And this element is entirely improper. This is the union practice of making it impossible for the struck employer to deal with alternative sources of labour who are anxious to compete for the jobs the strikers have just vacated.

Such an entry restriction can be accomplished in several ways. In the days of yore, organized labour would first brand their competitors as "scabs" or "strike breakers" and then use threatened or actual physical intimidation (mass picketing, trespass, sit down strikes, violence, arson) to make it impossible for the employer to hire replacement workers. In the modern era, unions have added to this tactic a plethora of legislation which also effectively drives a compulsory wedge between employer and "scab." The businessman must convince the Labour Relations Board that he is "bargaining fairly" with those who have left his employ (even though what he most desires is to ignore them and deal with others instead). He must give special considerations to those who have left him in the lurch by striking.

In Ontario, for example, according to legislation recently introduced, professional strike-breaking would be outlawed. That is, it would not be legal for the struck business to engage a separate firm for the purpose of replacing striking employees. It is claimed that this action would interfere with a legal strike. But notice, however, that this attempt to hire alternative workers only interferes with a strike in the second or illegitimate sense. No attempt whatsoever is being made to thwart the right of employees to resign en masse. On the contrary, this action, already illegal in Quebec and in British Columbia, attempts only to uphold the right of the employer to deal with alternative employees. Even worse, Quebec is considering legislation which would prohibit the employer from dealing with any alternative workers during a strike.

One argument of organized labour is that its present powers—or something like them—are responsible for past wage increases and are needed if wages are to continue to rise in the future. But this is false. On the contrary, gains in labour productivity—because of better skills, improved capital equipment, and industrial peace—are the causes of gains in take-home pay. This is proven by relatively declining wages in the heavily unionized "smokestack" industries compared to increased salaries in the less unionized computer, microchip and other "information" industries.

Another argument for the status quo is that the "scab" is stealing the job of the striker. This is also invalid. A job is an embodiment of an agreement between two consenting parties, employee and employer. It cannot be the possession of only one of them. A worker no more owns "his" job than does a husband own "his" wife. A striking union which forcibly prevents the employer from hiring a replacement is like a husband who divorces his wife and then threatens to sue her, or to beat her up, and any prospective new suitor as well if she tries to remarry.

A properly revised labour code, then, would allow strikes in the sense of mass refusals to work, or quits in unison. It would entrench this behaviour as a basic element of the rights of free men; but it would limit union activity to this one option. It would thus prohibit, to the full extent of the law, any and all interferences with the rights of alternative employees ("scabs") to compete for jobs held by union workers. *W.B.*

SCALPERS

Next to husbands, scalpers are the most misunderstood group in our society. This is a fact made clear by the assault on those who were buying up tickets for the entertainment at Expo 86. The scalpers, so it was said, were depriving others of tickets and should have been stopped. However, just a moment's thought shows that this accusation isn't true; scalpers actually perform a valuable service.

First of all, the actions of scalpers don't deprive others of tickets. The only way scalpers can retrieve their investment is by successfully selling their hoard to people who attend the events. On the contrary, scalpers distribute tickets more widely than they otherwise would be. In the particular case of Expo 86, the people to whom the tickets were spread were visitors to the fair who otherwise would have been denied tickets altogether. These people may pay a higher price than those who were tuned in enough to purchase the tickets at the first offering, but the scalpers are betting they will be willing to pay much higher prices. Their willingness to do so is an indication that the scalpers are performing a valuable service. While the name "scalper" implies the buyer is being unfairly treated, the fact is they don't have to attend the event. For that and other reasons, high scalpers' profits are not a sure thing.

Scalpers also help the organizers of events. Organizers must set ticket prices to ensure a full house. That means lower average prices for tickets and a "no return" policy for unused tickets. If there are scalpers, ticket buyers who are uncertain about their ability to attend will not be deterred by the no-return policy because they know they can sell to the scalper. Praised be the scalpers! *W.B.*

S

SCHOOL VOUCHERS

Very often, developments in the United States are a bellwether for Canada. That isn't always the case, but in general terms the Americans have tended to predate this country in important social evolutions. It was thus with some interest we noted that the Supreme Court in Washington upheld a Minnesota law that gives parents a tax deduction for their children's school expenses. The Reagan White House, of course, was delighted with this Supreme Court decision. It had long been advocating more choice in education and the removal of the current bias against parents being able to determine how their children are educated.

The Minnesota enactment permits all parents of school age children to take a tax deduction for actual educational expenses up to $500 per child for elementary school and up to $700 for junior high and high school. The law applies equally to public and private school expenses, although there is no tuition in the Minnesota public school system. The force of the law is to permit Minnesota parents to more readily opt out of the public school system. This is particularly important for parochial and other private school families because it effectively eliminates the double education expenditure these families would otherwise have to undertake. In most provinces in Canada, for example, a decision to send your child to a private school—whether of the upper-crust, conspicuous consumption variety—or the more pedestrian religious or ethnic schools—means a decision to bear a double cost for education. You pay for it once in your property or income tax and a second time in the form of tuition fees for the private school.

This kind of development would be an excellent change to implement in Canada as well. An increasing number of Canadians are deciding that the public school system either does not reflect their values or simply is incompetent in providing education and are, therefore, opting for private schooling.

Contrary to what many of us believe, that does not mean that more children of the rich are attending ritzy boarding schools. The average cost to educate a child in a private school is actually less than in the public schools. This indicates that many of these independent schools are run on a very austere basis indeed. Moreover, it is also interesting to note that the average parent of an independent school child, at least in British Columbia, is less wealthy than his public school counterpart. If parents were permitted to claim a tax deduction for tuition fees, more resources would be made available to the independents. That school system would provide a more equally funded and, hence, a more robust competitive challenge to public schools.

As we all know, there is nothing like competition to improve the quality and reduce the price of a product. At the moment, because there is no effective competition, we don't know whether our educational dollars are being spent well, whether the education system is producing the best product for the price, or whether, in fact, there isn't a better way to get the job done. It may be wishful thinking to hope that the recent Supreme Court decision in the United States will inevitably seep over into Canada, but as Robert Browning so aptly put it, "man's reach must exceed his grasp or what's a heaven for?"

However attractive, there are many misunderstandings about the voucher system. In order to clear up the record, it is important to consider the following points. First of all, it is not a new idea. Educators in California, in particular two left-liberal professors at the University of California at Berkeley, have been pushing the idea for nearly two decades. They have tried without success to have it passed as a proposition on the ballot in California.

Secondly, it does not mean that government will get out of the education field. In fact, the voucher would simply be a piece of paper representing the cost of educating a child in the public school system which would be given to parents so they could take it to the school of their choice. Once having received it, the school would redeem it from the government for the full dollar value.

Third, in British Columbia, we already have a form of voucher, since parents can choose which public school their child should attend and the government then transfers a set amount of money to that school. The only problem is that if the parents choose an independent school only 40 percent of the full cost is transferred to the school. The result is that parents who choose an independent school pay an additional amount for their child—once through taxes and once in tuition fees.

Fourth, the anticipated consequence of a voucher system would be an increase in the quality of education, more control over the education system by parents, and greater satisfaction by teachers who would have greater autonomy to devise teaching strategies and methods, even if the curriculum would continue to be set by the province as is the case for independent schools at the moment.

What needs to be explained is why the existing system of parental choice extends only to the range of public schools available and not to the independent schools. This is the essential question about vouchers. *M.W.*

SELF DEALING

Ottawa has allowed the takeover of Genstar Corporation (the owner of Canada Trust, the nation's seventh largest financial institution) by Imasco Ltd., the Montreal-based tobacco and retailing conglomerate, but it did so only after imposing severe restrictions on the merger. According to the stipulations set down, self dealing shall be prohibited, the management and boards of directors of Canada Trust and Imasco will remain forever separate, and Imasco will not be able to acquire other financial institutions. As if this were not a sufficient protection of the public interest, the government reserved the right to partially or fully reverse the takeover, or to force Imasco to divest all or part of its holdings in Canada Trust, in possible subsequent legislation.

The reason for this large-scale government intervention into the economy would appear to be the fear of an alliance of a financial institution and a non-financial business corporation, and the self dealing thereby made possible. Self dealing has been defined, variously, as a process where a conglomerate uses its trust company to unfairly benefit related firms even though this unduly risks its depositor's money, or where a parent company uses capital from its subsidiary to finance its own dealings regardless of the best interests of the subsidiary's depositors.

Based on the opposition to the merger vociferously made by members of all three parties, there would appear to be something particularly objectionable about a merger between a financial and a non-financial corporation. But there are several difficulties with such a contention. First of all, the concern is too general and overstated. *Any* merger may conceivably result in one party misusing the assets of another. There is thus no reason for the state to limit its misgivings to just those corporate purchases which combine financial and non-financial holdings. Of course, if two non-financial corporations form one larger one, no depositor's funds are put at risk; but there is as much of a public interest in protecting the property of shareholders as there is in protecting the property of depositors.

Secondly, the concern is biased. The critics of the Imasco purchase were visibly troubled by the prospect of the conglomerate pillaging the depositor's property. But the reverse, which they ignore, is equally plausible. The history of economics is littered with sorrowful tales of bank failures. Who is to say that in order to ward off such an occurrence in future no financial institution would engage in a raid on the non-financial membership of its conglomerate?

Thirdly, the property of depositors may be ravaged not only by the takeover of a non-financial conglomerate but by any one shareholder in the trust company or bank who attains a measure of control. For example, a 60 percent owner could arrange to lend $100, based on dubious collateral, to his grandmother. When the loan goes bad, he benefits by the full amount (his grandmother turns over to him the entire $100). True, his company loses all this money, but as a 60 percent owner he is out of pocket by only $60. Thus he gains a profit on the deal of $40—at the expense of the other members of the financial institution. In order to obviate just such a scenario, government has enacted legislation limiting control over banks to 10 percent, and has enmeshed trust companies in a welter of restrictions which limit the ability of owners to engage in this sort of fraudulent "sweetheart" deal.

The government has also organized a scheme of mandatory deposit insurance (*de jure* this is limited to a coverage of only $60,000, but *de facto* there has been no such limit in recent times). This sharply diminishes the creditor's incentive to insist upon the writing of efficient contracts to preclude such fraudulent behaviour. As a result, market institutions to accomplish this task have atrophied or have never come into existence at all. In the absence of deposit insurance and other government activities which retard marketplace incentives, if the investment community felt that a merger between financial and non-financial corporations would unacceptably increase the risks attendant upon self dealing, the depositors would desert any such trust company or bank in droves. This would make it impossible to even engage in merger negotiations in the first place.

Were markets allowed to work, there would be no need for any special government vigilance on behalf of the depositors against a merger with a non-financial business concern. One solution is to recognize that legislation which presently protects the depositor from other would-be predators within the financial corporation will presumably serve as well against any threat from a non-financial source. More radically, public policy should contemplate the removal of the first unwise government regulation, subsidized deposit insurance, which deludes marketplace participants into thinking they are safer than they actually are.

Since we have seen that there is nothing unique about a financial/non-financial corporate merger, the brouhaha about self dealing which emerged in the Imasco-Genstar purchase may be interpreted as a general criticism of the propriety of mergers in the private sector. The Fraser Institute's publication *Reaction: The New Combines Investigation Act*, subjects Canada's competition law to intense scrutiny. In the analysis of the 14 eminent contributors to this study, the visible hand of the Canadian government is far less able to protect the public from harmful and untoward mergers than is the invisible hand of the free marketplace. *W.B.*

SOAK THE RICH

Canada's income tax system is theoretically designed to tax people according to their ability to pay. And, for the most part, people in Canada do pay more tax if they are wealthy. In fact, statistics released by Revenue Canada show that those earning more than $40,000 per year, who earned 18.3 percent of the income declared in Canada, paid 29 percent of the total tax paid in Canada.

The reason that those earning more than $40,000 paid much more tax in proportion to their income is because Canada has a progressive tax system—the more you earn, the higher the percentage of your income that goes to government. However, there are some taxpayers, including 13,805 who had incomes greater than $40,000, who paid no income tax at all. In fact there were 239 Canadians who had incomes in excess of a quarter of a million dollars who got off scot-free. Naturally, this leads to cries of "tax the rich; plug the loopholes so that the rich pay their fair share."

Can such a policy be successful? The answer is "no," and that for many reasons. The first is that there aren't enough rich people to start with. As a consequence, even outright confiscation of all income above $40,000 would only yield $5.5 billion. To put that in perspective, if it were allocated to all those with incomes less than $40,000, it would amount to the handsome sum of $385 per taxpayer. Secondly, if you continuously attempt to get it from the rich, there will simply be fewer rich people from whom to get it. Confiscation of high incomes will eventually mean that people won't attempt to earn high incomes, or they will escape with their high incomes into the burgeoning underground economy which exceeds $50 billion.

High income individuals are only able to avoid taxation because of the tax incentives or loopholes which governments consciously build into the income tax system. Such individuals avoid taxes by spending their money on projects the government designates. Some economists have called these loopholes "tax expenditures" to indicate their true nature. Many observers have long suggested that tax loopholes be abandoned in favour of a simpler tax system involving no fancy deductions and exemptions but rather a flat rate of taxation. In effect, this would result in a lower rate of income tax for high income taxpayers but, of course, that is exactly the opposite route proposed by the get it from the rich movement.

In this regard, there has been a marvelous economic experiment in the United States. During 1981 the top rates of income tax in the United States were cut from 70 percent to 50 percent. The results of that policy change are now available and they are remarkable. The result of cutting the top rate of income tax was to increase the percentage of the total paid by high income taxpayers.

Canadian evidence just compiled and presented in the table below corroborates this international evidence. In 1981, the top rate of federal income tax in Canada was reduced from 43 percent to 34 percent. The result was to increase the share of taxes paid by the top 5 percent of income earners and increase the fraction of their total income that they paid in taxes. In 1981 the top 5 percent of income earners paid 9.27 percent of the total tax bill and an average tax rate of 25.23 percent. By 1984, the top 5 percent were paying 9.48 percent of the total income tax bill and faced an average tax rate of 27.17 percent. The most fascinating aspect of this development is that during the same time interval, the average tax rate faced by income earners at all levels actually fell from 10.65 percent to 10.63 percent.

Effects of the 1981 Tax Changes
Top 5 Percent of Income Earners

	1981	1984
Income Earned ($ million)	9,157.7	10,519.7
Tax Paid ($ million)	2,310.6	2,858.3
Tax Rate (percent)	25.23	27.17
Share of Total Tax Bill (percent)	9.27	9.48

Source: Revenue Canada Taxation, Taxation Statistics, 1983 and 1986, Summary Table Two; calculations and interpolations by the Fraser Institute.

Reducing the top rates of tax increases the effective tax rate of high income earners because they take less advantage of loopholes and hence pay more tax. They, along with everybody else, are better off because the taxes saved under current loopholes are often dissipated in legal and accounting fees, lost because tax-based investments are no good, or recovered from the taxpayers in future years. Reinforcing this effect is the fact that people actually work harder when they know they can keep more of what they earn with no strings attached.

In other words, the evidence from Canada, the U.S., and the U.K. speaks with one voice on the issue of fairness. If you want the rich to pay more of their income in taxes and you want them to pay a higher fraction of the tax bill, reduce the top rates of income taxation. *M.W.*

SOCIAL JUSTICE

There is no such thing as social justice. This term, used to justify legislative interventions ranging from affirmative action programmes to the progressive income tax, is increasingly seen as nonsense. Moreover, it is recognized that the pursuit of the mirage of social justice has led us and our society to perpetrate monstrous injustice on the individuals who comprise it.

Providing, as it does, the basis for a great number of the so-called social interventions by government, this concept is a very important one to debunk. There are grave injustices which can be perpetrated under the guise of seeking the higher good. In the first instance, it is very difficult to conceive of a "just society." One can conceive of, and there can obviously be, just behaviour by individuals. Individuals can be treated with justice or injustice. Moreover, one can conceive of a just set of laws or an unjust constitution. But how can one conceive of a just society apart from the justice or injustice which is visited upon the individuals which comprise it? Those who appeal to social justice to validate their actions and objectives explicitly reject the notion of individual justice. They must do so in order to pursue their collectivistic ambitions.

The most well-known expression of the just society is the attribution of positive rights to individuals. These are almost too familiar to bear repetition, but include such blanket statements as: everyone has a right to decent housing; everyone has a right to medical care; everyone has a right to a minimum level of income. While these are objectives to which we might all subscribe, they cannot be defended on the grounds that they serve justice. The reason is that achieving them requires specific injustices against other members of the society.

The only way to guarantee individuals the minimum level of anything is by demand that some people be forced to provide the resources to achieve this end through coercive redistribution. When this is conceived as a tax upon the rich to support the poor, its real import is disguised (although it would be difficult to suggest that taxing one individual at a higher rate than another could be construed as being just in the normal sense of that term.) However, when this process of taxation is put on an individual level, very obvious sources of injustice immediately arise. For example, individuals who, on moral grounds, oppose abortions are nevertheless coerced to provide the wherewithal so that other individuals can obtain an abortion. Two persons, equal in every respect, except that one of them saves a fraction of his income, are subjected to very different tax rates by the state since the investment income earned by one will attract taxation. Those who have risked their capital to start a business are taxed to provide subsidies to a competitor because the government wants to "create jobs."

Like its bedfellow, the public interest, the pursuit of social justice has left in its wake the wreckage of individual justice. This is an increasing barrier to economic progress. Unfortunately, many features of our society have been molded by the social justice principle. Among the more important of these are many aspects of labour relations, legislation, so-called consumer protection, and social welfare legislation relating to unemployment insurance, old age pensions, and so on. *W.B.*

SOCIAL SPENDING CUTS

So we won't be accused of simply engaging in generalities, let us indicate what this sort of policy really means. First of all, restraint in the size of government and in the tax burdens Canadians must bear is not compatible with continued growth in programmes like the Canada Pension Plan, nor with an indexed old age pension system, nor with ever larger subsidies to the unemployment insurance fund. More reliance on the private sector means more independence and more individual responsibility. It is useless and self-deluding for us to pretend we can restrain the size of government unless we are prepared to see cuts in social service spending. Likewise, there must be a cutback in the growth of expenditures on health care and education. These are the two largest sources of operating deficits in the provinces. Doing something about over-spending in these areas means doing less in those areas. It means allowing Canadians to be more self-reliant and more responsible for these basic expenditures.

We all know the standard response to these arguments. We can't cut back social services spending because it will mean that some Canadians will lose their economic security. We can't cut back health and education spending because low income Canadians will be neglected. These are tired arguments. They are arguments born of the old ideas which have led us to the current mess.

In the well-intentioned effort to provide a few Canadians with government-based economic security, we have produced a juggernaut which threatens the economic security of all. At no time in the period since the Second World War has Canadian economic security been more in jeopardy than now, and at no time has government taxed and spent more of our incomes. While the intention of government programmes in health and education was to expand access to these essential services, their production under the aegis of the public sector has brought us to a state of crisis which threatens the very lives of our sick, and periodically, the education our children receive. The health care systems in two of our largest provinces are on the verge of paralysis. In B.C., hundreds of hospital beds are being closed down.

For those who will see, the course of action is clear and involves less, not more, government spending. Conversely, the private sector must be relied upon, more and more, to provide these essential services. *M.W.*

SOUTH AFRICA BOYCOTT

It is easy enough to understand the venom of those opposed to the Botha regime. Apartheid is a state-sanctioned attack on the very basis of civilized behaviour. It prohibits, or at the very least sharply curtails, economic, political, and social interaction between consenting adults who happen to belong to different racial groupings. It is extremely unjust, highly immoral, and very inefficient from an economic point of view. It is reminiscent of Naziism, with its emphasis on racial supremacy. All in all, it is a blot on the record of humanity.

Why, then, is the case for a complete boycott of this misbegotten country to be termed "uneasy"? There are several reasons. The major sufferers of such a programme will not be the perpetrators of apartheid, who are the whites, and especially the Afrikaners, but rather the victims of this system, the blacks in the country. A boycott might still be justified if, in the view of the oppressed themselves, the short-run economic harm was more than offset by the long-run benefits that would accrue with the ending of this evil system. There are many black South African leaders, such as Bishop Tutu and Nelson Mandela, who maintain precisely this position. However, there are many more blacks who do not agree, as indicated by the position on boycotts taken by Zulu Chief Mangosuthu G. Buthelezi.

Bad as is apartheid, there are things far worse. Apartheid merely keeps people apart on the basis of race, assigning the better end of the stick to those in favour and the worse end to the others. But the downtrodden in countries other than South Africa are treated far more viciously than are the victims of apartheid.

People in Afghanistan are now being murdered by invasion forces from the Soviet Union. If a boycott against South Africa is justified, then even stronger, on moral grounds, is the case for imposing sanctions on the Soviets. Even apart from its foreign adventurism, the Russian treatment of the Jews is in at least one sense worse than that accorded the blacks in South Africa by the whites. There are no Jews attempting to gain admission to the Soviet Union. On the contrary, the traffic is all one way, the other way.

In contrast, the black migration patterns in and out of South Africa tell a very different story. Here, the blacks from the countries surrounding South Africa aspire toward entry into the only nation in the world which practises apartheid; there are no masses of victimized blacks who wish to leave and settle elsewhere in black Africa equivalent to the Russian Jews who would give their eye teeth to be allowed to go to Israel. The Jews, in other words, "vote with their feet" against the Soviet Union; the blacks, paradoxically, "vote with their feet" *in favour* of South Africa.

It could be argued that a boycott against South Africa might have an important effect, whereas one against the Soviet Union is doomed to failure. This is a pragmatic argument, unworthy of the distinctively moral fervour which surrounds the movement of opposition to apartheid. It is akin to a child fighting against a smaller and weaker opponent on the playground, while refusing to defend himself against the more powerful neighbourhood bully. It is like agonizing over the effects of secondary tobacco smoke, while ignoring those of AIDS. And on pragmatic grounds, if it makes sense to trade with the Russians, to engage in cultural, artistic, and athletic exchanges with them in an attempt to promote mutual understanding and win them over to our way of life, then this applies even more strongly to the weaker and more isolated country of South Africa.

Further, there are numerous black-run African nations which accord far more brutal treatment to their black minorities than is visited upon the South African blacks under apartheid. Idi Amin is only one of many black African rulers who engaged in mass murder of his own hapless and innocent citizens. Surely, the case for a boycott against these countries is far stronger than one against South Africa. There cannot even be the pretense that a boycott would fail to create disarray on pragmatic grounds. Many of these countries are already on the economic skids, a boycott might be all that is needed to push them even further down the road to chaos.

If a successful boycott would impact mainly on the victims of apartheid, against their will; if it is morally hypocritical in that it is not first instituted against the Soviets, or the tyrannical black African states, or because it is joined by the Indian government which presides over a caste system of its own; why, then, does the movement against South Africa attract so many otherwise moral people? One suspects that it is not so much the spectre of blacks being victimized in South Africa that is so disturbing to the protestors but the fact that these evil deeds are being perpetrated on blacks by whites. Given the history of imperialism, of the "white man's burden," and all that this implied, this thought is perhaps understandable. Yet, it is a profoundly racist view, and completely incorrect. It implies that whites are necessarily morally better than blacks; that it is unfortunate if blacks mistreat blacks, but that it is intolerable if whites mistreat blacks. How else can we explain the particular "moralistic" vigour with which the South African boycott is pursued while so much that is far worse is either ignored or dismissed? *W.B.*

SOUTH AFRICAN DIVESTITURE

As a result of, and in tandem with the anti-apartheid protest, clergy of all major faiths in Canada have come out strongly in favour of a policy of divesture of securities in companies located in South Africa and those doing business in that country as well. Since apartheid is an evil and the Republic of South Africa engages in that practice, they urge, on moral grounds, that all investors sell any such stocks they may own.

There are several difficulties with this programme. First of all, the action is logically inconsistent. Based on ecclesiastical reasoning, holding shares in these corporations is morally proscribed. How, then, can they in good conscience sell them to other people? To do so would be to knowingly encourage the purchasers to adopt an evil stance—the ownership of these securities.

Let us not misunderstand the precise economic implication of offering shares for sale; it is one of encouraging others to buy them. This can be shown dramatically by assuming that at the current price, whatever it is, demand is insufficient for the entire offering. What will happen then? Prices will have to fall so all shares supplied to the market can be taken up. Since there can be no clearer economic inducement to purchase an item than to lower its price, we see that if morally motivated people offer South African securities for sale they are encouraging others to engage in the evil of owning them. The offer of sale, then, is like first preaching about the evils of alcohol consumption and then cajoling other people into making purchases of one's own whiskey stocks.

But the problems do not end here. Let us assume that religious authorities are fully successful in convincing everyone of the moral impropriety of engaging in South African corporate ownership. If they are, no one would be willing to take any position, no matter how small, in these shares. How, then, will the churches be able to sell their own securities in such firms? The answer is that they will not be able to do so. This leads to the paradox that if clerics are successful in their mission of convincing all market participants to avoid ownership of corporations identified with apartheid, they will dry up the pool of potential purchasers and make it impossible for them to sell these shares of stock. The two-part programme is thus internally inconsistent. To the extent that one goal is accomplished, the attainment of the other is rendered impossible.

One conceivable way out of this quandary is to urge not that the shares be sold to others (endangering their moral standing) but that they be shredded, burned, mutilated, or otherwise destroyed. But many clergymen are reluctant to accept this course of action, deeming it "impractical." By this response, however, they expose their own hypocrisy. They are willing to act morally, but only if it is costless. They uncannily resemble the person who decides to make a charitable contribution to a good cause, then pulls back suddenly, remembering that this course of action will at least slightly reduce his own wealth.

Even this is not the end of the story. Let us assume that there are at least some ecclesiastics willing to put their money where their convictions are and destroy, not sell, their ownership positions in companies tainted by apartheid. Will even this extreme action harm commerce in South Africa? On the contrary, this will do the very opposite; it will help the very people against whom this disinvestment policy is aimed! How is this paradoxical result achieved? If there are 1,000 shares in a firm and 100 are destroyed by their clergy-owners who oppose its investment policies, this will only increase the value of the 900 which remain for these will now account for the entire book value of the enterprise.

According to the Bible, it is very difficult to pass a camel through the eye of a needle. In like manner, it is not easy for the stock owner of a South African firm, or of a Canadian one which does business there, to harm the apartheid system. Indeed, every effort to do so through commercial means either involves a denial of the underlying moral stance which motivates the attempt, or boomerangs entirely, ending up benefiting this unjust system of racial separation. The moral of the story is that benevolent intentions are not sufficient for sound public policy. Needed, as well, is an appreciation of the economic realities which are often subtle and complex. *W.B.*

SOVIET PLANNING (see Planning)

Public planning or central planning, as it is commonly understood, is a relatively recent development. It first arose in the Soviet Union as Lenin attempted to operationalize the doctrine which he, following Karl Marx, had developed. The Communist doctrine forbade, among other things, private trading and the use of money because of their association with capitalism. Unfortunately, in eliminating these, Lenin also destroyed all legal market activity. This meant that Communism was left without a doctrinally acceptable economic mechanism. As a direct consequence, the vague, transitional phase of "state capitalism" envisaged in theory became, in fact, little more than an emulation of the German war economy as Lenin struggled to cope with the famine and economic stagnation which followed the abolition of the market. Under this system of confiscation and arbitrary allocation, things deteriorated even further.

The extent to which the Russian economy collapsed under the heavy hand of the state is not often appreciated. It will suffice to indicate that by 1920 industrial output had declined to 14 percent of prewar levels. As 1920 drew to a close, it seemed inevitable that the Soviet economy would completely collapse. Lenin, in a desperate effort to forestall disaster, instituted the New Economic Plan (NEP) in 1920/21.

The New Economic Plan involved a reinstatement of private trading and small-scale private enterprise and a capitulation from the objectives of the Bolshevik Revolution. However, the upsurge in economic activity was to be short-lived since the respite was used to begin the process of institutionalizing central planning. In what could not have been foreseen as perfect irony, the first Five-Year Plan was launched in 1929.

The story of the application and evolution of central planning in the U.S.S.R. is a story of bloodshed and human misery. It is a chronicle of incompetence and malfunction, of famine and defeat. It is certainly not a record that would attract emulation from those who seek economic prosperity. It would seem more than passing curious, therefore, why anybody would recommend the adoption of such a system. *M.W.*

SPECIAL INTERESTS

What do hairdressers and lawyers and architects and surgeons have in common? The answer is that they all primarily have the interests of the consumers at heart. (And if you believe that, you'll believe anything!) At the annual meeting and convention of the British Columbia Hairdressers Association, President Ann Harrison informed one and all of the absolutely critical need for the hairdressers association to maintain prices in the face of price cutting by members. In her view, price cutting represented a clear threat to the quality of the service offered by hairdressers. As the famous Don Jabour case adequately attests, hairdressers and lawyers are no different in this regard. Their claim is the same: prohibiting price competition protects the consumer interest.

Mrs. Harrison's remarks are not idle chatter. The actions and activities of hairdressers in the province of British Columbia are subject to the provisions of the Hairdressers Act of 1929, which explicitly prohibits the advertising of price. So, for example, if some uppity hairdresser should seek to compete with fellow association members by indicating a willingness to work for less, the association would descend with the force of law upon the errant brother or sister with great alacrity.

Special interests have managed to chisel away at our rights as consumers by the restrictive legislation they have been successful in passing. There should be no real question as to whose interest is being served by a law which prohibits competition among suppliers of a service on the basis of the price that they charge, particularly in the case of a service like hairdressing. At the very most, a consumer would sample a service only once to discover whether it was worth the price or not. There may be some modest element of consumer protection in setting standards and the withdrawal of licence from those inclined to put purple dye in their client's hair in a fit of pique, but it is highly questionable whether this minimal insurance feature is worth the price being paid for it.

We must not single out only hairdressers; it is time that we began to question many of these so-called consumer protection Acts, particularly as they affect associations of professionals. *M.W.*

SPECULATION

Since time immemorial speculators have been vilified for high and rising prices. This view is incorrect; in fact, the opposite is true. The result of speculation is a reduction in the rate and extent of price rises from what would have prevailed without it.

To see this clearly, let us consider the uncontroversial example of widgets and then, having established the basic principles for the classic case, apply them to the special and more sensitive issues of land and housing prices. Suppose that in the absence of speculation, the future supply of widgets is as in the Biblical story—seven fat years followed by seven lean. Given similar demand in the two periods, the years of ample supply would result in low prices and the era of short supply in high prices.

Enter the speculator. What will he do? If he has any sense, he will follow the sage counsel of profit-seeking—buy when prices are low and sell when they are high. His initial purchases will, to be sure, raise prices above the low levels that would otherwise have obtained in the first period as his additional speculative demand is now added to the demand to buy widgets for consumption purposes. But his subsequent sales will reduce prices from the high levels that would have occurred, but for his efforts, in the second time interval. This is because speculative sales, when added to other sales, depress prices further than all other sales would have done by themselves.

The speculator will be seen by people to be selling at high prices in years eight through 14. People will thus blame him for these escalated prices, even though they would have been still higher in his absence. But the speculator does far more than merely iron out prices over time. By dampening price oscillations, he accomplishes something of crucial importance: the stockpiling of widgets during the years of plenty when they are least needed, and the dissipation of the widget inventory during times of shortage, when they are most useful.

Furthermore, the speculator's actions in the market signal to all other businessmen that an era of short supply is expected in the future. His present purchases raise widget prices and, hence, the profitability of producing them now. This encourages others to do so before the lean years strike. The speculator is the Distant Early Warning System of the economy.

But, as in the days of yore when the bearers of ill tidings were put to death for their pains, modern day messengers, the speculators, are blamed for the bad news they bring. There is talk of prohibiting their activities outright or of taxing their gains at 100 percent confiscatory rates. Such moves would deprive society of the beneficial effects of speculation.

There is only one possible fly in the ointment. If the speculator guesses incorrectly and sees years of plenty ahead when belt tightening is really in store for the economy, chaos will result. Instead of stabilizing prices and supplies of widgets, the speculator will destabilize them. Instead of hoarding during the fat years and reducing inventories during famines (and leading others to do so as well) he will encourage needless saving under adversity and wasteful profligacy in good times.

The market, however, has a fail-safe mechanism to prevent just this sort of disaster. The speculator who guesses wrong will buy high and sell low, incurring losses, not profits. If he continues to err, he will go bankrupt, usually very quickly. Professional speculators who have survived this rigorous market test of profit and loss can be relied upon to forecast the future with far greater accuracy than any other conceivable group, including seers, crystal-ball gazers, bureaucrats, politicians, mystics, marketing boards, or swamis.

Now let's consider the effect of speculation on land and housing prices. As in the case of widgets, the speculator is observed to be selling at high prices, to be holding land off the market until yet higher and higher prices are reached. But if we carefully trace out the effects of such activities, we can see that the only time the speculator can raise prices is when he *buys*—and he bought when prices were low, before the increase in demand. We can likewise see that the only result of speculative sales is to *decrease* prices. No matter how expensive the level at which the sale take place, prices would have been higher still in the absence of this additional land and housing supply. As well, the speculator can function as a distant early warning line in the market. His initial purchases can encourage the construction of additional dwelling units. At higher home prices, more profits can be earned in building, lumber, cement, wiring, and so on.

By definition, additional land cannot be created (barring reclamation from the sea, as in the case of Holland) but space can be converted to housing from other uses, such as farming and industry. But the housing and land markets in Vancouver, for example, where prices have been soaring, have been hemmed in by a bewildering array of government activities—all seemingly aimed at worsening the local housing crisis, not solving it. Speculators would love to convert Fraser Valley farmland worth a few thousand dollars per acre at best to home-building parcels worth hundreds of thousands and even millions per acre. They are prohibited from doing so by an agricultural land reserve policy. Only a small percentage of Vancouver's foodstuffs is grown in the Fraser Valley, yet government has made a fetish out of trying to preserve this status quo, even though virtually everyone would prefer vast savings in their mortgage and rent payments.

Land developers would be more than willing to provide additional housing on a highly concentrated unit-per-acre basis, but they are discouraged from doing so by zoning legislation that severely restricts such things as lot size and floor space ratios and by tax reforms that have taken capital cost allowance privileges off the provision of residential accommodation while maintaining them for movie production and other non-essentials.

Last, but not least, rent controls in many provinces have diverted what limited funds and land space are available to real estate away from the rental sector which needs it most. It is in this sector that the highest concentrations of single-parent families, the handicapped, minorities, and people on low and fixed incomes are found.

The hated speculator would love nothing more than to "exploit" these people—by providing for their needs! But when rent controls take away the profit potential and increase the downside risk, they reduce the incentive to do so. Where bureaucrats tread, landlords, developers, and speculators fear to go. *W.B.*

SUBSIDIES

Government subsidies to industry should be opposed on a number of grounds. The first arises from a consideration of the functions which the market process performs for society. The most basic of these functions is that of information retrieval. The market answers to the following questions. What should be produced? How should it be produced? By whom should it be produced? Where should it be produced? When should it be produced? This information retrieval function is particularly important when we consider the future.

The future is a collective noun describing ignorance and uncertainty. It is not something which even the most intelligent and insightful human beings can know anything about with certainty. It is not something which exists out there and which, if we study carefully, we can come to know. It follows that there is much uncertainty about which products and services ought to be produced in the future.

Some people think they do know the future. It is a characteristic of entrepreneurs that they feel they have isolated a "sure thing," just the product which consumers will want and be willing to pay for and which will make the entrepreneur a very rich person. Entrepreneurs invest their own money and try to convince others to do likewise. They take a chance that the dream will come true. If it does, everybody will be better off. The entrepreneur will be rich, as will his co-venturers. Consumers will be better off because they have a new good or service to purchase, and society will have enjoyed a net increase in economic welfare.

On the other hand, perhaps the entrepreneur will be wrong. Consumers will not want the product at the price for which it can be produced. Instead of profits, the entrepreneur begins to realize losses. For a time, the businessman and his financial backers won't know whether this is due to the normal process of placing a new product or whether they have made a mistake in their assessment of consumer demand. Initially they will continue to finance the venture. In fact, the normal pattern is that new businesses have a negative cash flow, and it is to underwrite this that the entrepreneur needs up-front capital. At some point the entrepreneur will realize that a mistake has been made and cease operating. Typically, that will be when he has exhausted his supply of capital and cannot get access to more. Potential suppliers of capital in the private sector have better opportunities and opt not to continue to fund what is judged a failure.

Surprisingly enough, when a venture of this sort fails, society is also better off. In supplying the product, the entrepreneur was using valuable resources in a combination which consumers did not value. In some sense, society was making a net loss on each item produced. Stopping production halts the waste. Society also gains from the knowledge that has been accumulated. It now knows that product X is not one that should be produced at that time. This trial and error process is repeated hundreds of times every day across Canada. And, in this way, the market gropes cautiously and imperfectly into the future—learning and coping.

A very different pattern emerges under government. The "government entrepreneur" will have very strong ideas about what consumers want and will tend to be adamant in his views—just like his private sector counterpart. However, government has, for all practical purposes, no natural limitation on the capital it provides to underwrite a particular venture. Moreover, the decision-making process will involve political as well as economic variables. Governments are concerned first about very parochial political issues. Accordingly, the decision to support a firm making losses may depend on where it is located or how that locality typically votes. This problem is an obvious consequence of public sector institutions.

Government aid of this sort causes direct losses of resources and compounds these losses by providing incorrect signals to the market. The latter problem is of particular concern because, if widespread, it can affect whole cities and regions. The decision to support a textile or auto manufacturer conveys certain messages to the firm's employees and to the suppliers. Employees and their children stay in a particular area because they think they are gainfully employed. Suppliers think they have a market for their product and may expand. Suppliers of secondary services may do the same.

In the end, of course, the subventions to the firm will be terminated either because the government can no longer afford them fiscally or politically, or because the government changes and the new lot have different supporters to whom they must cater. When the collapse finally comes, the social disruption is greater and the resource costs to society of a much larger scale than if the firm had been allowed to go bankrupt in the first instance.

This example is not meant to imply that the private sector always supports winners and shuns losers—certainly not. Participants in the market are human and have all the usual human failings. Some firms which should collapse are supported, and conversely, some which should be supported cannot find the capital to continue. At the same time, governments will from time to time provide money to enterprises which are successful. The central point is that on *average* the market systematically rewards and advances those individuals who can successfully provide what consumers want while weeding out those who do not. The reward system from the governmental point of view is quite different. The political system rewards those who can successfully extract benefits from one group and confer them upon another. Whether the recipient firm is producing wealth for society or not, governments will tend to provide the subsidy as long as that action produces more votes on balance.

Consideration of this redistribution activity of government leads naturally to the second major reason we are opposed to government aid to industry. It has to do with the fact that there is no such thing as government aid to industry. Government aid, along with that other characteristically Canadian phrase "public capital," conveys an entirely misleading impression about what is happening when governments involve themselves in the market.

Governments have no money to give to anybody—nor do governments have capital. What governments have is a coercive power to redistribute money or capital—to take from one group in society and give to another. This insight provides a whole new meaning for former Prime Minister Lester Pearson's comment that politics is the art of accomplishing very delicate acts with very blunt instruments. The instruments are the legislative clubs with which the government beats the long-suffering taxpayer.

When considering transfers to business, we have an obligation to consider from whom the money comes. The answer is that it comes from taxpayers, either now or in the future. On average, the taxpayers forced to provide the subsidies via the tax system are the same people who, as consumers, decided not to support the troubled industry by purchasing its products. Of course, not one in a million consumers will recognize this fact. This is why government's actions don't produce riots in the streets or, what would be worse, defeat at the polls. The other reason governments don't have to worry about these possibilities is that it simply isn't worth any individual taxpayer's effort to get exercised about the $1.00 per year which he or she is forced to provide to some trucking firm or other. But the bottom line is that subsidies to the "corporate welfare bums" are bad public policy and ought to be ended. *M.W.*

SUNDAY SHOPPING LAWS

Sunday shopping prohibitions are completely unjustified. The usual argument in their behalf is that Sunday is the Lord's day. This is open to interpretation, however, as Jews and Seventh Day Adventists celebrate Saturday and Moslems view Friday as the holy day. Moreover, there is simply no need to compel the entire society to refrain from commerce on the Sabbath just because some people, even a majority, want to celebrate this day in more quiet pursuits. Surely churchgoers can live their own way of life without imposing it upon all others?

Many people claim that without such legislation, shopkeepers and, in turn, their employees, would be forced, if only by economic factors, to remain open on Sundays despite their own personal wishes in the matter. There are several grounds upon which to object to this charge. First, this is not in keeping with the little evidence available on the subject. Far from supporting the law, most small merchants have been vocal in their opposition. Secondly, while some employees may not wish to work on weekends or evenings, others may prefer to do so. Department stores usually hire additional help for the Christmas rush, ofttimes with additional pay; there is no reason to believe they will not be able to attract adequate numbers of willing employees on Sundays should they be so disposed. Third, and more basically, this is exactly what is meant by aphorisms such as "consumer sovereignty" or "the customer is always right." In a market economy, the buying public should call the tune. Retailers who do not wish to dance to this tune are either in the wrong business or voluntarily agree to earning less in profits than full service to the public would entail. A law which prohibits Sunday store opening is an attempt to protect some unwilling merchants from the needs of their customers.

Further the Sunday shopping law breeds a disrespect for law and order in general. It is very unpopular; tens of thousands of people have signed letters of protest. More importantly, the law has been widely violated by thousands of irate storekeepers. In the otherwise law-abiding Victoria suburb of Saanich alone, 118 separate charges have been laid. Violators in this case are not your average lawbreaker, and their widespread disobedience threatens to lead to the devaluation of law-abidingness everywhere.

As well, the Sunday shopping law is shot through with capriciousness. In Vancouver, there is talk of exempting Gastown and Chinatown, but then "Japantown," "Punjabtown" and the Granville Island Market, with as much or more right to special treatment, would be left out. Moreover, fresh fruits and vegetables have been judged as permissible but not shelled peanuts and tinned juices. Are the former, not the latter, "works of necessity and mercy" as required by the antiquated 1907 Lord's Day Act?

Sunday shopping laws, like many of the other commercial enactments of government, are an assault on the freedom of individuals garbed in the cloak of the public interest. Surely the best way to determine whether people want to shop on Sunday and whether merchants want to earn the profits associated with serving the public on Sunday is to allow people the freedom to make these choices. The Sunday shopping law, like many other laws, is based on a very peculiar idea of what a consumer is—a person intelligent enough to elect a government but who needs a law to tell him when he should buy his groceries. *W.B.*

SUPPLY SIDE ECONOMICS

The relatively esoteric concepts of incentive effects and marginal tax rates began to impact heavily on the political consciousness in the United States shortly after Arthur Laffer drew a curve on a napkin in a Washington restaurant. In it he sketched out the relationship between the tax revenues a government collects and the tax rates it levies on its citizens.

Laffer's central point was that the higher the tax rates people must pay on additional income the less likely they are to earn that additional income. In fact, at some point on the upward spiral a government will find that increasing the tax rates further actually reduces the total revenue collected. The increase in revenue from increasing the tax rate is more than offset by a reduction in the total income available to be taxed. This occurs because high tax rates reduce the after tax income associated with a given amount of income-producing effort and because they increase the return from tax avoidance.

That is Laffer's central point and the one which ultimately motivated Ronald Reagan to bring about a net tax reduction in 1983 in the United States and to reduce the highest marginal tax rate from 70 percent to 50 percent, and then to 35 percent. Other countries, including the U.K. and Canada (partly), have followed suit. *M.W.*

T

TARIFFS

Tariffs can only harm us. It is by no means a foregone conclusion that without tariffs the Japanese will always be able to out-compete us. Where there is the will there may be a way, as long as free competition is allowed. Western auto producers may one day be able to assert their previous pre-eminence.

But suppose that tariffs were removed and the Japanese-made autos, selling at a fraction of the price of ours, swept all before them. Even under such a scenario, all is not yet lost. To cut costs even further by reducing transportation expenses, the Japanese may open factories of their own here, employing Canadian workers. Canadian suppliers of spare parts or accessories to an expanded Japanese operation may then prosper.

But what if the Japanese, under a regime of complete free trade, organized auto production entirely on a domestic basis, not using Canadian manufacturers even as suppliers? Such a state of affairs would still be in the best interest of Canadians. Why? Let's say that Canadians could then buy an automobile of given quality for $5,000, rather than $15,000 when produced domestically under the old regime of tariffs. The first effect would be that Canadians who purchase cars will have an extra $10,000. Some of this wealth will go for increased domestic consumer purchases, creating additional employment here. Some will be saved, helping to keep interest rates down, making it easier to start new concerns and to expand old ones.

The purchase price of the automobile goes to Japan. What will the Japanese do with this money? Why, turn around and spend much of it on items we producc more effectively than they, such as wheat or barley or coal or lumber or oil or natural gas or maple syrup or any of dozens of other products produced on farm, forest, or in mines. This will create more jobs and not just any old kind of employment. It would create jobs that are highly productive. After all, the path to wealth is by allocating labour to its most productive uses. There are few better ways of accomplishing this than by specializing in what we do best, allowing the Japanese to do the same, and then exchanging our best efforts for theirs.

So far we have been assuming that Japan has an advantage in the production of cars and that Canada can out-produce it when it comes to products of forest, farm, and mine. Let's assume that not only is Japan a better producer of automobiles, but it can out do us in other products as well. It still does not follow that Canada would be better off with protective tariffs.

Suppose, for example, that with given resources, Japan can produce 10 times as many cars as we but only twice as much wheat. When Japan sells us cars, it will still use some of the proceeds to buy our wheat. Even though Japan has an absolute advantage over us in all products, we have a comparative advantage in wheat. To draw a parallel, consider a person who is not only the best lawyer in town but also the best typist. If lawyers make $200 per hour and typists earn $10 per hour, does it pay the lawyer to hire a typist, or to do both jobs himself? Of course, he is better off sticking to his comparative advantage and specializing in the practice of law.

In just the same way, even if the Japanese can produce more cars and wheat than Canada, unlikely as this is, it will still find it in its own interest to specialize and trade with us. So let's stop this ill-advised negotiation of "voluntary" trade barriers with Japan so both of us can get on with what we do best. *W.B.*

TARIFF RETALIATION

British Columbia was hard hit by the U.S. imposition of a 35 percent tariff on shingle and shake imports. The immediate response has been to call for retaliation in the form of a tariff on products imported from the United States. What this amounts to, in the most basic terms, is that the U.S. has shot us in the foot tradewise and many are proposing that our reaction ought to be to shoot ourselves in the other foot. That is what retaliation would do, because tariffs increase prices and reduce choices for Canadians.

Many people regard this position as simply maddening because the natural human reaction is to react against attack—particularly when it is unprovoked and unjust. But this very fact must cause us to think carefully about how we respond. The truth is that the 35 percent tariff will do great damage to the Americans as well. It will raise the price of shakes and shingles by an amount almost as large as the tariff, and that price will be paid by American consumers. The reason the tariff was imposed, in spite of its costs, is because of the political situation in the U.S. In calculating our response, we cannot ignore the fact that as they were shooting us in the foot, the Americans also, in effect, shot themselves as well.

How can we deal with a country bent on such-self injury? The answer is that we must ignore their assault and press on with even greater resolve to negotiate a free trade agreement with a legally binding process for resolving such trade irritants outside the political process. At the very least, we should use this current difficulty to silence once and for all those who argue against a free trade agreement on the grounds that jobs will be lost. *M.W.*

TAX BURDEN

Ever since 1975 the Fraser Institute has been working on a project called the Canadian Tax Simulator. This is a computer package that enables us to simulate the total tax burden faced by the average Canadian family. We analyse some 26 tax categories, 21 different sources of income, and the activities of three levels of government. The result is a complete, if somewhat distressing, picture of the tax and income situation of the average Canadian family.

In 1986, the average family earned an income from all sources of about $33,500. On such an income, the family paid a total tax bill of about $17,400. If you happen to have committed the Canadian Tax Act to memory, you will immediately see that this is nearly three times the amount of income tax that a taxpayer in this bracket would pay. The reason is that the tax bill of the average Canadian family is now composed mostly of taxes other than the income tax. Property taxes, import duties, amusement taxes, licence fees, energy taxes, transit levies, direct and hidden sales taxes, profit taxes, social security taxes, liquor, tobacco, and excise taxes, as well as a host of other too numerous to mention now make up two-thirds of the total tax bill. That tax bill now makes up 51.9 percent of total income for the average family and absorbs a greater chunk of their budget than the total of food, shelter, and clothing combined.

That's a complete turnaround since 1961 when the biggest problem Canadians had was feeding, clothing and sheltering themselves. Now the biggest problem is the extent to which we are taxed. *M.W.*

TAX EXPENDITURES

Does the government subsidize the people of the country by neglecting to tax them on all their earnings? That, in a nutshell, is the essence of the dispute over tax deductions, tax credits, tax concessions, tax expenditures, loopholes, preferences, and tax shelters. Examples include multi-unit residential buildings, capital gains exemptions, oil drilling, and movie and film investments.

There are two schools of thought on this issue. According to one viewpoint, whenever government fails to collect a tax that would otherwise be due (under an alternative law) it is equivalent to a subsidy. This oversight reduces its revenues by this amount, and this is the same as if the government had first taxed the money away from us and then given it back in the form of a subsidy.

Let's use the exemption for charitable donations as an example. Mr. A contributes $100 to the XYZ Foundation. Because of his tax bracket, he can save $25 on his total tax bill. What is that, according to this line of thought, but a government grant of $25 to Mr. A (and indirectly to XYZ)? Had government not allowed the exemption, it would have cost Mr. A roughly $125 to donate the same $100 to XYZ. The difference? A subsidy from all the taxpayers, ultimately to XYZ. It is just as if government had given away $25 of its revenues.

Nor are we talking peanuts here. According to the finance department, which publishes an annual accounting of such tax expenditures, the cost of loopholes in the personal income tax alone was $23.4 billion for 1980. The following statistics are reported by W.T. Stanbury and John L. Howard in *Probing Leviathan* (The Fraser Institute, 1984): corporate tax concessions were 67 percent of all such taxes collected in 1973, 75 percent in 1974, and 69 percent in 1975. Based on these findings, Stanbury and Howard estimate that had cash subsidies been used instead of forgone tax revenues, the federal budget would have been almost 50 percent larger than it was in 1979.

But there is a second school of thought on the question of tax expenditures. In this view, the tax expenditure philosophy rests on the implicit and illegitimate premise that government really owns the entire gross national product; that the public sector could, if it wished, claim this entire amount for itself; that when it does not do so, it in effect gives back to the citizens money which rightfully belongs to it, the state; hence, the concept of tax subsidies.

But this is not the proper relationship between the citizen and the state in a democracy. The individual, not the government, owns what he earns. In the classical liberal, limited government society, the citizen gives up part of his income to ensure the provision of certain essential goods and services, but only he is the rightful claimant of the remainder. The government does not "give" it to him by refraining from taxing it away from him. It is his own money. To fail to tax is thus not to subsidize.

Let us consider an analogy. During the era of slavery, which ended in North America in 1865, how could we describe the relationship between the white slave holders in the Confederacy and the blacks who were still living free in Africa? If we adopted the tax subsidy way of looking at the world, we should have to say that the slave masters were subsidizing the unenslaved black Africans by refraining from enslaving them. A manifest absurdity, since the whites had no right whatsoever over the lives of the blacks.

A second difficulty arises in the compilation of statistical measures of "tax expenditures." Such attempts depend on an arbitrary and illegitimate distinction. It is the distinction between the tax revenues uncollected by government as a result of specific tax enactments (MURB, AHOR, RHOSP, tax write-offs for oil drilling, films, capital gains) and all other untaxed income.

If tax expenditures are merely potential revenues the state chooses not to collect, then all untaxed income is a tax subsidy. Tax expenditures could be simply calculated, without fuss or fanfare, as GNP minus total tax revenues. Apart from destroying jobs in the economics profession, such a measurement would have the drawback of rigourous honesty. It would lay bare, once and for all, the essence of tax expenditures and their fatal flaw. *W.B.*

TAX FREEDOM DAY

We hope you work extra hard on Tax Freedom Day, because for the first time in nearly six months you will have been working for yourself. Until roughly noon on that day, you were working for the various levels of government—it took you until then to accumulate enough income to pay the total amount of taxes you are obliged to pay to the various levels of government. (For the exact date on which Tax Freedom Day falls for each of the provinces and for all of Canada, consult the Fraser Institute publication *Tax Facts*.)

We are not just talking about personal income taxes or property taxes or sales taxes. Also included are the 51 different categories of tax that you pay as a Canadian: the profit tax you pay via your retirement savings plan, the business tax you pay when you have a meal in a restaurant, the various sales and excise taxes hidden in the price of many of the products you buy, the natural resource taxes, royalties, and the licence fees government collects on your behalf on your resources but which you never see.

Some years ago the Fraser Institute began to compile a collection of statistics on the total tax situation faced by the average Canadian. We've been publishing these statistics now for seven years and for three years have been highlighting our findings in the declaration of Tax Freedom Day. Evidently, it is not a day which will ever receive an official government proclamation to mark its passing, but we believe it is an important indicator of the relationship between government and its citizens.

You don't have to be an economist to realize that government is spending an enormous amount of money these days, some of this admittedly to provide services which many would find desirable to have provided even if government were not doing this. What many of us have not recognized is the extent to which this expansion of the government sector is eating into our ability as individuals to control the incomes we are responsible for producing. Incidentally, if you are thinking about the impact of the Canadian deficit—which, remember, is only taxation deferred to a future year—you may be interested to know that the average Canadian would have had to work until August 15th to pay the tax bill this year if, instead of financing its expenditures by deficits, the Government of Canada had simply increased tax rates to balance the budget. Perhaps that explains to some extent why deficit financing is so popular with governments.

Happy Tax Freedom Day! *M.W.*

TAXI LICENSING

New York City has done it again. Always the biggest, and sometimes the best, the Big Apple has just set another sort of record.

For the first time in its history, a taxi medallion has been sold for a cool $100,000. This is in U.S. currency, of course, in Canadian dollars its $125,000. (The situation in this country is serious but not as critical. The value of medallions in our cities is still far less, so perhaps there is time to learn from the mistakes committed south of our border.)

The reason for this startling event in Gotham is not too difficult to explain. The number of medallions (licences to drive a cab) in New York City has remained frozen at 11,787 ever since 1937! But in the last 50 years Gotham has grown quite a bit and, with increased affluence the taxi-riding public has increased by even more. As a result, the value of a legal permit to pick up and deliver passengers on the streets of New York has skyrocketed and has now reached its present six-figure height.

This situation is highly problematic for several reasons. First of all, the consumer—especially when it rains or during the late evening and early morning hours—is ofttimes forced to go without taxi service. This phenomenon, no doubt, is in large part responsible for the jokes New Yorkers tell about the difficulty of finding a cab when you want one. (But it is not much of a joke for the city's minority group members of all races and personalities who are often discriminated against by cab drivers.

Secondly, there is the plight of the would-be new entrant to the taxi business. Imagine the barrier he faces. Not only must he be able to purchase an automobile and keep its gas tank full, he must somehow come up with an even $100,000! This, of course, all but rules out any immigrant, young person, or minority group member. At best, such people can get jobs in the industry driving cabs owned by others, but ownership of their own taxi business is simply beyond the means of all but the very rich.

New York's feisty Mayor Ed Koch has come up with a plan to increase the number of medallions by 1,200, or some 10 percent of the total. But the taxi interests, and the major banks which hold the mortgages on these permits, have howled in anguish and outrage, and it is not hard to see why. If we assume that all taxi licences could sell at the $100,000 price, the total book value of the 11,787 medallions is $1,178,700,000 or almost $1.2 billion.

Any large-scale increase in the number of cabs permitted on the streets would eat into these values and create vast losses for many in the industry.

What should be done? The status quo defends the property values of the medallion owners, but it violates the public interest, inconveniences the consumer, freezes out new entrants, and enhances discrimination against minority group members. No matter what decision is finally arrived at, the interests of at least some people will be harmed. Increasing the medallions by 10 percent, or by any other amount, might slightly alleviate some of the symptoms of the problem and could be seen as a reasonable compromise, but it would only perpetuate a patently unjust system. The only just solution is to end the system of entry barriers to taxi driving in one fell swoop. This could be done by announcing that, henceforth, no medallions are necessary for taxi ownership. Anyone can own and drive a cab, provided only that safety and insurance requirements are met. This would ensure that customers were supplied with cabs and that all those wishing to own and drive cabs would at last have this opportunity.

Wouldn't this solution be unjust to all those who in good faith purchased the now worthless taxi medallions? It would be no more unfair to the present cab owners than it was unjust to free the slaves without compensating the slaveholders.

Legislative sittings have been called "futures markets in stolen property." Anyone who makes a purchase in this "futures market"—such as the owner of a taxi medallion or of a slave—deserves to lose his entire investment when the scheme is finally exposed as the theft it is and the legislation is repealed.

Another common objection to a completely free market in taxi cabs is that there will be too many such vehicles on the road. If anyone is free to enter, goes the argument, everyone will. This objection misunderstands a basic premise of economics. Profit tends to equalize across all industries. If so many cabs entered the field such that none of them could move, much less make a living, many would be forced to leave. This would occur until the remuneration that could be earned behind the wheel tended to equal that which could be earned elsewhere, with due consideration given to the skills needed, the working conditions, and so forth. The market has its own system of checks and balances. Government is hardly needed to ensure that there are not too many participants in any one industry and too few in another. *W.B.*

TECHNOLOGICAL UNEMPLOYMENT

There is a new piece of nonsense making the rounds these days. It goes something like this. New technology means more productivity. More productivity means that you need fewer employees. herefore, high tech means more unemployment, more social distress, and is something which must be managed very carefully by government to ensure there is a minimum amount of social dislocation. Government will have to create a lot more jobs to employ those displaced by the new technology.

The historical experience in Europe and in North America simply does not support this view of the world. One of the best pieces of evidence to refute this theory of the impact of technology is the Japanese experience. In the course of the last 30 years, productivity per employee in Japan has been rising at an average rate of 6 percent annually. At least some of that productivity increase has been due to the very highest of technology employed in industries which have been technological laggers in North America. If this theory about the effect of technology on employment was correct, you would expect the Japanese to have a very severe problem of joblessness. Quite the contrary is true. Japanese unemployment levels are typically around 3 percent—a level that we in North America can only dream about.

Why has the seemingly inevitable consequence of job-displacing technological advance not had its effect in Japan? The reason is simply that technology does not in total displace employment. Increasing productivity means that for the same cost more can be produced. It also means that the same goods can be sold at lower prices. To the extent that increased productivity is passed along to consumers in terms of lower prices, they will have more income to spend on things other than the commodities which are now being produced more efficiently. This explains why the

Japanese have become the world's consummate consumers of every conceivable kind of gadget and implement.

While the Japanese have been growing by leaps and bounds at rates which see their productivity double every 11 years, Canadian productivity growth has been dismal and has scarcely doubled in 30 years. Unless there is a return to the kind of productivity increases technology can provide, especially in our world competitive industries, we will simply stagnate. The real threat from technology is not that we will lose jobs by adopting it but that we will lose out because our competitors abroad adopt it and make our manufacturers uncompetitive in world markets. *M.W.*

TIP TAX

As people become more ingenious in evading taxation, governments (with their voracious requirement for revenue) must become ever more aggressive, intrusive, and coercive in their pursuit of errant taxpayers. The Province of Quebec has made clear the extent to which governments may be prepared to go in this regard. While in Sweden the authorities have pressed ordinary citizens into the role of squealer on their fellow citizens, the Province of Quebec has indicated that it may enlist restaurant owners as tax collectors.

The problem is restaurant tips. The government is worried that waiters and waitresses are not declaring their tips as income and, hence, are not paying their tax. In Quebec, the provincial government collects all the taxes and administrative questions of this sort are a provincial as opposed to a federal matter. Under Bill 43, waiters and waitresses will have to calculate their tips every week and report the amount to their employer who will deduct the amount owing from their salary and remit the taxes to government. Another provision of the Bill would have the restaurateur levy a tax of 8 percent of sales directly on his employees—giving up any pretense of voluntary assessment. Restaurant owners and workers alike have not been amused by these developments. Their hostile demonstrations in Quebec City have caused the government to proceed with caution but, of course, the tax remains.

The interesting question that arises in connection with this and much of the other brouhaha that has arisen about taxation in the country is the whole question of voluntary assessment. To what extent do people really support the programmes and expenditures of government which allegedly are being undertaken on their behalf? Some economists who specialize in an area called public choice have long maintained that the ballot box is a very poor means to reflect the actual preferences of citizens about how they want their money spent—even their tax money. The problem is that it isn't selective enough. One has only one vote to cast and this has to cover, in the case of the federal government, more than $100 billion worth of expenditures on different and varied programmes.

Does the fact that government is having to use ever more intrusive and coercive measures to collect the tax bill reveal something, per chance, about how people feel about government? If people felt they were getting value for money in the expenditures and activities of government, wouldn't they feel less inclined to object to paying their tax bill? Negative reactions to the tax requirements of government do, indeed, reflect public sentiment about those programmes and activities. It is no coincidence that the increasing attention being focused on taxation is occurring at a time when there is an evident decline in people's acceptance of a grandiose role for government in our society.

It is important to remember that the great historical surges in the rights of the individual, such as the Magna Carta and the American Constitution, were precipitated by taxation not supported by popular sentiment. Modern governments would be less than perceptive to ignore emerging developments in this respect. *M.W.*

TRANSFER SOCIETY

Nowadays, it is unfortunately the business of politicians to redistribute income from one group in society to another. Politicians are quite regularly elected on platforms which involve providing benefits to particular special interests and, in fact, most of the concern of political parties and government bureaucracies is to handle the flow of funds from the paying group to the receiving group. For the most part, the collection agency in this redistribution process is the tax department. Government passes laws which enable it to take money from citizens as taxpayers which it returns to them in a variety of other guises.

You may be wondering why this process works. Why are people willing to be bought with their own money? The answer is simple. The taxes collected by government are spread across many taxpayers. Each of us individually contributes only a small amount to any particular transfer which goes to a particular group or individual. For example, Mr. Macdonald's $800 a day salary (for the royal commission on the economy) cost each person the princely sum of only three-quarters of one cent. It doesn't really pay anyone to get on a soap box to complain about this three-quarters of one cent in the same way that it doesn't pay us to complain about the four or five cents or the $2 or $10 taken from us to provide subsidies to industrial concerns which are friends of the government. Moreover, some of us, each of us in our own way, perceive that we are benefiting from some of these transfers. Each will have their own special concern which we perceive as being supported by government, and we are very happy to participate in the process of taking money from others via the tax system to support our own pet project. In this sense, politicians in an election campaign curry favour and win votes by promising to pay to one group or special interest what they will, upon being elected, take away from taxpayers in general or from some other politically less important group.

It is not at all surprising that in this process of sloshing money around between citizens some of it is conveyed to people who may have a political affiliation with the government. We don't like it when we lose thereby, however, we are all guilty of engaging in precisely the same kind of process when we demand political support for our own pet hobby-horse. *M.W.*

TUITION FEES

Few subjects attract more attention than the issue of educational funding. The most prevalent issue in this area is what will happen to educational funding in the light of fiscal restraint. In provinces like British Columbia and Ontario, actions or policy proposals involve a tightening of the allocations to the university system as well as an indication that students will be required to pay a larger fraction of the total cost of their education.

The upper middle class are not amused by this development. At first encounter, the issue appears to be a concern for social values. Education is a valuable asset, not only for the individual who acquires it but for the community at large. More funding ought to be dedicated to education simply because it is a demonstrably valuable feature for the population.

However, it does not follow that simply because education is valuable, spending more public funds on it will increase society's welfare or even the welfare of the student. It is difficult, if not impossible, for administrators either in the university system itself or in the Treasury to know whether extra dollars dedicated to education are contributing more to individual or societal welfare. The value of a "soft" course like a Bachelor of Fine Arts is often "objectively" viewed as less valuable at the margin than a "hard" course like a Bachelor's degree in Engineering. But, if the recipient of the Fine Arts degree has in mind a career in rock music, folk singing, painting, or sculpting (for which the general populace is willing to amply reward the individual, particularly as our society spends more and more of its time in diversions and entertainment), the dollars invested in that particular soft course may yield a higher rate of return both for the individual and society. Ultimately, it is only the individual who can assess the probability of success and therefore the desirability of making an investment in education.

While it is almost a matter of dogma that those who oppose education cuts are on the side of enlightenment and a future for our children and those who oppose them are troglodytes, neither of these positions can, in terms of the marginal dollar of expense, be justified by an appeal to the facts. From a long-term point of view, society's and the individual's interests will be best served if the individual receiving the education is the one who decides how and in what direction extra dollars should be applied.

Another reason for the conundrum surrounding post-secondary education funding is the widespread belief that continued public sector involvement makes education available for low income students who might otherwise be prevented from acquiring an education. While that may, to some extent, be true, calculations in the Fraser Institute study *Who Benefits from Government Spending?* suggest that at least 70 percent of those in attendance at post-secondary institutions come from families whose incomes are above the national average.

Moreover, about 70 percent of those who receive a post-secondary education will themselves have an income above the average, and half of them will find themselves in the very highest income group. In other words, to the extent that educational funding is a redistributive process, it redistributes income from those whose incomes are below the average to those whose incomes are above the average. Viewed purely as a redistributive device, post-secondary education institutions are a very imperfect and, from the point of view of the primary objective, very inefficient (even more inefficient than the so-called universal programmes), not to say perverse.

Many of those who are aware of this, support the system anyway on the grounds that lower income Canadians benefit from the activities of those with higher educations. The better educated the populace is, the more advanced the society will be and, therefore, the better off everybody will be. A kind of cultural trickle-down theory! By its very nature, this hypothesis is difficult if not impossible to test. It is, however, interesting to inquire what distribution of benefit between the individual who receives the education and society as a whole supporters of such a proposition have in mind. At the very maximum, this split would be a fifty-fifty proposition with society benefiting 50 percent and the individual benefiting 50 percent from the education he or she receives. Students, however, are currently asked to pay only about 15 percent of the cost of education.

It would appear that there are three very good reasons for insisting that university students pay a higher fraction if not the entire cost of their education. First, it would ensure a more certain efficiency in the allocation of resources to the education sector. Secondly, much of the public expenditure on education now amounts to a very regressive system of redistribution. And, thirdly, insisting on a higher fraction of user-pay would more closely approximate the distribution of benefit between the individual and society. *M.W.*

U

UNDERGROUND ECONOMY

It has finally been made official. What economists and others have been saying for years has been recognized by the United States government. An increasing amount of economic activity in North America is occurring in the "underground economy," that is to say, economic activity which occurs beyond the scrutiny of a country's statisticians.

The Economic Studies Branch of the U.S. Census Bureau has released estimates suggesting that in the United States the underground or unobserved economy amounts to about $222 billion. That places the estimate of the U.S. government, which must be regarded as an absolute bottom, low-ball estimate, at about two-thirds the size of the entire Canadian economy. In other words, day-in and day-out in the United States there occurs unobserved economic activity roughly equivalent to two-thirds of the income produced in all of Canada.

This estimate of the Census Bureau follows a variety of estimates provided last year by the U.S. Department of Commerce on the extent of illegal drug activity in the United States. The Department of Commerce estimated, for example, that marijuana was America's fourth largest cash crop. However, while illegal activity does comprise some of the underground economy, it is not the largest portion nor is it the most significant reason for its existence. On the contrary, the most important reason is the system of regulation and taxation imposed by governments. People don't declare their moonlighting income because of the high tax rate to which it is exposed. People and businesses barter because in this process they can avoid monetary transactions which lead not only to taxation but also to regulation of their activities. While the U.S. Census Bureau estimates of the size of the underground economy now provide official recognition of the extent of this avoidance behaviour, there is not yet any indication that governments understand its implications.

In Scandinavia, the size of the underground economy has grown to such proportions that government has passed a series of tattle-tale regulations applying to income taxation. Now, on their income tax returns, Swedes must report payments they have made to others. This is, of course, to entrap the greedy cleaning lady who goes about her business without due regard for the income requirements of the state. The very necessity for such laws points to the fact that the citizenry will no longer voluntarily support the level of taxation and the extent of regulation for which governments have developed an appetite.

In the Canadian case, estimates of the size of the underground economy made in the Fraser Institute book *Probing Leviathan* suggest that it ranges from $38 to $60 billion per year, and is growing by leaps and bounds. It remains to be seen whether that growth will lead to the same kind of big brotherish intrusions into private affairs which have begun to evidence themselves in Scandinavia. Maybe the increased activity of Revenue Canada and their tax auditors, which has recently received notoriety, is the leading edge of such developments.

The development of an underground economy is a very healthy sign that markets will survive even the most blundering and abusive activities of governments. Its existence should be acknowledged as a safety valve for the economic process. Its size and growth should also indicate to governments the extent to which, political rhetoric apart, their actions do not enjoy the popular support of citizens. Those who seek shelter in the underground economy are, in effect, refugees from a tax and expenditure process which they no longer wish to support. *M.W.*

UNEMPLOYMENT INSURANCE

The plight of those who are less fortunate economically takes some of the joy away from the high level of economic affluence enjoyed by Canadians. Constant reminders of food lines and unemployment rolls in TV broadcasts and radio stories of food lines and unemployment rolls force one to reflect on the plight of the less fortunate. Even though our enjoyment is not at their expense, the existence of their misery dilutes our happiness.

While we should feel sympathy for the disadvantaged, it is also important to have a perspective about their plight and realize that there is a certain natural tendency in the media to focus disproportionately on that aspect of our society. The extent to which we can be misled by reporting of the "facts" is brought forcefully to our attention when we realize that very few individuals, having exhausted their unemployment insurance benefits, take refuge on the welfare rolls. It caused something of a national commotion when it was revealed that only 7 percent of those who exhausted their benefits under unemployment insurance found themselves on welfare. The other 93 percent either miraculously found jobs at precisely the time their unemployment insurance expired, had no need of income support in the first place, or found other means of sustaining themselves.

It was the view of professional observers that a very high proportion of those exhaustees found work once their unemployment insurance benefits ran out and that this was the single most important explanation for the failure to observe a swelling of welfare rolls when people were terminated under the unemployment insurance programme.

This statistic is particularly important when interpreting the machinations of certain social critics who point to the fact that our actual unemployment rate is a very low estimate of the total amount of unemployment because of the so-called discouraged worker effect. That is, that some people simply give up looking for work after they have tried and tried to no avail to find work. The unanswered question is how do those people sustain themselves when they leave the unemployment insurance rolls? Very few of them are forced to avail themselves of welfare. The most important implication of the transferal figures is the fact that for a very large number of people unemployment is a choice, an option preferred to other possibilities which are less onerous than the task of applying for social welfare assistance.

While nothing about these figures should lead us to be complacent about the problem of unemployment, they should serve to provide a certain perspective on the plight of the unemployed and to remind us that the generous provision of unemployment support does cause some people to choose to be unemployed. This choice is not made in preference to the dole but in preference to some other option they have available to them.

A dramatic instance of this phenomenon occurred on Canada Day of 1984. The unemployment insurance fund produced an unexpected benefit for some Ontario residents in that many were invited to pick strawberries free of charge on the property of Norfolk Region Berryfarmers. The public was invited in free of charge because otherwise the berries would go to waste as local farmers found it impossible to get enough labourers to pick the crop. According to the local farmers, the reason for the problem was the fact that new unemployment insurance regulations require farmers to complete Record of Employment forms for all employees. Many of the usual berry pickers apparently weren't interested in work if it involved reporting the fact.

One farmer, Mr. Peter Shabatura, found that less than a third of the normal 350 workers he needs to pick his berries were showing up daily. Mr. Shabatura finally solved his problem by advertising that he was not going to fill out the required forms, an action with which the neighbouring farmers have all concurred.

UIC forms themselves are designed allegedly to help the workers. New regulations permit farm workers the same eligibility as other workers for unemployment insurance. Farm workers are now eligible for benefits if they work 15 hours or earn $77 a week from one employer instead of the previous requirement that they were insurable only after earning at least $250 and working 25 days for the same employer. Apparently, most farm workers aren't interested in the paper trail implied by the new regulations.

It is not until we contemplate why workers would not want the government forms filled out that we begin to see the real lesson from the farmers' experience. Undoubtedly, some workers simply can't be bothered to work if that involves paying unemployment insurance premiums. On the other hand, that is a very small imposition for a couple of week's work, and it would ultimately entitle the worker to unemployment insurance compensation at the end of the picking season.

It seems most likely that the "formo-phobics" must have been motivated by other considerations. Migrant workers or people in the country illegally, for example, would not want their work activity reported. But others, and these just might be the majority, are people already receiving government assistance in one form or another. They would stand to lose those benefits or, even worse, be convicted of fraud if the fact that they were working was to be recorded.

There is an increasing amount of evidence that the social support programmes in the country are, in fact, maintaining many individuals who do have other sources of employment. Take, for example, the exotic dancers in suburban nightclubs south of Montreal who were recently found to be collecting welfare cheques while working. Of 53 women investigated in conjunction with liquor licensing and other aspects of nightclub operation, 25 were charged with fraud for failing to declare their incomes as dancers to provincial welfare officers.

Any suggestion that many of the recipients of welfare benefits might not need them is bound to lead to branding the speaker as a redneck. But it is true that every time there is an opportunity to get indirect evidence on the extent to which the system may be abused we do in fact find abuse. At what point will there be enough evidence to suggest that the social welfare system is becoming a hammock for a variety of individuals who most taxpayers would not agree to support in indolence if they had the opportunity to make the decision? *M.W.*

U U U U U U U U U U U U U U U U U U U U U U

UNFUNDED LIABILITIES

What do the Workers' Compensation Board, Canada Pension Plan, and the Canada Public Service Pension Plan all have in common? The answer is that they all have unfunded liabilities. Great, you say—what's an unfunded liability? Basically, it is a complicated deficit.

Unfunded liabilities are calculated by first working out what the total benefit payments of a plan will be for the foreseeable future, assuming that no new claimants are added. Having in this way calculated the total liabilities of the fund, actuaries then calculate what the current contribution rates will produce in income to the fund over the same period of time. The difference between total liabilities and total accumulations of income is what is referred to as the unfunded liability.

Unfunded liabilities are common to public and private pension plans, but in the case of the latter the unfunded liability must be covered by increased contribution rates over some reasonable period of time. In its periodic review of a company's pension plan, the actuary may discover an unfunded liability. In order to cover it, the firm must increase its contribution rates to the plan so that over a period, perhaps 15 years, the unfunded liability would be eliminated.

Public funds and plans are not typically subjected to the rigours applied to private arrangements, however. For example, the Workers' Compensation Board, the focus of considerable agitation, will not increase contribution rates in spite of the acknowledged existence of an unfunded liability of half a billion dollars or more. There may be a whole range of reasons why such increases are not being made, not the least of which may be that even current rates are economically infeasible. The fact of a very significant deficit is quite typical of public bodies of this sort. *M.W.*

UNION BOYCOTT

It's not a pretty story. Alderman Bill Sorenson of North Vancouver City voted to contract out the municipal garbage collection services to private enterprise. To add insult to injury—at least in the eyes of Local 389 of the Canadian Union of Public Employees—he also voted for a wage freeze covering all city employees. The union didn't take long to strike back.

Sorenson is the operations manager for the North Shore Community Credit Union, a local banking facility. As it happens, Local 389 of CUPE holds deposits with this credit union. In response to Alderman Sorenson's votes on city council, the Union withdrew $25,000 of its funds from banker Sorenson's employers.

This decision to withdraw funds was no mere coincidence. It was motivated by spite—an attempt to get back at a part-time politician by attacking him in his role as a private citizen. As a result of this act, Mr. Sorenson resigned his seat on city council—it isn't clear if he did this rather than face firing or a request to resign from his employer.

According to pundits, this sorry spectacle was a threat to democracy. Said one editorialist, "it was a mean, cheap tactic on the part of a trade union, and no credit to the labour movement as a whole." Mean? Yes. Cheap? Yes. Petty? Again, yes. But let's put things in perspective. The union, and all other depositors for that matter, have every right in the world to withdraw funds at any time they wish for whatever reason seems sufficient to them. That, after all, is the meaning of a demand deposit. Such an arrangement is the embodiment on a contract between two mutually consenting parties, the depositor and the lending institution. In choosing to withdraw $25,000 even for this spiteful reason, CUPE Local 389 was completely within its moral and legal rights. The $25,000 is owned by the union. It and it alone has the sole right to determine its place of investment. Neither Mr. Sorenson, nor the credit union for which he works, has any right to determine where, how, or whether this money shall be invested. Certainly, their rights have not been abridged by the decision of the proper owners to withdraw the money from the care of the bank.

Not only has the union every right to withdraw its funds for this reason, but other groups in society act in the same way—

without the wailing and gnashing of teeth visited upon CUPE. Does anyone really doubt that corporations deposit and withdraw their funds in accordance with what they perceive as their best interests? Certainly, church groups have publicly withdrawn holdings from banks which have invested in South Africa. Consumers continually pick and choose amongst the stores they will shop at, partially on the basis of boycotting merchants who displease them, sometimes on the most subjective of grounds. Why should unions be singled out for opprobrium for stewardship of their own money?

Then there is the difficulty of legally prohibiting such behaviour. How could government stop this practice without telling everyone how to spend and invest private property? Any attempt to stop such practices would surely involve us in the scenario warned against by George Orwell in his book *1984*.

Contrary to the political commentators, this act of boycott is a credit to the union movement as a whole, certainly when compared to other acts which are essential ingredients of organized labour. Canadian unions, as a matter of institutional arrangement, are commonly allowed to invoke the coercive power of government in order to pursue their own commercial goals. This is practically a defining characteristic. Organized labour is one of the few institutions in our society permitted to use the threat of fines and/or jail sentences to prohibit competition.

This is a reference, of course, to the manner in which competitors to union jobs are treated. They are branded as scabs and pariahs. Canadian law forces the employer to "bargain fairly" with the union and thus prohibits him from dealing with those who would compete for the jobs of organized workers. Even though mutually agreeable contracts could be made between employers and "scabs" for the jobs and pay scales rejected by striking workers, our labour legislation forbids such an occurrence.

So there we have it. On the one hand, a union boycott which violates no rights but which is roundly condemned by commentators, and on the other hand, the union practice of restricting entry to employment which is a patent violation of the rights of every non-union, would-be competitor for these jobs. Yet this immoral practice is condemned by practically no one, and even enjoys the prestige and protection of Canadian law. *W.B.*

UNION EXPLOITATION

Unions depict themselves as a protection for the working class against the inroads of the marauding capitalist. For this purpose, so they say, they must not only have the money to conduct collective bargaining but also to represent the general interest of workers in lobbying for particular legislation and supporting political parties that represent the interest of workers.

There is an implicit assumption that unions do in fact represent the interests of workers. However, a study of unionization in the United States calls into question the accuracy of this assumption. The study suggests that in areas of the United States where the unionized percentage of the labour force is large, or where the union/non-union wage premium is large, workers are less likely to be employed. Moreover, those who are employed are more likely to have a part-time job than in areas where unionization is less strong. These effects were more likely to be experienced by females and young men than by prime age males. It is, of course, true that education and basic economic conditions were more important factors explaining employability, however, the fact that unionization has any effect on the employment levels of these two groups suggests that unions are not the universally positive influence that is sometimes suggested. *M.W.*

UNION FREE ZONES

A union free economic zone is only one variant of an idea that is now sweeping the world. In the general case, a free enterprise zone is a special geographical area in a country within which the usual prohibitions—red tape, regulations, intervention, and bureaucracy—do not apply. Government involvement is limited to providing for the public safety—protecting the persons and property of the inhabitants. As well, there are limited free enterprise zones, where only one or a few industries are freed of government interference. There are free banking zones, free insurance zones, free gambling zones, free trade zones where tariffs do not apply, and union free zones, where unions are not allowed.

What are the advantages of union free economic zones? Simply this. They will help create additional employment. The major economic cause of unemployment is government mandated wage rates in excess of productivity levels. If the union demands $17 per hour but the worker can only produce goods and services worth $13 per hour, something has to give. Either the employer will refuse to comply in the first place or will eventually be driven bankrupt. This is perhaps the entire *raison d'être* of labour unions—to drive wages up and up in strict disregard for the productivity levels where wages would otherwise be set.

Our union legislation was enacted in the first place because many people thought that without unions wages would be set at levels dictated by employers. In point of fact, this is untrue. Wages are determined by employee productivity and competition between employers, not at the whim of the boss. We know this because we cannot otherwise account for rising wages before the advent of unions in the late 18th century, or in industries untouched by organized labour—such as domestic service, legal secretaries, and computer programmers, and in places such as Hong Kong, the Philippines, and the southern and southwestern states in the U.S. where unions are weak or nonexistent.

Were union free economic zones instituted, those who favoured unions would merely stay away. Outside these zones, they would still be able to avail themselves of the benefits they perceive are afforded by unions. In contrast, only those hardy souls who were willing to take their chances in a geographical area where present labour codes did not apply would enter the union free zones.

Critics claim that free enterprise zones exist only in the Third World, in countries which have dictatorships, or something close to it, and which suffer from extreme poverty. In fact, this claim is at complete variance with the facts. Free enterprise zones of one variety or another are by no means limited to the impoverished nations of the Third World. On the contrary, there are hundreds located in Europe, the U.S., and the Far East. According to a study on this subject published by the Fraser Institute entitled *Free Market Zones*, as of 1980 there were roughly 90 such zones in Europe, 80 in Latin America, 60 in the U.S., 50 in Africa, 35 in thc Far East, and 20 in the Middle East. Since 1980 the numbers have grown. For example, the People's Republic of China had four zones in 1980 and has announced the creation of 14 more.

Canada is practically alone in not having even one free enterprise zone. This is particularly regrettable given their success elsewhere in the world. *W.B.*

UNION POWER

One of the most vexing aspects of the modern economy is the relationship between wages, unionism, and unemployment. For their part, unions maintain that they are society's bulwark against the actions of rapacious capitalists in the ruthless pursuit of profit. They offer the view that the standard of living enjoyed by the average worker is in large measure due to the union's ceaseless effort to keep wages in line.

Economists, on the other hand, in observing the economic forces at work in the country's labour markets, have a different view. They have observed that in spite of the growth of unionization there has been little or no effect on the relative share of profits and wages in the gross national income pie. Economists have inferred that unions have their effect on wages by effectively restricting the supply of labour to particular occupations. By ensuring that all workers in a particular occupation are unionized and that the members adhere to union disciplines, the competition which might otherwise be provided by people willing to work for less than union wages is pre-empted. In raising the wages of their members, unions are successful only because the wages of excluded workers are lower. In the end, total wealth falls due to the misallocation effect, and the existence of minimum wage laws translates the exclusionary activities of unions into unemployment.

While the theoretical niceties of all of this leave most of us cold, two events provide some concrete evidence on the matter. The first event was the suspension by the federal Minister of Finance, Marc Lalonde, of the application of the federal Fair Wages and Hours of Labour Act in the provinces of Nova Scotia and Ontario. This act by the finance minister was prompted by his government's intention to keep costs on federal projects in line with the government's six and five restraint programme in the face of four recent construction wage settlements providing for increases well above the guidelines.

The Fair Wages and Hours of Labour Act provides that firms tendering for federal construction projects have to pay workers no less than wages currently reigning in the region or province. The effect of the law was, of course, to eliminate the possibility for wage-cutting non-unionized construction firms to compete for federal construction contracts. Correspondingly, it limited the employment prospects for those non-union members excluded from employment in construction by the high wage levels set by their unionized counterparts. The fact that the federal contracts were open to effective competitive bidding had a dramatic effect on the cost of federal projects. It also gave a boost to low-cost non-union firms in the private sector which then had access to public projects long denied them. Because of the threat this poses to their preserve, union reaction to the federal government's move was prompt and negative.

The other piece of evidence arises in the mind-numbing action of the unionized employees of the British Columbia Place Stadium taking strike action in support of higher wage demands. Mind-numbing because the 260 employees were selected from a cast of nearly 5,000 applicants for jobs from janitors to ticket-takers a matter of only a few months before. The wage and working conditions offered by management were indicated in general terms, and the workers accepted those conditions in taking the jobs. At the time, Stadium management was negotiating with the Service Employees International Union, which became the bargaining unit for the employees because they had represented the handful of tour guides employed during the construction phase.

The major issue in the dispute was money. The union sought a base rate of $7.00 an hour; B.C. Place had offered $5.70 per hour which was 50 cents above the highest wage offered to employees when they accepted their employment six weeks before.

The B.C. Place labour dispute is not an unusual situation. It is often difficult for a union and an employer to reach a first contract. What is interesting about it, however, is the fact that the unionization and the strike threat came so quickly after the initial employment of the workers. Because of this, the source and impact of the union's power can be clearly observed without the obscuring presence of complicating temporal or other factors.

If Stadium management had the power to declare their inability to reach an agreement with the workers and simply declared the jobs open, there would have been a landslide of applications as there was in the initial hiring period. It is also clear that the only reason the union can demand higher wages—wages higher than the employees themselves willingly accepted a matter of weeks before and higher than would be necessary to attract employees to fill the position—is because the union in this instance has the power to exclude those other willing workers.

As noted above, it is conventional to view unions as a bulwark against the rapacious behaviour of management. The union's role assumes entirely different proportions if we view it from the stance of those excluded workers. From that vantage point, it is much less clear that unionism is reflecting the interests of workers—as opposed to the minority of workers who happen to be members of the union.

These examples provide evidence in support of the economist's view of the impact of unionism and strong corroboration for British Labour thinker Lady Barbara Wootton's view that "it is the business of unions to be anti-social; its members would have a just grievance if their leaders and committees ceased to put sectional interests first." At some point this more accurate perception of union's role in society will become widespread and challenge the mythology informing private and public attitudes toward unions at the present time. When that day of enlightenment comes, the country's Labour Code will have to be brought in touch with reality. *M.W.*

UNION VIOLENCE

There is a conspiracy of mumbles in Canada which is regrettable and surprising. This refers to the apparent implicit agreement not to talk about the violence being directed at individuals in labour disputes. An article in a local newspaper reported an incident wherein a Prince George employee of a Canadian Tire store narrowly escaped injury when a person or persons unknown allegedly fired a shot at her car. The bullet, which entered the drivers side door of clerk Betty Johnson's automobile, was stopped by a metal brace inside the door and came to rest six inches from her body. In the same dispute, a mechanic was caught under a store employee's car apparently tampering with the brakes. Black paint had also been dumped on cars. The owner of the Canadian Tire store has avoided suggesting any union involvement in the incident and union officials, of course, deny any union involvement. It's probably just a coincidence that this violence is occurring while the union is seeking its first contract with Canadian Tire.

A recent strike by teachers provided many instances of intimidating telephone calls, slashed tires, and scratched automobiles. The strike by Hydro gas workers also produced a number of incidents involving professional tampering with gas serving lines. Again, probably just a coincidence. There was no coincidence about the violence used against replacement workers in the recent, highly publicized postal strike. Similarly, there is no denying the video tapes of violence in the Gainers and Superstore strikes in the last few years.

The intriguing thing about these incidents is that they are typically given only the scantiest attention by the media. The abovementioned story about the Prince George employee appeared in a small spot on page 13. Perhaps it is just a coincidence that the report did not bear the by-line of the individual who had written it but was rather attributed to a staff reporter. Again just a coincidence.

One can't suggest that a particular union attempting to get a particular contract with a particular employer is engaging in acts of violence, but one is entitled to ask, "who would benefit from such acts of violence?" Employees refusing to join their fellow employees in striking and the owners of such a struck organization have no interest in perpetrating violence against the firm or against those who work for it. People who do have something to gain are the unions who seek to represent the employees and union leadership in general which seeks to aggrandize its power base in the community. For violence to occur, there does not have to be a plot by union leaders. Individual union members, in the misguided belief that their actions are justified by their industrial dispute, are probably the culprits. But equally to blame is an attitude of tolerance by law enforcement officials who themselves have set aside labour dispute violence as a different and unpoliceable form of behaviour.

It is a comedy of the absurd against the backdrop of this violence to read the conditions governing employers in their communications with employees during a certification procedure. An employer is forbidden from communicating with his employees during the course of a certification drive. He may not use any of the economic facts about his organization to attempt to convince employees that it is not in their interests to form a union because it is not in the interests of the firm and, therefore, not in the interest of their long-term employment. The employer may not do this because it was felt by the drafters of the provincial labour codes that this would provide intimidation of the employees.

As provincial governments approach the issue of redefining and rewriting their labour codes, they must bring an element of rational pragmatism to their deliberations. They must treat the real world as it is and not as some wide-eyed idealists would like it to be. Certainly, a more enthusiastic effort will have to be put into the matter of policing union violence which is the oldest and, evidently, one of the most effective intimidators around. *M.W.*

UNISEX PENSIONS

What is equal treatment of men and women with regard to pensions? Under most private pension plans, for an equal amount of money paid in, women are given smaller pension benefits. On the face of it, this is an inequity crying out to the deity for retribution, not only because of the obvious discrimination but because of its blatantness and its boldness. Insurance companies actually have the audacity to print documents indicating that yearly benefits for women are less than for men! How, in this modern era, could an insurance company ever hope to get away with such a miscarriage of justice?

The U.S. Supreme Court recently dealt with this issue, but it wasn't an open and shut case. Four of the justices voted against conviction while four voted in favour. The fifth and deciding vote in favour was cast by Justice Sandra Day O'Connor. In setting down her judgment that the payment of unequal pension benefits to men and women violated the 1964 Civil Rights Act, Justice O'Connor separated herself from the other four by indicating that this judgment should not be applied retroactively.

The reason the decision was split is because the whole affair is an absurdity. What are the facts? The facts are that men don't live as long as women. On average in Canada, for example, a male can expect to live 70 years; a female, on the other hand, can expect to live 77 years. If they both pay the same amount in total premiums into a plan, and the terms of the pension are that the benefits will be paid until the person expires, the fact that a woman on average is expected to live longer must influence the total amount of money that in each particular year she can draw out. That is a simple fact of arithmetic. That is why a smaller yearly pension benefit is received by a woman who has paid exactly the same amount into a pension plan as a man. But on the average, the total amount paid to women will be the same, because they live longer.

This judgment by the Supreme Court in the United States reflects an attitude which is increasingly prevalent in Canada as well. Here, as well, gender may not be used as a determinant of classification regardless of the characteristics which may be associated with it. In making the determination in the case of pensions that such reliance on gender-related facts constitutes discrimination, the U.S. Supreme Court has revealed a literal-mindedness and meanness of intelligence.

To get the full flavour of this judgment we have to extend its implications into related areas. Take, for example, life insurance, which is very similar in many respects to pensions. Insurance companies are not satisfied with discriminating only on the grounds of sex—they charge men and women of the same age different premiums for the same amount of life insurance. Further, they add insult to injury by inquiring about the age of the person to be insured. A $10,000 life insurance policy for somebody at age 20 costs considerably less than a life insurance policy for the same amount for an individual age 75. Imagine, discriminating against senior citizens.

Absurd you say. Nobody would ever think of linking age-related differentiation as a problem related to discrimination. Why then is it that in several jurisdictions in this country higher automobile insurance rates for those less than 25 years of age who have a demonstrably higher incidence of accidents have been judged to be discriminatory—and therefore eliminated? If it is discrimination to charge different age-related rates on such a frivolous service as automobile insurance, surely it is a travesty to permit it to remain in the area of life insurance. Why charge a 75-year-old higher insurance rates just because the incidence of death amongst 75-year-olds is higher than the incidence of death amongst 20-year-olds?

The preoccupation with discrimination and civil rights, while admirable in intention, must be informed by intelligence and circumspection or it will lead us into a vortex of fallacy. Our own Canadian Civil Rights Commission had already, well in advance of the Supreme Court of the United States, made clear its view that providing different benefits for men and women under a pension plan is discriminatory. If it is increasingly the case that our judiciary and our quasi-judicial boards and panels are to make their decisions in isolation from the facts, they will surely perpetrate more injustice and bring to our society more inequity and plain, ordinary, garden-variety evil than they set out to cure. *M.W.*

UNIVERSALITY

At long last Canadians are beginning to debate some of the central questions surrounding that multi-billion dollar monument to fiscal folly called the federal deficit. While in due course it can be expected that all the stones in it will have to be turned over to reveal the ghosts of budgets past, the most pressing question is what will be done about the so-called universal programmes? While family allowances and old age pensions make up a relatively modest fraction of the federal budget, they are an entré to consideration of the whole gamut of social affairs spending which accounts for 40 cents of every dollar spent by the federal government.

It is not surprising that those opposed to spending cuts have started the debate with a stand in favour of old age pensions and family allowances. These two programmes have readily identifiable fan clubs to whom boosters can appeal. Also, of course, they are highly emotional programmes and politicians are attracted by the heat of emotion like moths to a bright light. But Canadians must not permit themselves to be distracted from the main issue by this hovering cloud.

The main issue is not universality but the pendulous size of the federal deficit. Because of the immense size of the deficit, there will have to be expenditure reductions. The only question is, which expenditures will be reduced and who will bear the burden of restraint? The Fraser Institute has long argued that it makes no sense whatsoever to make payments to Canadians whose incomes are above the average and at the same time regard them as social welfare expenditures; or even, social expenditures. It is surely the height of anti-social behaviour to make payments to those whose incomes are above average as long as the crushing weight of total government spending forces the collection of taxes from those whose incomes are below average.

Universality has the advantage that it eliminates a means test for beneficiaries, but since we must tell all every April on our income tax return anyway that justification has a hollow ring. Besides, what Canadian would feel demeaned by having to indicate that they had an income below the average of $30,000 per year?

Those who lead the cheering section in favour of universal programmes claim to have the interests of the weak and disadvantaged at heart. They should recognize that failure to effectively deal with the problem of the universal programmes may well mean failure to come to grips with the deficit itself. Such a failure will have catastrophic effects on the economy, with the most adverse consequence falling on the shoulders of those who are weak, disadvantaged, and least capable of coping. It is ultimately for that reason that we must dispense with political posturing about universal programmes and get down to the boring, unglamorous, but critical business of controlling federal spending—particularly spending on those who don't need it. *M.W.*

USER FEES

The federal government was concerned with provincial attempts to augment their health care revenues and impose an element of pricing in health care services by levying user fees. This is perceived as a threat to the universality of access which, in the view of some, is the cornerstone of the Canadian health care system. Therefore, the federal government enacted the National Health Act which prohibits user fees. But, is the health care system really jeopardized by fees or extra billing?

It must first be said that government is rising to the defense of a mirage. We do not have universal access to the best possible standard of health care in Canada; we do not have universal access to all medical treatments. We simply can't afford such a system any more than we could afford to provide every Canadian with the best possible standard of housing or automobiles. Kidney and heart transplants, for example, which cost about $200,000 each, cannot be provided to all Canadians who, at this moment are suffering acute kidney and heart failure. Some will receive the replacements, others will simply die. Some nameless, anonymous surgeon or committee of medical bureaucrats will survey those requiring the procedure and, on their best judgement, will select the lucky transplant recipients.

So, there is no universal access where it counts. Everybody cannot be and, as a matter of fact, is not accorded the best possible standard of health care—especially if their lives depend on it. Often, the more crucial the medical procedure, the more expensive and, with increasingly tight medical care budgets, the less available it is. As if that were not bad enough, medical specialists now freely admit that there is a widening gap between the services available in the major hospital centres in this country and those available in the United States—particularly where treatments developed in the last ten years or so are concerned.

There is almost universal access to less crucial medical procedures such as visits to the family doctor—a large number of which are simply not necessary—X-rays, laboratory tests of a pedestrian nature, and other conventional procedures. There is also universal access to hospital beds, though queues are becoming commonplace. In a paradoxical fashion, however, the very existence of this limited universal access provides the biggest single threat to the medical system as we have known it. The reason is simple economics—cost.

Funds used to provide universal access to a growing number of family doctors for the treatment of a hangnail are not available to finance other, more essential, medical services. Funds used to support universal access to hospital beds are not available to purchase kidney transplants or scanning devices or cancer-detecting mammographs. In health care, as in other aspects of life, "both" is not an acceptable answer to the question "which one would you like?"

How does all of this relate to the contentions between the federal and provincial ministers of health? It lies at the core of the issue. At the moment, Canadians have a medical insurance system with first dollar coverage; there is no deductible provision. In consequence, people use more of the universally accessible services than they otherwise would. By imposing user fees, the provinces were, in effect, attempting to impose a deductible feature which would simultaneously raise extra revenue and reduce the extent to which people used the non-essential aspects of the health care system. Since both these developments would increase the amount of money available for life-preserving procedures like kidney transplants, they would have the effect of improving access—where it counts. By directly addressing the unpopular question of user fees, the provincial ministers of health are contributing to the preservation of the health care system whereas the federal government is posing a threat by its opposition.

Unfortunately, the provinces are unlikely to go as far as they should. They could, for example, eliminate about 30 percent of the total health care budget (a saving of some $600 million in the case of B.C.), by changing the form of the health system to a catastrophe protection system—an insurance system that would only protect people from financial ruin as a result of health problems.

The $600 million saving in B.C. would accrue if the provincial government only stood ready to cover medical costs in excess of $1,000 for a given illness. The first $1,000 of medical costs would be borne by the patient. At the moment, such a programme is unthinkable for no other reason than that we have become inured to the notion of free medical coverage.

While we have a healthy disrespect for their monopoly power, nevertheless we do want to applaud medical associations for their stance against the federal government's attempt to eliminate extra billing, or a doctor's right to charge an amount for his services above the amount provided under the province's medical plan. It should be clear that what the government would be eliminating is not extra billing but extra paying. Patients have a choice in all Canadian provinces between doctors who charge an ordinary fee and those who charge more. Patients may choose to patronize those doctors who charge a higher amount than the government fee, and it is with the behaviour of those patients the government is attempting to interfere.

From an economic point of view, extra paying on the part of patients is simply an indication that the government's medical fee schedule is inappropriate. But more importantly, the drive to eliminate extra paying is part of an overall drive to entirely eliminate user charges from the medical care system. This is not in the long-term interests of maintaining high quality medical care in Canada. While it may be a politically attractive idea to offer medical care as a free good, we all know it isn't free. We also know that as long as a lack of user charges encourages us to believe it's free, we're going to use too much of it.

Moreover, international evidence strongly indicates that planning for the future of health care systems requires thinking the unthinkable. For example, the move by the senior unions in the British Trade Union Congress to have their members receive care in private hospitals would have been unthinkable ten years ago. That was before the British National Health Service really began to collapse under the weight of universal access. The British solution must be seen as the greatest threat to our health care system. Unable to remain within the universal system and extra-bill, doctors simply created a parallel private system whose superior treatments were available only to the wealthy. Patients who can afford to do so will be driven, by deterioration in the public system, to private hospitals as the U.K. experience clearly shows. *M.W.*

V

VALUE ADDED TAXES

Economists are generally in favour of the value added tax. In the first place, it has the great advantage that since it applies to just about every item of consumption, it is as neutral as can be hoped for. That is, it does not encourage consumers to prefer one kind of good or service over another simply because the tax applies to one and not the other. For example, the value added tax applies to both laundry services and washing machines. The manufacturers sales tax, on the other hand, applies only to the latter. Accordingly, the manufacturers sales tax provides relative encouragement to purchase laundry services and penalizes purchases of washing machines.

Some economists prefer value added taxes to income taxes because they tax consumption. To the extent that this is true, they tax people on the basis of what they take out of the economy in the form of consumption rather than on the basis of their productive effort as measured by the amount of income they earn. Value added taxes, by comparison with income taxes, also avoid the double taxation of savings which is common to income tax regimes. (After tax income which is invested produces income which is then taxed.)

These theoretical advantages of value added taxes are often not realized in practice, however, since they are most often adopted as an additional tax rather than as a substitute for other forms of tax, including those on income. Such is likely to be the case in Canada, and it is difficult therefore to ignore the possibility that the value added tax is not being proposed because of its apparently superior economic characteristics but rather because of its political characteristics.

It was Colbert—Louis XIVs Finance Minister and the reputed instigator of the famous response, *"nous laissez faire"*—who remarked that the art of taxation consisted of extracting the maximum number of feathers from the goose while eliciting the least amount of hissing. It is within Colbert's theory of public finance and not the modern theories of Musgrave and others that we must search for the *raison d' être* of the value added tax. Pre-eminently, the value added tax is a hidden tax. Its incidence will be felt in the higher prices Canadians will face for the goods and services they consume. Since prices seem to rise all the time anyway, not one in a hundred Canadians will be aware of the fact that they have been subjected to an increase in their tax bill. Accordingly, there will be no hissing as the tax extracts 4 or 5 percent of the Canada goose's feathers.

Such an approach to taxation is a well-worn Canadian tradition. Much of current government revenue comes from a variety of "hidden" taxes. At the moment, nearly 30 percent of federal government revenue comes from taxes which are not specifically identified as such when we pay them—excise taxes, import duties, energy excise taxes, other energy taxes and, of course, the manufacturers sales tax, which is the federal government's most important revenue source after the personal income tax.

As we contemplate relying even more heavily on such hidden taxes, it is instructive to observe that the U.S. federal government has consistently avoided them. In the United States, 92 percent of total federal tax is in the form of direct, visible taxes. When the U.S. recently considered and rejected the use of a value added tax, one of the determining arguments was that it was a hidden tax. There may be a connection between such a stance and the widely held belief that the U.S. is inherently more conservative than Canada. Could it be that when the tax cost of programme expansion is more obvious, there is less appetite for the programmes?

Louis XIV did not have a conspicuous interest in the furtherance of democratic choice making. His M. Colbert could therefore ignore the public choice features of his theory of the optimal forms of taxation. In well-functioning democracies, the hissing of taxpayers should not be ignored or avoided but taken as an indication of what government ought to be doing. Instead of adopting a new hidden tax, the federal government should limit spending on the programmes that necessitate the goose plucking in the first place. *M.W.*

VISIBLE MINORITIES

We have just completed our application to the CBCs "Visible Minorities Training Program." Yes, there really is such a programme. The reason for its existence was recently summarized by its co-ordinator as follows: "Approximately one out of 12 Canadians is Inuit, Indian, black, brown or Asiatic. There can be very little argument that this fact is not reflected in the increasingly important area of broadcast journalism, a situation most observers consider unhealthy in a society dedicated to the ideas of equal opportunity for all. Through its training programme, the CBC is attempting to better reflect the multi-cultural reality of this country and to enrich the field of radio and television broadcasting with the diverse viewpoints and ideas that will result from the equitable presentation of all our people."

When we read this our hearts leaped with joy—finally we'll get our just deserts. No longer will we be neglected and rejected by the moguls of state radio. Finally there is some recognition of the anguish we have felt as night after night for all of our adult lives we have had to endure the silent agony of our deprivation. You see, we are members of that long-trampled minority—bald economists who advocate free markets.

Imagine what we have suffered as year in and year out we have had to watch the carefully coiffured anchormen for which CBC is famous drone out their peculiar rendition of the news without a thought for how that might make us feel. Not only have they flaunted their hirsuteness, but they have revelled in an utter disregard for our philosophical attitudes.

Oh, it is true, from time to time, that obscure sports events have featured bald commentators. It is even true that upon occasion a conservative commentator has found his way to the recording studio. But, until the establishment of the Visible Minorities Training Program we had naturally assumed those lapses to reflect a lack of vigilance or simple incompetence on the part of CBC programme directors. (Yet another reminder that efficient management in government agencies may not necessarily be in the public interest.)

As of this writing, our enthusiasm has begun to wane, however. Perhaps, optimism isn't warranted. While, it's true, we are bald free enterprisers from British Columbia (and that should make us shoo-ins for a minorities' position), there is a potential problem with our colour. We are both fair-skinned and, other than the red coloration around our necks, virtually indistinguishable visually from other bald Canadians. However, with the right camera angles, our visual minority status could be appropriately displayed.

A more worrisome aspect, however, is whether the whole programme can succeed. Will the Visible Minorities Training Program really be successful in overcoming the barriers within the corporation, particularly when it comes to the philosophical minorities? Our experience in this regard has not been good. Two years ago we went to some trouble to arrange for a CBC Journal interview with another bald conservative—a member of the American Chapter of BALD (Baldies Against Lawful Discrimination). As a matter of fact, not only was he a bald conservative, he was a short, Jewish bald conservative—from Chicago. As you will have guessed, it was Nobel Prize winning economist, Milton Friedman. The interview was taped as planned, and Friedman was magnificent. His mirror smooth pate vastly outshone the coiffured eminence on the other side of the camera, and he dealt with every question in a superbly cool, conservative fashion. Most importantly, he was persuasive, even convincing in dealing with the issues.

Now, there's nothing the CBC likes less than a convincing conservative, and we were permitting ourselves a silent chuckle at the prospect of them airing the Friedman interview. But we had chuckled too soon because this film clip never appeared. A unique opportunity for Canadians to hear the views of one of the leading minds and outstanding baldies in the world of economics was simply frittered away.

And that was not a unique experience. On another occasion the same programme filmed a debate between a Winnipeg lawyer and one of us (Mike Walker) on the subject of rent control. Late in the day they called to say that they couldn't use the material. Why? "Because it was too one-sided." "You dominated the discussion, they said." "It simply wasn't good television."

Who are they kidding? They tried to claim that the fact that the Winnipeg lawyer had a full head of hair and was a left-leaning NDPer had nothing to do with it! No, it isn't reasonable to think that this Visible Minorities Training Program is going to work. It's silly to think that us bald conservatives will ever get fair representation. Perhaps if we hurry we can intercept that application before our secretary drops it in the mail. *M.W.*

VOLUNTEER SECTOR

One of the aspects of our economy which never gets measured by Statistics Canada is the very large amount of voluntary work. Every year, church, civic, and service organizations engage in billions of dollars worth of effort to accomplish benevolent ends.

Unfortunately, in the past several decades the extent of volunteer work has been declining. This is due to the arrival on the scene of professional help-providers, paid for by government out of tax revenue. Recently, there has been recognition of this displacement effect, and some of the more farseeing policy-makers in Canada are attempting to reinvigorate the voluntary sector by consciously planning for a reduced role for government. Retractions of government services in Saskatchewan and British

Columbia have, in part, been designed to this end. They have, of course, been roundly criticized by many observers as simply the reactionary manifestation of a niggardly-minded policy focusing on financial as opposed to human consequences.

However, a 1983 report issued by the Swedish Secretariat for Future Studies indicates that we all have good reason to be concerned about the fate of the voluntary sector and the effect the past actions of government are having upon it. The report, *Care and Welfare at the Crossroads*, deals with paying for the care of the aged, the handicapped, and the young or ill. The rather startling conclusion of the study was that the Swedish state ought to initiate a programme that would compel Swedes to engage in volunteer work. Sound paradoxical? You bet; but forecasts suggest that by the end of the century an impossible fraction of Swedish GNP will have to go into taxes to support current care programmes.

Being unwilling to reduce the wages of care workers or tolerate a reduction in the quality of care, the marvelously inventive Swedes have decided to invent a voluntary sector. Yes, invent a voluntary sector, because in Sweden no voluntary sector as such exists today. What did exist has been displaced by a tax-financed government service. Even the church, believe it or not, is financed by the government.

In re-inventing a voluntary sector, the Secretariat was, however, concerned that the voluntarist principle may not be entirely reliable and, therefore, proposed that upon creation of the voluntary sector participation in it be made compulsory. In case you are thinking that this Swedish Secretariat for Future Studies' recommendations are pie-in-the-sky idealism, you should know that in the past most of the recommendations of the Secretariat have ultimately been reflected in Swedish law.

Hopefully, we in North America can learn something from the Swedish experience, and our government policies and programmes will begin to have a higher regard for the volunteer sector and do more to encourage it rather than to destroy it. However, this does not look as if it will come to pass. For years now, the leaders of government employee unions in Canada have been extolling the virtues of a larger governmental sector, allegedly because they are concerned about social welfare, about the plight of the poor or the handicapped—those who need the assistance of their fellow man as organized through government.

A British Columbia Government Employee's Union resolution presented at the national convention of provincial government employees shows a slightly different side to that concern. The BCGEU is asking provincial employees across Canada to stop contributing to charitable groups that in any way take part in replacing government services to the disadvantaged because of cut backs or downsizing programmes across the country. United Way organizations are clearly concerned by this gesture. Half of all the unionized employees in Canada belong to public sector unions. That represents a significant chunk of potential funding for charitable causes.

Of course, the reason for the move on the part of the government employees unions is because they realize that agencies funded on a voluntary basis by Canadians simply can't afford to pay the high wages which charity conducted under the aegis of government can afford. Besides, what with the jobs of government employees at stake, concerns for the sick, the handicapped, and the disadvantaged simply have to take second place. *M.W.*

W

WEATHERMEN

The nation's weathermen, it is claimed, are poorly trained, their reports are unreliable, and they provide inconsistent services to those such as boaters, fishermen, farmers, snow removal crews, and members of the public who rely upon them for important economic and even safety considerations. Despite these cutting criticisms, only superficial reforms are commonly recommended. According to a recent government report, the status of the Atmospheric Environmental Service would remain safely where it has always been—in government hands.

Yet, here is a prime candidate for privatization. Instead of one monolithic monopolistic public sector forecasting service, an entire industry of competing firms would provide a far better product for the Canadian people and especially for those whose livelihoods—and even lives—depend upon this service.

For one thing, with competition, we would have *different* prognostications of the weather. Under such a procedure, some firms could be expected to outdistance their competitors. This would provide an incentive to all to improve their skills—and an overdue exit for those who could not keep up.

For another thing, under a private sector weather service, the financing would be radically altered. Under present circumstances, we all pay for weather reports through the tax system whether we want them or not, whether we listen to them or not, and weathermen are paid no matter how inaccurate their forecasts. With competing private forecasters, only those who wanted them—newspapers, radio, TV stations, and other special interest groups—would have to shell out. There would be more incentive to get the forecast right—for a change. *W.B.*

WE OWE IT TO OURSELVES

One of the arguments frequently advanced to support the proposition that the government of Canada ought to spend its way out of the current uncomfortable levels of unemployment regardless of the effect on the deficit and the national debt is because, "we owe it to ourselves." When we sit down and work out the total burden of the national debt, we discover that the sum of the IOUs equals the sum of the IOMes. Therefore, why worry about the debt?

This is an attractive and seductive way of looking at the problems posed by the government's failure to balance its budget. It is often alleged that because we owe it to ourselves there is no practical limit on the extent to which we can engage in this debt-creating exercise. A moment's reflection, however, shows that this is incorrect. The reality is that most of the debts that we have in Canada we owe to ourselves.

When Mr. A borrows money to finance his mortgage, he borrows part of it from himself—from his savings account, from his pension fund, from his rainy day money, even from his chequing account to some limited degree. And, of course, he also borrows it from Mr. B and others to the extent that they have money on deposit in the institution from which he borrowed his mortgage.

But does the fact that we owe our mortgages to ourselves change the fact that if we have invested the mortgage money in a house with rotted foundations or, worse still, blown it on a trip to Pouce Coupe, or are unable to meet the payments because we owe so much for the new car and the investment in Acey Deucey Mining Corporation mean we don't have problems? Of course not. Don't be misled by this simplistic theory that since we owe the debt to ourselves it poses no burdens for our future. *M.W.*

WHEAT BOARD

The Canadian Wheat Board sits like a gigantic spider perched on top of the grain industry. By raising and lowering prices for the various grains, the CWB seeks to impose its own views of "orderly marketing" (the mandate given it in the Canadian Wheat Board Act of 1939). But here is the rub. By the very nature of things, the relevant supply and demand conditions will not exist until some time in the future, and much can change between the time of planting and harvest.

If we make the heroic assumption that deep in the bowels of the CWB there exists a foolproof crystal ball, able to predict future market conditions for grains with uncanny accuracy, then Canada is a most fortunate country to be so blessed. It would be nice, even in the absence of such a magical device, could we assume that while admittedly imperfect, the CWB was always the best prognosticator of future events. If either were true, we could be sure that prairie planting decisions were always in accord with future world conditions, and that mistakes would be nonexistent (or minimal).

Unfortunately, neither is the case. Far from being perfect or even the best prognosticator, there is good and sufficient reason to believe that in the CWB Canadians have placed a very inefficient decision-maker in charge of their farm planning.

First of all, there was the scandalous LIFT (Lower Inventory for Tomorrow) programme of over a decade ago, when farmers were ordered to reduce wheat production—right before the onset of a world-wide shortage of wheat. Second is the problem that even in the absence of gigantic snafus such as LIFT, there exist no independent criteria as to the forecasting ability of the CWB. The Wheat Board tries to promote orderly marketing, but how do we know whether or not it succeeds?

Now there is nothing at all wrong with trying to adjust present crop choice decisions to future market conditions. Let that be perfectly clear. Indeed, one of the hallmarks of a successful farming operation (perhaps as important as having the proverbial "green thumb") is this very ability. So the question is not whether to plan for the future; it is rather, which institutional arrangement is likely to succeed better—one in which each farmer makes these decisions for himself, or one in which the economic czar (CWB) makes them on behalf of the entire economy.

The history of agricultural economics speaks out clearly on this matter. All the economic evidence available indicates that decentralized market arrangements are far superior to those of central planning. Nor is this a mere coincidence. The benefits of market decision making are striking. One, there is a criterion of success, profit. Those farmers better able to anticipate future demands will tend to choose the right crops to grow. Other things equal, they will earn more profits than their less prescient colleagues. Two, other farmers will tend to follow the patterns set by the most highly successful operations in the industry. This will increase the ability of the farming community to anticipate future needs. Three, the prosperous farmers will be able to buy out their less successful brethren and so come to account for a greater and greater proportion of total acreage over time. This process will tend to shift acreage from those who do not anticipate future needs well toward those who do. Again, it will raise the overall efficiency of Canadian farming. Four, the collectivized method of central planning is like putting all the eggs in a single basket. When an individual farmer fails to see how the land lies ahead, he damages himself and only those foolish enough to follow his lead. But when a mistake is made by a bureaucrat armed with the power to affect the choices of thousands of farmers, calamity of the LIFT magnitude can ensue.

Sound public policy would therefore indicate that the CWB be stripped of its powers to set grain prices and thus encourage the growth of certain grains at the expense of other alternatives, not because this is not a task that needs doing but because the impersonal marketplace composed of thousands of decision-makers can do this job far more effectively than can a handful of political appointees. *W.B.*

WORKERS' COMPENSATION

Several years ago, Workers' Compensation Board bureaucrats shut down Janron Enterprises Inc., a Langley, B.C., kitchen cabinet manufacturer, owned by husband and wife team Ron and Janet Coles. Their crime? Failure to pay a WCB account of $5,000.

As firm sizes go, this was no big deal. Janron employed only 12 full-time workers and had a monthly payroll of only $18,500. But in that recession, with thousands of small firms going belly-up and millions of unemployed, it is more than passing curious to see a government agency deliver the death blow to a struggling debt-ridden but still viable enterprise.

It even makes us wonder whether workers' compensation ought not be put on a voluntary basis. If you were a Janron worker, would you rather have a job and make your own compensation arrangements with a private insurance company—or be unemployed? *W.B.*

WORKERS' CO-OPS

From the Toronto area comes news of a form of enterprise that may well solve both the problems of unemployment and low wages—at least in the area of small businesses. The basic idea is that of a workers' co-op in which the firm is owned by the workers. Typically, such co-ops emerge when the original business has failed or is on the brink of failure and the employees buy the assets in order to save their jobs. An important feature of these worker co-ops is the fact that once the employees are typically highly motivated, they see more clearly the linkage between their productivity and the success of the business and therefore their own economic future. Moreover, since many of these worker co-ops are owned by the people on the factory floor, so to speak, they have a direct stake in terms of the profit they share. Simultaneously, workers increase their productivity and demand wages that are compatible with the survival of the firm.

This recipe is not suitable in every case, nor has it worked in every instance. The failure of two packing plants sold to the employees by Gainers in Quebec and Ontario make that clear. On the other hand, worker co-ops are not incompatible with free enterprise either, as is sometimes implied. The very essence of free enterprise is the voluntary combination of workers, capital, and know how to achieve economic production. Co-ops are just one of the ways in which people combine their talents and capital to pursue their own interests and solve their own unemployment problems. *M.W.*

WORK SHARING

Working sharing seems to be the "in" thing. According to its advocates, unemployment is caused by people working too many hours. If they would just reduce their work week to 32 hours, there would be plenty of jobs to go around for everyone. Some people estimate that the 32-hour work week could create more than 780,000 additional jobs in Canada, halting unemployment dead in its tracks.

Superficially attractive as this idea is, it is deeply flawed. It flies in the face of the historical fact. Modern rates of unemployment were almost unknown during the industrial revolution, and yet the work week commonly lasted for 60, 80, and even 100 or more hours. Surely, if the long work week created unemployment, our rate of joblessness would have been reduced as the length of the work week fell; instead, the unemployment rate has risen as the work week decreased to 40 hours, and even fewer in some cases.

Modern day Japan is another refutation of this thesis. The Japanese work 41 hours per week, and have an unemployment rate of only 2.7 percent. In contrast, the Canadian work week is shorter than that of the Japanese, and our unemployment rate is roughly 10 percent.

The work-sharing hypothesis also commits the lump-of-labour fallacy. In this view, there is only so much work to be done in society. There is a definite upper limit to employment opportunities. If some people do more than their fair share of work, there will be less left for everyone else. Hard work, responsibility, and great efforts are thus not virtues, as tradition would have it. Rather, these qualities are evidence of greed. Ambitious and untiring workers are hogging the available jobs.

These are dubious propositions. There is no particular upper limit to the amount of work. Over the long sweep of time, the scope for employment is continually rising. As long as people are unsatisfied with what they have, want more goods and services, and are willing to work for wages that reflect their productivity, there will be room for additional employment possibilities.

At one time in our history, almost all labourers in Canada were tied to the farm; we needed them to feed ourselves. Now, thanks to vast gains in productivity, only about 5 percent of the workforce is in agricultural employment. We not only can feed ourselves far better than ever before, we can feed people in the rest of the world as well. Where did the additional non-agricultural jobs come from? If the amount of work to be done had a strict upper limit, almost all our labour force should be unemployed instead of barely one-tenth. The same analysis applies to the knitting mill, automatic elevators, the computer, and other labour-saving technology. At one time or another in our history, it was feared that numerous jobs would become obsolete because of these innovations.

Unemployment, in reality, is created when employees price themselves out of the market by demanding wages in excess of their productivity levels. This is precisely what will result from work-sharing schemes when proportionate wage decreases are resisted, as they almost always are. Fewer hours, at the same weekly pay, translates into higher hourly remuneration. Work-sharing plans of this sort will thus exacerbate unemployment, not cure it. *W.B.*

Y

YELLOW DOG CONTRACT

The dictionary defines yellow dog contract as "a contract in which workers agree not to join a union." Behind this somewhat laconic definition lies an ideological thicket in which bloody battles have been fought. At one time in our labour history, the pro- and anti-union forces contended mightily over the legitimacy of such contracts. The courts have now spoken out clearly; it is incompatible with Canadian labour law to offer or accept an employment contract which stipulates that the employee is not now a union member and shall automatically forfeit his job should he join one in future. The interesting question, however, is whether or not such a ban is justified. There is nothing in economic theory which deals with such questions (welfare economics) that can be used to defend this prohibition.

The reasoning for this surprising conclusion stems from an analysis of contracts. A contract is an agreement between two consenting parties. When both partners are adults and judged to be of sound mind, it must be concluded that each entered into the agreement because of all the options he saw as open to him this one seemed to be the most advantageous.

Consider first the case of two delivery truck drivers, the proverbial pie man and milkman. The former, with hundreds of pies in his possession but nothing to drink, values a quart of milk he is to receive in trade far more highly than the pie he must give up. And the latter, practically swimming in milk, drools at the prospect of a pie, so much so that he contemplates a gain in welfare even though he must part with a quart of this beverage in order to obtain his goal. Each, at least in the *ex ante* sense of expectations, anticipates a gain in welfare from the trade. Were this not the case, the two voluntarily consenting adults would scarcely agree to it. This reasoning applies regardless of their respective wealth positions; it does not matter one whit who is the richer: whether they benefit from the trade depends solely on their expectation that, rich or poor as they are, this commercial interaction will benefit them.

And so it is with the yellow dog contract. The worker who accepts it does so because, as far as he knows, this is the best option open to him. Ditto for the employer. The economic welfare of each, in other words, is improved by this contract, otherwise there would not have been two parties who consented to it. If no one agrees to such contracts, the law prohibiting them is hardly necessary. Again, the prior conditions of the participants is completely irrelevant to this issue. Be the previous situation of the employee ever so impoverished (or wealthy), he still gains by engaging in an act which in his view constitutes an improvement.

An objection to the foregoing may be couched as follows. Granted (for the sake of argument, anyway) that the worker can enhance his lot in life by signing a yellow dog contract. But he can gain still more if this provision is prohibited, for he will have to be employed in any case and can then avail himself of union membership if he so chooses.

One difficulty with this line of reasoning is that it is by no means guaranteed that all workers who would have been employed in the presence of a yellow dog contract (or in the absence of a union) will still be employed when it is banned (if unions are allowed). There is strong evidence showing that the extent of unionization is highly correlated with unemployment. For example, in 1960 the unionization rate in both the U.S. and Canada hovered around the 30 percent mark, and the unemployment rate for each was similarly close, at around the 7 percent level. By the mid-1980s, unionization in Canada had risen to over

40 percent of the labour force, while in the U.S. it had declined to just under 20 percent. As a result, an unemployment gap opened up between the two countries, with Canada's some 4 percent higher than that prevailing in the U.S.

A more basic problem with this objection is that it proves far too much, for the same could be said of *any* mutually agreeable contract. By setting aside a condition harmful to the interests of only one side, the other will certainly benefit (if the contract goes through, which, as we have seen, is by no means certain).

Let us return to our milk and pie example. Each gained from the trade, but if the government had stepped in on the side of the pie man and mandated that he should only have to give up one-half a pie for the quart of milk, he would be even better off than in the original agreement. However, were such a price control imposed by government, in all likelihood the pie man would not have been able to trade at all. Thus, paradoxically, his position would have been worse rather than improved by the government intervention ostensibly in his behalf. *W.B.*

Z

ZONING

In the view of most concerned professionals, zoning legislation is a necessary bulwark against chaos in urban land use. Without zoning, it is contended, external diseconomies will abound: pickle works will come to rest cheek by jowl with single family homes, glue factories beside country clubs, and oil refineries in proximity to family restaurants. Moreover, it is feared that rapacious land developers will erect profit from and then abandon buildings, placing undue strain on the capacities of municipal services. Further, the unzoned city will be one of haphazard construction, falling property values, instability, disregard for neighbourhood "character," irrational allocation of property—and a haven for unscrupulous speculators.

The zoning idea has a certain appeal. What, after all, could be more simple and obvious? If land usage seems imperfect, all that is needed is the enactment of a set of laws compelling proper behaviour. There are, however, grave flaws here. Consider Exhibit A, the City of Houston—which has never enacted zoning legislation. The very existence of a large North American city (an area in excess of 500 square miles and a population of 1.6 million) which can function normally and continue to grow without zoning is a major piece of evidence against the traditional view that zoning supposedly protects against chaos.

The reality appears to be either that there are a few significant inter-dependencies and externalities in urban property markets, or that "one man's meat is another man's poison." For instance, the presence of commerce in an otherwise residential neighbourhood is interpreted in a positive way by some people and in a negative way by others.

We must not lose sight of the fact that market mechanisms exist naturally to eliminate such externalities that would arise from the proverbial glue factory on the corner of Portage and Main. Quite simply, land prices in the top neighbourhoods are too expensive for the glue factory; they effectively prohibit any but the most valuable, concentrated uses—such as large office buildings or high-rise residential dwellings. And, in the more marginal areas from which industrial users cannot be precluded, the evidence is that the local inhabitants look upon them as a blessing, not a curse, because of the jobs they bring.

In Houston, the market has tended to create a reasonably well-ordered pattern. Because of private "marketplace zoning," we find no filling stations at the ends of cul-de-sacs; ship-channel industries are, naturally, located along the ship channel; large supermarkets, bowling alleys, movies and department stores are placed at or near major intersections, not in quiet residential areas.

In the absence of zoning, the post-1973 oil price rise would have had great repercussions on the urban/rural settlement pattern. Since fuel is an important input in commuting, we could have expected rising gasoline prices to have reduced the demand for suburban and country living. With fewer people in the country and more in the city, and with an all-round decrease in commuting distances, society would have economized on this suddenly more-expensive fuel supply. But with zoning legislation in all major North American cities, this fuel conservation process was stultified. Settlement patterns depend upon many other factors as well, but building height limitations, minimum acreage requirements (for single family units), the prohibitions of multiple apartment residential units from many zones, and so on have all interfered with the orderly process of relocation.

Moreover, the days of three-district zoning (residential, commercial, industrial) with two or three pages of regulations have long since passed. Today's ordinances are continually growing to accommodate more detailed regulations of use, lot size, building height, and bulk; more reasons for granting varianccs, bonuses, and special exceptions; and much more complicated procedures for appeals and reviews. Things have come to such a pass that no self-respecting set of zoning regulations dare appear in a tome of less than 500 pages.

The real issue here is between private and governmental zoning. What has been criticized above is government zoning, not the private variety. What is private zoning? The most well-known example is Houston's system of deed restrictions. (Neighbours contractually tie each other to continued or similar land usage. These voluntary agreements thus preclude the arrival of a factory—unless all or a previously stipulated number of signatories desire it.) But private zoning also takes place every time a glue factory is priced out of a residential neighbourhood, or whenever the gas station locates on a major thoroughfare, not in a side street, in its quest for customers. The same process is at work in shopping centres. It is difficult to imagine two "incompatible" tenants adjacent to each other in a shopping mall. Any inclinations toward such mall-zoning tends to be rigidly suppressed by the market.

In contrast, when the bureaucrat makes a mistake he does so on a vast scale. He negatively affects millions of people, virtually none of whom will be able to connect him with their suffering. He need not lose any of his personal funds, since he deals with other people's money. The public zoner can rest secure in his immunity from the "dollar vote" of the consumer, while his private counterpart, the land developer, is dependent for his very existence on continually satisfying customers. *W.B.*

INDEX